Research Strategies

Finding your Way through the
Information Fog

William Badke

5th Edition
2014

iUniverse LLC
Bloomington

Research Strategies
Finding your Way through the Information Fog

iUniverse books may be ordered through booksellers or by contacting:

iUniverse
1663 Liberty Drive
Bloomington, IN 47403
www.iuniverse.com
1-800-Authors (1-800-288-4677)

ISBN: 978-1-4917-2233-6 (sc)
ISBN: 978-1-4917-2234-3 (e)

Library of Congress Control Number: 2014901316

Printed in the United States of America.

iUniverse rev. date: 2/4/2014

Acknowledgements, etc.

Thanks to EBSCO Publishing for permission to use screenshots from their databases.

See the Research Strategies Website for updates, live links, keys and teaching aids: **https://sites.google.com/site/researchstrategiesweb/**

See the Research Strategies Textbook site for courses, syllabi, rubrics, etc.: **http://acts.twu.ca/Library/textbook.htm**

Meet me on Facebook; search for: **Research Strategies**

Contents

Preface   xvii

1.   Welcome to the Information Fog   1
    1.1 Before there was print   3
    1.2 Reading and inscription   4
    1.3 The printing press   5
    1.4 Enter the World Wide Web   8
    1.5 Information today – The state of the art   10
       1.5.1 Books   10
       1.5.2 Journals and magazines   14
       1.5.3 Government and corporate documents   16
       1.5.4 The World Wide Web   16
       1.5.5 Web 2.0   17
    1.6 Primary and secondary information sources   18
    Clearing the Fog – What's all this talk about academic
information?   19
    1.7 Warning - Not all information is informative   20
    1.8 For further study   21
       Study guide   21

2.   Taking Charge   22
    2.1 Wrestling with a topic   24
    2.2 Elements of inadequate research   25
    2.3 The key to great research   26
    2.4 A model for research   29
    2.5 Getting started in research   30
       2.5.1 Getting a working knowledge through reference
sources   30
       2.5.2 Excursus: Wikipedia, the professor's dilemma   33
       2.5.3 Full text reference tools   35

2.6 Finding a good question   36
    2.6.3 Thesis statements   37
    2.6.4 Research questions - The bad and the ugly   38
Clearing the Fog – Research is a conversation, not a soliloquy   40
2.7 The preliminary outline   42
2.8 How about a few good examples?   44
    2.8.1 "The thought of Erasmus of Rotterdam"   44
    2.8.2 "Teenage Alcoholism"   44
    2.8.3 "Climate Change"   44
    2.8.4 "Behaviorism as a model for social engineering"   45
2.9 For further study   45
    Study guide   45
    Practice with research questions   46
    Assignment for a research project of your own   46
    Teaching tool   47

3.   Database Searching with Keywords and Hierarchies   48
3.1 What's a database?   49
3.2 Keyword searching   50
    3.2.1 Database basics for keyword searching   50
    3.2.2 Boolean searching   52
Clearing the Fog – What's the best way to choose keywords?   59
3.3 Keyword searching with hierarchies   60
    3.3.1 Hierarchies   60
    3.3.2 Clustering search tools   64
3.4 Keyword searching – The good, bad, and ugly   65
3.5 For further study   66
    Study guide   66
    Practice with keywords and hierarchies   67
    Suggested key to practice with keywords   68
    Assignment for a research project of your own   70

4.   Metadata and the Power of Controlled Vocabularies   71
4.1 It's all about the metadata   72
4.2 Understanding metadata   73
4.3 Metadata in practice – The database record   75

4.4 Controlled vocabularies 77

4.5 Library of Congress Subject Headings 78

Clearing the Fog – Subject headings are not keywords, no they're not. 84

4.6 Working the angles—Identifying controlled vocabularies 85

    4.6.1 Library catalogs 86

    4.6.2 Other databases 87

4.7 Getting more creative—combining controlled vocabulary and keyword searching 88

4.8 Keeping on track with controlled vocabularies 90

4.9 For further study 91

    Study guide 91

    Practice with controlled vocabularies 91

    Suggested key to practice with controlled vocabularies 92

    Assignment for a research project of your own 93

5. Discovery Searches, Library Catalogs and Journal Databases 94

5.1 Discovery Searches 95

5.2 Library catalogs 97

    5.1.1 Making the catalog work for you 98

    5.2.2 E-Books 100

Clearing the Fog – How to create in-text citations from e-readers when page numbers are missing 102

5.3 Journal databases 104

Clearing the Fog – Do you know the difference between an article and a journal? 104

    5.3.1 Some background on the journal scene 106

Clearing the Fog – Some tips on journal article citations 109

    5.3.2 Introduction to journal databases 110

Clearing the Fog - Please stop treating academic databases like Google – You're hurting their feelings 114

    5.3.3 RSS feeds from journal databases 116

    5.3.4 Table of contents alerts 116

5.4 Approaching journal databases – Tips and hints 116

    5.4.1 Be prepared for challenges. *116*

    5.4.2 Read the interface. 117

5.4.3 Be aware that databases tend to be something
of a black hole.   117
5.4.4 Resist the urge to fill the search box with words.   117
5.4.5 Think about staging (faceting) your search.   118
5.4.6 Look for controlled vocabularies and advanced
searches.   118
5.4.7 Think before you search.   118
5.4.8 Retrace your steps.   119
5.4.9 When in doubt, use the instructions.   119
5.4.10 Remain calm and get help if you need it.   119
5.4.11 Sometimes problems arise because you're
using the wrong database.   120
5.4.12 Check out the possibilities of interlibrary loan.   120
5.5 Citation searches, related articles and reference lists –
Alternative ways of searching   121
    5.5.1 Citation searches   121
    5.5.2 Related articles   121
    5.5.3 Reference lists   122
Clearing the Fog – What's a doi?   122
5.6 Trying out a live journal database   123
5.7 Varieties of the journal database   126
5.8 Final pep talk   127
5.9 For further study   127
    Study guide   127
    Practice with journal databases   128
    Assignment for a project of your own   128

6.   Internet Research   130
6.1 A brief introduction to the Net   132
6.2 Google Scholar and other free academic search engines
on the Net   133
    6.2.1 Why start with academic search engines?   133
    6.2.2 Google Scholar (http://scholar.google.com)   133
Clearing the Fog – Google Scholar may be more valuable
for what surrounds a citation than for what is in it.   137
    6.2.3 BASE (http://www.base-search.net/)   138

6.2.4 Microsoft Academic Search
(http://academic.research.microsoft.com/)   139
6.2.5 CiteSeerX (http://citeseerx.ist.psu.edu/)   139
6.2.6 Scirius (http://www.scirus.com/srsapp/)   140
6.2.7 getCITED (http://www.getcited.org/)   140
6.2.8 Others   141
6.3 Search engines for the rest of humanity – Google and
friends   142
6.3.1 Searching by search engine, using keywords   142
6.3.2 A basic introduction to the best search engines 144
Clearing the Fog – While you are searching Google,
Google is searching you   148
6.3.3 RSS feeds from search engines   152
6.3.5 The coming semantic search engines   152
6.4 Searching by subject tree   153
6.5 Portals   153
6.6 The Hidden Internet   155
6.6.1 What do we mean by "Hidden?"   155
6.6.2 What's in the Hidden Internet?   155
6.6.3 How do I find information on the Hidden
Internet?   156
6.7 Evaluating information from the Internet   156
6.8 Some more Internet addresses valuable for research
purposes   159
6.8.1 Reference sources   159
6.8.2 Searchable library catalogs   159
6.8.3 Phone directories   160
6.9 For further study   160
Study guide   160
Practice with the Internet   160
Assignment   161

7.   Other Resources and Case Studies in Research   163
7.1 Seeing where you've been   164
Clearing the Fog – Step by step may not always be the
best approach, but it can help you find your way   165
7.2 ERIC   166

7.3 Government documents   169
7.4 Doctoral dissertations   170
7.5 Bibliographic managers   171
    7.5.1 EndNote (http://www.endnoteweb.com/)   171
    7.5.2 RefWorks (http://refworks.com/)   172
    7.5.3 Zotero (http://www.zotero.org/)   172
7.6 Consulting with friends, mentors and librarians   173
    7.6.1 What are good friends for?   173
    7.6.2 Consulting professors   173
    7.6.3 Encountering librarians   174
7.7 Case studies in research   174
    7.7.1 "Arctic Ice Issues Resulting from Climate
    Change"   174
    7.7.2 "The First Crusade"   180
Clearing the Fog – Research is like a box of chocolates   184
7.8 For further study   185
    Study guide   185
    Practice with resources introduced in this chapter   185
    Assignment   186

8.   Learning How to Read for Research   188
8.1 Reading for the connoisseur and the glutton   189
    8.1.1 Be ruthless   190
    8.1.2 Get to know the material without reading it all   191
    8.1.3 A final word on analytical reading   195
Clearing the Fog – On using more than the first three
pages   196
8.2 Evaluation of research resources   196
8.3 Note taking   198
    8.3.1 The determined photo-copier/printer/e-doc
    highlighter   199
    8.3.2 The value of going all digital   201
    8.3.3 The quoter   202
    8.3.4 The summarizer   203
    8.3.5 The paraphraser (*not recommended* in most
    cases)   204
    8.3.6 Which method is best?   205

8.4 Further notes on note-taking 205
Clearing the Fog – What if I'm not an organized person? 207
8.5 A gentle warning about the horrible crime of plagiarism 208
    8.5.1 Why get stressed about plagiarism? 209
    8.5.2 About getting caught 210
    8.5.3 International students and plagiarism 211
8.6 For further study 212
    Study guide 212
    Practice / Assignment 213

9.   Organizing Your Resources to Write your Paper 214
9.1 Your notes, photocopies and printouts 215
    9.1.1 Organizing digital notes 215
    9.1.2 Organizing your paper-based notes 216
9.2 Your bibliography 217
Clearing the Fog - How can I learn to read citations well? 218
9.3 Your subject index 220
9.4 A Second Method for Note Organization 223
9.5 Indexing your notes for larger assignments 226
9.6 For further study 227
    Study guide 227
    Practice/Assignment 228

10. Tips on Research Writing 229
10.1 The final outline 230
    10.1.1 Step one: The research question/thesis
    statement 230
    10.1.2 Step two: Preliminary outline headings 231
    10.1.3 Step three: Organizing the headings 231
Clearing the Fog – What about creativity? 236
10.2 Some tips on research writing 237
    10.2.1 Introduce your paper well 237
    10.2.2 Be focused at all times 238
    10.2.3 Always describe before you analyze. 238
    10.2.4 Avoid ridicule. 238
    10.2.5 Be logical. 238
    10.2.6 Be explicit. 239
    10.2.7 Aim for clear writing rather than erudition. 240

10.2.8 Watch out for flawed arguments. 240

10.2.9 Know when to quote and when not to quote 242

10.2.10 Know some basic principles for quotations. 243

10.2.11 Know the uses of footnotes/endnotes/citations. 244

Clearing the Fog – Becoming a better academic writer 246

10.2.12 Watch your conclusions. 247

10.2.13 Give your final paper a professional look. 247

10.3 For further study 248

Study guide 248

Practice/Assignment 249

APPENDIX ONE – A Research Paper Clinic: More Tips and
Troubleshooting for Development of Great Research Papers 250

A1.1 Research questions 251

A1.1.1 Why many research projects miss the target 251

A1.1.2 Getting focused by asking the right question 252

A1.1.3 The question that isn't there 253

A1.1.4 The fuzzy question 254

A1.1.5 The multi-part question 256

A1.1.6 The open-ended question 258

A1.1.7 The question that will not fly 259

A1.1.8 Thesis statements 260

A1.2 Practice with research questions 260

A.2.1 The questions: 260

A.1.2.2 Suggested key for the questions: 261

A1.3 Types of research papers 263

A1.3.1 Descriptive paper 263

A1.3.2 Analytical or investigative paper 263

A1.3.3 Persuasive paper 264

A1.3.4 Literature review 265

A1.4 The outline as a research paper guidance system 266

A1.4.1 Why worry about an outline early in the
research process? 266

A1.4.2 Steps to a good outline 267

A1.4.3 Practice with outlines 270

A1.4.4 Suggested key for practice with outlines 271

A1.5 Building the substance of the essay 274

A1.5.1 Intent and direction 274
A1.5.2 Building the paper 274
A1.5.3 Using sources well 275
A1.5.4 **Avoiding theft of other people's work** 277
A1.5.5 Practice with essay structure 279
A1.6 Bibliographic style 280
A1.6.1 Style software 281
A1.6.2 Crib sheets 283
A1.7 Conclusion 286

APPENDIX TWO – This Textbook and Information Literacy
Competency Standards for Higher Education (ACRL) 287

Index 289

Preface

Everyone does research. Some just do it better than others.

This book is definitely for you if you are:

> ➤ a university student whose term papers have been patented as a cure for insomnia;
> ➤ a Dilbert of industry who's been told to do a feasibility study on the expansion potential of winter ice cream bar sales in Nome, Alaska;
> ➤ a simple honest person trying to find the truth behind the advertising so that the next car you buy won't be like your last disaster-mobile, the car that made you *persona non grata* at the automobile association.

Are you ready for your next research project? Really ready? Do you have the skills and strategies to get the job done efficiently and effectively without panic attacks and the need for a long vacation when you're done? Do you have confidence that you can start with a topic about which you know nothing and end with an understanding of it that is neither trite nor superficial? Are you prepared to enjoy the experience? [Yes, I did say "enjoy."]

If the previous paragraph has left you feeling somewhat queasy, this book is for you. Even if you think you have significant research skills, you can learn better ones if you take the time to read on. You have the privilege of living in the information age, with boundless opportunities all around you to find out anything about anything. But faced with a humongous number of Internet sites, not to mention academic and commercial databases of increasing size and complexity, knowing how to navigate through the information fog isn't something you can pick up easily on your own. Truth to tell, there is a ton of studies telling us that most people have vastly higher opinions about their research ability than actual tests of that ability can demonstrate.

Yet you can hardly call yourself educated if you don't have really good skills to handle complex information systems and do research effectively, not in a world in which most careers are built more on what you can find out than what you already know.

Who am I to try to teach you about research? Just someone who has taught the strategies in this book to thousands of anxious university students, both undergraduate and graduate, for close to 30 years (making me a dinosaur?), and who likes nothing better than to walk people through the information fog. I am Associate Librarian for Associated Canadian Theological Schools and Information Literacy at Trinity Western University. Being the author of a number of books and scholarly articles myself (see my bio at **http://www.acts.twu.ca/library/badke.htm**), you can rest assured that I've devoted a lot of my life to doing research and not just teaching it. So I understand what you're going through.

One caution: This book is about *informational* research. It won't teach you how to do a science experiment or determine the best way to train a rat how to ride a bicycle (though it will help you do a literature review). But if you need to identify a problem, and then acquire and use information to address the problem, this book is for you.

Learning how to do research does not have to be painful. It can be fun. Honestly. Personally, research gives me so much pleasure that my family has to kidnap me out of the library whenever they want to go on an outing or buy groceries. You can have the same joy that I have. Read on.

Updates to the textbook will be posted at: **https://sites.google.com/site/researchstrategiesweb/home/updates**

See the Research Strategies Website for live links, keys and teaching aids: **https://sites.google.com/site/researchstrategiesweb/**

See the Research Strategies Textbook site for courses, syllabi, etc.:
http://acts.twu.ca/Library/textbook.htm

Meet me on Facebook. Search for: **Research Strategies**

1

Welcome to the Information Fog

We are living in the middle of a revolution. Not since the creation of the printing press (and maybe not ever) has our concept of information been so disrupted. The driving force of the information revolution is the World Wide Web, which has given us access to more knowledge than ever before in human history.

Information used to be scarce, thus creating a demand for experts who knew things and could share those things with the rest of us. Now we have Google, the information candy store, which makes information abundant and challenges the role of the expert. "Information candy store?" Yes. Google serves up lots of enticing stuff right there at our finger-tips, most of it looking good enough to devour. The down side of a candy store, if there ever could be a down side, is that candy tends to be loaded with empty calories.

No, I'm not down on Google or Bing or whatever search engine suits your fancy. We won't be Google-bashing here. But there is so much more than Google. The revolution in information has led many of us to believe that Google is god, or at least the ultimate information source. But nothing is that simple. Fact is, we live in an era in which there is untold opportunity to go beyond Google. And we also live in an era that is much more complicated than it used to be.

At one time we thought we knew what information was. Now we're not so sure. These days we're buried in data, and defining what is and what is not genuine information is getting to be more of a challenge all the time.

Information is supposed to inform. That means it has to be reliable, relevant, current, and so on. There was a time when people believed that, given the right information, we could solve any problem the human race encountered. They thought that the power of reason could be used in a totally objective way to wade through all the data and come up with the right answers, even with the truth. Now we're no longer even sure what the questions are (and we can't remember last Tuesday).

To be sure, we've always known that some of what passes for information can't be trusted. That's why we have law courts to determine the truth of a matter, though the best liar often wins.

We've come to understand over the past hundred years that information is colored with subjectivity: What we know depends on how we interpret our information base. Even the best authors of information bring their own biases into the mix. Thus, for good or ill, we are no longer as trusting when it comes to interacting with information. It's like buying a Rolex from a man in an alley – it might be a real Rolex coming from somebody down on his luck, but, unless you know Rolexes, you could well be getting a knock-off.

I'd like to take a bit of time to trace the events that have led us to this place. Textbooks, after all, are supposed to lead you on a journey through history and philosophy-of-whatever before they get to the good stuff. But in the case of information, the next few pages really are essential to doing good research. Believe it or not, you need to understand our world of information if you want to do intelligent research within its often foggy terrain.

So how did we get here, to an age dominated by the World Wide Web?

1.1 Before there was print

Throughout the entire history of humanity, knowledge has been passed down from one generation to another. Before this was done in written form (and in non-literate societies today), *speech and demonstration* were the source of humanity's information - historical tales told around campfires, children learning about agriculture by doing it with their parents, and so on. These were "traditional societies." I use the word "traditional" not in the sense of 1920s country music and picket fences, but in the sense of knowledge viewed as a *tradition* to pass down from generation to generation, often for the very survival of the society.

Here's an example of why these kinds of societies need traditional information: When I lived for a couple of years in Africa, people would point to this plant or that one and tell me, "You could eat this." It happened often enough that I finally asked someone why it was so important for me to know what plants I could eat. He explained that during the recently ended civil war, the people had been forced from their city homes into the jungle. They were starving, because no one knew what was edible and what was deadly. Their ancestors had once carried this knowledge with them, but these city dwellers had stopped passing it on to their children, and the knowledge had died.

So the former urbanites, now living in the bush, cooked various plants and fed them to their chickens to see if the chickens would cluck or croak. And gradually they rebuilt their knowledge base. "We have decided," my friend told me, "that we must never again forget what we can eat, so that's why we tell one another what is edible."

3

Their traditions had meant the survival of their society. If you forgot what you could eat in the jungle, you might have to choose between potentially poisoning yourself and starving.

Clearly, though, traditional information has to be reliable. Thus, in societies that depend on their traditions, knowledge is passed down only by people qualified to do so, and unregulated production of new information is not encouraged. There is an emphasis within traditional societies on memorizing the information that exists rather than using existing information to create new knowledge. The development of new knowledge in such cultures is a deliberate and slow process performed with care and authorized only by experts in the existing tradition. Otherwise, the next plant you eat could well be your last.

1.2 Reading and inscription

The development of *written* language brought a number of changes to the world:

➢ Knowledge could be preserved in print. Thus there was less of a need to pass it on orally (though the oral element remained important in daily life), let alone a need to memorize huge amounts of information. Memorization continued, to be sure, but you didn't need to know everything, because it was possible to look it up if you had access to written documents.

➢ Since the knowledge base was more secure, people could pay more attention to discovery, thus hopefully adding to the knowledge base.

➢ The keepers of knowledge (i.e., the tradition experts who actually had the books = the librarians) were more elite than they had been in an oral society. Now only the people who could read could stay close to the tradition. What is more, there were few copies, because everything had to be transcribed by hand. Thus a small group of people in society controlled the knowledge base, and these people (recognizing that knowledge is power) generally worked against the forces of discovery (who tend to take the power away from the people who control the knowledge base). As long as access to documents was controlled, most people continued to rely more on oral tradition. The full transition from oral to written cultures took many centuries.

1.3 The printing press

The Chinese actually invented the printing press centuries before the Europeans did (as was the case for many things, including gunpowder), but it was the Europeans who used it to revolutionize the use of information in society. In 1447, Johannes Gensfleisch zur Laden zum Gutenberg (Gutenberg for short) created a moveable type press, a development so revolutionary that the A & E Television Network in 1999 named him #1 in its list of "People of the Millennium." The printing press was such a big deal because:

> From a "preservation of the tradition" standpoint, it meant that multiple copies could be produced, thus making the tradition more secure (previously, it would have taken only one match lit by a careless monk to burn the single manuscript that had everything you needed to know – sort of a medieval hard-drive crash, only more permanent).

> More people could actually get their hands on the knowledge base, thus creating a better-informed society that was not as dependent on oral tradition. The elitism of knowledge was undermined as "holders of the tradition" found they no longer had an exclusive right to control who saw the knowledge base and who added to it.

> The possibilities of discovery were greatly increased, because so many more people had access to existing knowledge. It was thus much more likely that new knowledge would be built on the foundation of the old.

Knowledge multiplied in the centuries that followed. In fact, the major discoveries and inventions that make our lives what they are owe most of their existence to the printing press. Yet there were pros and cons to this invention. The pros are obvious, the cons not as much.

First, on the con side, the printing press was only as useful as the population was literate. We are still working on that problem.

Second, a new form of elitism developed, and whether it was good or bad remains a matter of debate. It came from the fact that production of new information depended on two things: bright people to make the discoveries and money to publish their words. The bright people created the elitism of universities and the money people determined what would be published and what would not.

The money issue also put a limit on who could get his or her ideas into print. Publishers, wanting to be sure they didn't lose their shirts, added "gatekeeping" processes to their requirements. Gatekeepers ask two key questions: First, is the information worthy to be published? This is a value judgment, usually based on level of scholarship or reliability or entertainment value, but sometimes focused on the aims of the publisher or the desires of the marketplace (thus the existence of romance novels). Second, will it sell? Many a worthy manuscript goes into the trash simply because the publisher doesn't think there's an audience to sell it to. Alternately, there might be a small audience that has to pay a large amount for each copy published (as with most scholarly books).

Gatekeeping is a good thing when it helps to preserve quality. No one wants our knowledge base to be filled with shoddy stuff that no one can trust (or so the wisdom of commercial publishing would tell us). On the other hand, gatekeeping has been used to censor valuable information, keeping it away from the very people who need it most. This has prevented perfectly good ideas from seeing the light of day, simply because someone viewed those ideas as unacceptable or there wasn't a good market for them. Thus gatekeeping has tended to maintain the status quo or promote certain biases, because new, radical concepts (or concepts the publisher doesn't like) are not as sure to sell as the tried and true. On this, see Brian Martin, *The Politics of Research,* **www.uow.edu.au/~bmartin/pubs/98il/il07.pdf.**

Certainly, people have always been able to self-publish material that the gatekeepers rejected, but distributing self-published books can be a tough game. Would-be buyers often ask, "If this is such a good book, why didn't the commercial publishers want it?" Thus self-published material tends to stay more or less underground, though much of it is of high quality.

More recently, several very entrepreneurial self-publishing companies have made it possible to produce your own book at minimal cost and without the need to stock thousands of copies in your basement. You even have the opportunity to publish it in multiple e-formats as well as print. Thus the self-publishing of books has come into its own, so much so that we now find that there are more self-published books on the market than there are commercially produced titles. Still, getting a self-published book into the hands of purchasers remains an uphill battle, even if you can upload your own book to Amazon Kindle for free.

Along with the rise of the printing press came the development of the "subject discipline," allowing people to specialize in particular fields of discovery. The idea of a "discipline," a defined subject area within which discovery is made, has its good points (the main one being the ability to focus narrowly to provide more depth of research) and its bad points (the main one being the separation of knowledge into categories that don't talk much with each other). But the fact is that most advancement of knowledge these days is done within disciplines.

What does that mean for people doing research?

➢ Each discipline has its own "language" which is more than just its technical words but also involves the ways in which that discipline communicates information. A historian has a different mode of expression than that of a physicist (or an expert in the sex life of nematodes).

➢ Each discipline has its own method of doing research. While method, even in the humanities, has some connection with the scientific research process, there are distinct features that make research in English literature different from research in Korean history or in the biology of nematodes.

7

> Each discipline has its in-crowd, its elite group of highly regarded scholars. Knowing which writers and which works are the most highly regarded is very important to doing research without looking like an outsider.

1.4 Enter the World Wide Web

A revolution even more revolutionary than Gutenberg's has happened within our own generation – the creation of the World Wide Web, a popular subset of the larger Internet. In the short span of time since the early 1990s, the WWW has blown the lid off much that we've known about information since the beginning of time. Why? Because it has pushed aside most of the boundaries that once prevented us from having all the information our knowledge-greedy little eyes could want.

It comes down to one basic fact - ***On the WWW, anyone can publish almost anything he or she wants to say, without impediment***. Let me unpack this a bit:

> On the WWW, gatekeepers are no longer required. They still exist, and they still have great value, but we can publish without them. Whether or not it's always advisable to do so is another issue, but for the first time in human history we can have our say without anybody editing our words or stopping us outright. The Internet, for good or ill, is the greatest vehicle for free speech the world has ever known.

> We can publish and acquire information at a level never before possible. The Web enables us to have access to so much, in fact, that we can easily become overwhelmed by it. As far as getting our own message out, we have a potential audience that can number in the millions. This means that information is no longer scarce but cheap and plentiful.

> What we lose (perhaps) is certainty. If anyone can publish on the WWW, we no longer have many of the normal checks and balances that once kept the world

from being inundated by nonsense. This isn't a new problem, because even with gatekept print material, readers should always be exercising discernment. But we now have the challenge that, for a large portion of Web-based information, no one except the author has done any gatekeeping at all. This is a classic two-edged sword - if anyone can publish on the Net, then we have an amazing resource for freedom of speech and the democratic way of life. The old elitism is gone. But it also means that *we, the readers, have to become the gatekeepers to an extent never before seen, due to the lack of external quality control.* This demands that we enhance our evaluation skills.

➢ One more concern – if we are not careful in our gatekeeping, the whole concept of authority can disappear. What do I mean by "authority?" Simply the fact that every field of knowledge has its experts, its wise voices, its people who understand that field better than the rest of us, because they have immersed themselves in it. We might want to resist authority, but the people who really know a subject area are assets who we can't afford to ignore.

The WWW tends to level out authority. A Google search can bring you the work of an expert in the field as well as a website produced by Ms. Jackson's third grade science class. To fail to discern the difference is to miss the power of getting our information from people who really know what they are writing about. This is not to say that every great scholar is right all the time. But ignoring that scholar in favor of a website on the same topic from your uncle Frank is going to put you at a disadvantage. Right now, the average person selects the first five results from a Google search and does very little evaluation of their relative quality. For more on this, see the excellent article by MaryBeth Meszaros, "Who's in Charge Here? Authority, Authoritativeness, and the Undergraduate Researcher," *Communications in Information Literacy* 4.1 (2010): 5-11. **http://tinyurl.com/ln6r49m**. She has a bit of fun at my personal expense, but I forgive her.

You might also want to look at the white paper produced by the anti-plagiarism service, Turnitin, which compiled data from millions of student papers to show that most of you are not really using high quality resources (don't you just love it when data reveals the real you and it's something unflattering?): **http://pages.turnitin.com/ sources_in_writing_sec_2012.html**

Before you accuse me of being overly simple-minded (something I've heard a lot), let me point out that it's not as "either-or" as I may have implied, so that you either have to love the Net or hate it. You see, the WWW is really less a content-provider than a *vehicle* for information. Thus it is also used by publishers who still demand rigorous gatekeeping procedures. Commercial E-Books and scholarly articles are carried for a fee by the same system that provides us with a free copy of Aunt Bertha's remedy for lumbago. Many of these resources are part of the "hidden" or "invisible" Internet (found behind password gates so that only authorized users can see them), but they have as much of a home on the WWW as your cousin's jumpy YouTube video of river-rafting last summer.

1.5 Information today – The state of the art

Let's look at the status of some of the main sources of information today:

1.5.1 Books

Book publishing is continuing, with no hint of a slowdown in the process. The big story in recent years has been the rise of the e-book. To say that the move to the e-book has been confusing/frustrating for both publishers and readers alike would be an understatement. In a short period of time, traditional hardcopy book publishing has been challenged like never before, starting with the creation of Amazon Kindle, followed shortly after by the Sony Reader, Barnes & Noble nook, Kindle Fire, the iPad, numerous Android tablets, and so on. I don't intend to spell out the wondrous features of each, but we need to understand what is going on here, if we are going to be able to make sense of the options and opportunities facing the e-book future.

First, Kindle, then Sony Reader, NOOK, Kobo, etc. introduced a fairly old technology called "e-paper" but in a new way. E-paper is not a LED screen (as in tablets and cell phones), but something much more physical. Imagine a multitude of electronically charged particles squashed between a screen and a back plate. One type of charge will make these particles move toward the screen, making them appear white. Another type of charge will move particles to the back plate, making them look dark. Thus, if you program a book into the system, the particles get various charges that form dark areas and white areas - letters and background - making it possible to read words off the screen. The particles themselves are not light-emitting pixels, but real pieces of matter, so there is no glare.

One serious drawback of e-paper is that it is a lot like regular paper and thus is unable to function interactively like a screen on a phone or tablet. While some readers will allow you to do note-taking and highlighting, etc., the e-paper book readers lack the ability to function easily within the world of the Web the way an iPad or Android device can. The development of color e-paper readers since 2010 shows that the medium is still advancing, but it certainly has its limitations. The Kindle Fire was the first Kindle to be a tablet that doesn't use e-paper.

Another path to e-book success is typified by the Apple iPad and various Android tablets, which use LED technology that enables all of the standard interactivity features found in smartphones and laptops. (Of course, by the time you read this, you'll be using iPad10, and there will be 1267 similar products. Such is the speed of change in this area). The creation of these types of devices has paved the way for the so-called "enhanced e-book" that will embody, not just text, but video and audio clips, even gaming.

E-book interfaces will change over time as books move from static text to interactive experiences. From pages that will allow flipping similar to print books, but with additional options to make the flip even better (**http://www.youtube.com/watch?v=rVyBwz1-AiE&feature=youtu.be**) to amazingly interactive adventures in reading and viewing (**http://www.youtube.com/watch?v=LV-RvzXGH2Y**), the e-book is due for a format revolution.

Meanwhile Google Books, though slowing down, continues to digitize large libraries of books, some of which are deliverable to your device for free, as long as they are not in copyright. Google, under its commercial name, Google Play, will sell you some of these, in whole or in part, in electronic form or even as cheap paperbacks (what irony - Google digitizes a paper book, then prints it and sells it as a paperback). Aiding e-book to paperback production is the Espresso Book Machine® which, looking somewhat like a snack food vending machine, will create a paperback book from a digital master on the spot at low cost (**http://www.ondemandbooks.com/hardware.htm**).

Large scale book digitizing projects are growing. Beyond Google Books, on a less commercial front, the Open Library, which is devoted to free access to public domain (out of copyright) books and to proper cataloging of them, has close to 2,000,000 books available for online viewing (**http://openlibrary.org/**). The Open Content Alliance (**http://www.opencontentalliance.org/**) is quietly snagging key contracts to supply out of copyright and open access e-books to major libraries and library systems that are uncomfortable with Google's growing control in the e-book market. The Digital Public Library of America (**http://www.dp.la/**) has emerged out of The HathiTrust Digital Library and boasts millions of volumes. See its great new search interface at **http://dp.la/bookshelf**.

As of the end of 2007 (the last date for which statistics are available), the Universal Digital Library Million Book Project (**https://archive.org/details/millionbooks**), another non-commercial enterprise, with backing from Carnegie Mellon University and other groups, had 1.5 million book titles digitized. Items not in copyright are available in HTML, TIFF and a type of PDF format. Those under copyright offer only an abstract. A significant feature of this collection is the number of Chinese, Arabic and Indian language titles in it. The project has now been taken over by the Internet Archive. The Online Books Page (**http://digital.library.upenn.edu/books/**) offers over a million books for free, though most are out of copyright and thus old. The Oxford Text Archive (**http://ota.ahds.ac.uk/**) offers several thousand carefully chosen books important to academic study. One of the oldest enterprises offering free e-books is Project Gutenberg (**http://www.gutenberg.org/wiki/Main_Page**)

which has over 40,000 titles of its own and offers a further 100,000 free titles through its affiliates. Finally, Directory of Open Access Books (**http://www.doabooks.org/**) opened in 2012 and offers over a thousand peer reviewed academic books for free from close to 40 publishers.

What about the grand dream that every book will one day be online for anyone to read? Well, I think you can put that one to rest alongside the story of the baby alligators, once dumped into the sewers of New York, that have become twenty foot student-eating monsters. Even if all the books in the world were digitized, the full text of anything in copyright would only come to you at a cost. Authors like to get paid, and well they should, because they are all wonderful people who deserve it. Thus it is futile to believe that any book you want to have can be accessed electronically for free. Publishers won't give away their books any more than music producers want to give away their songs, though it has happened anyway (and book piracy may one day make a liar out of me). As well, many older books are not commercially viable for digitization unless they end up in a project like Google Books.

Even with all these efforts, though, the e-book is still struggling to find its way. Students, for example, still generally prefer a print textbook to digital one (though having no textbook at all is their first choice, sigh...). Don't expect that everything you need will soon be available to you electronically at home in the middle of the night while you're munching on a pickle and desperately trying to finish that research project before the doom of morning strikes.

There is another growing movement, fed by newer "print on demand" technology, which supports self-publication without the enormous cost and distribution problems that once existed. You can now, for $1000 or less, publish your own book (even having it editorially reviewed) and have it distributed through normal book distribution channels without the need to have 5,000 copies in your basement. You can also publish e-books yourself through Amazon (Kindle), Scribd, and so on. Other than offering some editorial help, most such options have little if any real gatekeeping to them. Does quality suffer in the process? Possibly, though even without gatekeepers a lot of self-published authors are putting out high quality material that traditional publishers did not consider marketable.

1.5.2 Journals and magazines

The end is near for most paper versions of scholarly journals, magazines and newspapers. Virtually all scholarly journals now have electronic versions and offer subscribers the option to get a subscription in print or in electronic form. As the popularity of electronic versions grows (and it definitely is growing), more and more journals will appear electronically only.

Does all of this electronic publishing diminish quality? No. Most scholarly journals continue to use the gatekeeping process of *peer review*, by which submitted manuscripts are evaluated by scholars in the subject discipline in order to determine whether they are worthy to be published. This is a key distinction between a scholarly journal article and what you might find through the average Google search. A website on a topic may be as electronic as the journal article on the same topic, but the journal article has been evaluated by experts before it ever sees the light of day. Maybe those experts were biased or missed something important (like faked lab results), but on average the peer review process does provide more confidence that the article is reliable than you would have from a website on the same topic written by your Aunt Kate.

Before we get too far into this, though, we need to answer the more foundational question: *What is a scholarly journal?* The answer is not as simple as it once might have been. In general scholarly journals are publications from universities, academic societies and publishers devoted to producing academic work. The articles in them tend to be short on pictures and long on citations and reference lists (or bibliographies). In general, they are not accessible through a Google search and require you to search specialized academic databases available through academic libraries.

A serious challenge to the availability of scholarly journals has been price. The average annual journal subscription can range from fifty dollars to the cost of a new Toyota Corolla or more. In fact, the most expensive journals top $30,000 per year. Only the major universities can afford this kind of thing, thus limiting who can get access. A number of public bodies that fund research have done a double take and said, "Wait a minute. If we fund the research out of public money so that scholars can publish articles (getting paid nothing for doing so), and then publicly funded universities have to pay through the nose to acquire the journals that present the research we've already paid for once, where is the justice in it all?" Thus, increasingly, funding bodies are demanding that articles based on the research they have paid for must be made available online at no cost a set number of months after being published in a journal.

This open-access journal movement is growing in opposition to the outrageous costs of scholarly journals. Many new journals are being published directly online (after proper peer review) and are available for free to anyone who wants to read them. In this we have the best of the gatekeeping approach of traditional publishing and the free dissemination of information provided by the Internet. For searchable databases of open access journals, go to Directory of Open-Access Journals (over 4000 journals covered: **http://www. doaj.org/**), Open J-Gate (**http://openj-gate.org/**), or Electronic Journals Library (**http://rzblx1.uni-regensburg.de/ezeit/index. phtml?bibid=AAAAA&colors=7&lang=en**). Cornell University has **arXiv.org**, a collection of hundreds of thousands of papers in the sciences, computer science, and finance. Two highly touted public open access sites for academic resources are Public Library of Science (PLOS - **http://www.plos.org/**), which has created its own super journals, and the similar Open Library of Humanities (**http://www. openlibhums.org/**), still under development. (There are, of course, fakes and charlatans out there who produce supposedly "academic" online journals that are anything but. Several scholars have published lists of such predatory enterprises to help you be aware of them, for example, **http://scholarlyoa.com/individual-journals/**.)

The pay vs. open access distinction may not mean much to you if you are a student in higher education, because your institution provides journals as part of those incredibly high tuition fees you pay. Once you have graduated, however, and no longer have access to the same databases, open access journals may well be a lifeline. Unrestricted availability of journals will increase over the next couple of decades due to open access initiatives. The Compact for Open-

Access Publishing Equity (COPE - **http://www.oacompact.org/**) represents a movement within universities to provide scholars with funds to publish own their journal articles within open access venues, thus taking funds from expensive journal subscriptions and using the money to support open access.

I am noticing, as well, that an increasing number of scholars are self-archiving their published articles, putting them up on their own websites. A good tool to find such self-archived material is Google Scholar (**http://scholar.google.com**).

Despite this growing trend toward open access (available for free) journals, the majority of journals and magazines are not accessible full text through a Google search. Using a search engine on the Net generally gets you a very different class of information than does using a journal database through an academic library database. That is why using a search engine like Google or Bing for a large portion of your academic research will greatly limit your ability to do good work.

While not quite in the category of "journal articles," there is a growing interest in materials put into institutional repositories (think of electronic filing cabinets full of all kinds of academic information from in-house studies to dissertations). A great tool for finding such stuff is *Open*DOAR – The Directory of Open Access Repositories (**http://www.opendoar.org/**).

1.5.3 Government and corporate documents

Governments and other corporate groups continue to publish vast amounts of information. Due to the convenience of the WWW as a vehicle, more and more government information is moving to an online environment, where it is usually freely available. For directories to such resources, go to the International Government Information site at **http://www.lib.utexas.edu/government/world. html.**

1.5.4 The World Wide Web

We have already looked at advantages and challenges of the Web. Ongoing issues include use of the Web for highly negative purposes (terrorism, child pornography, etc.), quality challenges which become evaluation skill problems, the need to catalog the more important websites in order to provide better searchability, a demand for search engines that are better able to identify the information we most need, and a requirement for increased instruction for users so that they can optimize the Web experience.

1.5.5 Web 2.0

Web 2.0 is really a concept rather than a defined area of the Internet. If you imagine the average web page to be a publication, a one-way communication from the author to the reader, Web 2.0 forms those parts of the WWW that are interactive. We can include here social networking sites, blogs, wikis, online office tools like Google Docs, RSS feeds, forums, chat, messaging, e-mail, and so on. As a concept, Web 2.0 doesn't mean too much unless we look at what it does for information.

Take the wiki, software that enables you to create web pages that others can edit. One scholarly use for a wiki is in collaborative research projects where several people contribute to an article or some other piece of writing. Another is embodied in Wikipedia, an online encyclopedia that is shaped and revised by its users (and its smaller but more upscale cousin, Citizendium). More recently, sites like Draft (**https://draftin.com/**) are bringing a level of sophistication to collaborative writing, enabling each partner to save his/her own drafts of work done together.

Blogs offer opportunity for one person to post ideas and others to comment on those posts. Forums and chat enable two or more people to share information that can then be revised as the discussion proceeds. Social networking websites like Facebook, LinkedIn and Twitter are enhancing opportunities for people to group-think about information that is of interest to them.

Web 2.0 assumes that connectivity and collaboration create better ideas and make a better world than did one-way communication. This, of course, is not a new insight. Those pre-literate people who recounted their history around the campfire so many centurie ago were doing the same thing, but without our technology. need to be careful, however, not to put Web 2.0 above Web 1.0 traditional publishing as if collaboration gives our informati edge or credibility that one-way publication could not do. Certainly, a meeting of minds can often result in something better, but that is only the case if the collaborators actually know what they are talking about in the first place.

Truth to tell, much of what you find on Web 2.0 is simply the same old shallow thinking you find in a lot of person to person conversations. Information is no more valuable than the ability of its authors to know something about their subject and to think well. One thing a researcher must guard against is the assumption that because a number of people believe something, it is actually to be believed. Shared opinion is not fact. To move to a level of certainty you can live with, you need to evaluate information by acceptable standards.

[Some people are now discussing Web 3.0, which is essentially artificial intelligence -the ability of our technology to learn our preferences and anticipate our needs. While not yet a reality in most situations, 3.0, also sometimes called "The Semantic Web," will be a growing interest in the information world].

1.6 Primary and secondary information sources

Books and articles that come right from the context of a subject, straight out of the horse's mouth, so to speak, are *primary sources*. Books or articles that comment on the work of pioneers in a subject are called *secondary sources*.

Here are some examples:

Primary	Secondary
Text of Homer's *Iliad*	A modern scholarly study of Homer's *Iliad*
A scientific report written by the researcher	Someone else's analysis of the report
ʳsthand account by a witness of 9/11	Book on 9/11 by someone not there
ₑt person's account of street life	Analysis of research about street people
ʰhe Trials of Galileo	Commentary on the Trials of Galileo

Your professor may well want you to consult primary sources on your topic. The key to figuring out what is primary and what is secondary is to ask whether it is an eyewitness account, comes from the subject's time period, is written by a key scholar who developed the subject area, is a direct report of an experiment done by the author of the report, and so on. If so, you have a primary source. It's right from "the horse's mouth." If not, you likely have a secondary source. Secondary sources, in general, comment on, analyze or explain the material you would find in a primary source.

Clearing the Fog – What's all this talk about academic information?

[This is the first of a number of vignettes in this book that will answer specific issues in the research process. Each will come under the moniker of "Clearing the Fog." I hope you find them helpful.]

When Dorothy from the Wizard of Oz discovered she was now in the Land of Oz, she told her dog Toto, "We're not in Kansas anymore." If you've recently come into (or come back to) higher education, one of the first things to recognize is that this isn't Kansas, this is Academia. It has new rules, new players, new sources of information and new ways of doing research.

Some students decide that, if Google and Wikipedia were good enough for Kansas, they're good enough for Academia. But most soon discover that these tools just don't work very well for academic information. Why do I mean by "academic" in this sense? I could tell you that it's written by people with higher degrees (Ph.D.) or that it's peer reviewed (checked out by other scholars in the field before it can be published) or that it has to have notes and bibliographies.

But let's get the inside story: A piece of information is Academic if it is accepted as Academic by those in the field (like your professor). Each scholarly discipline has its favored sources of information, favored scholars, favored rules for doing research, favored rules of evidence, and so on. So your professor will tell you to make use of academic or scholarly or peer reviewed literature, and anything else will probably give you problems. In this environment, Google and

Wikipedia are far less helpful than the sophisticated academic search engines you'll be learning about in this book.

Many of us see a piece of information as acceptable if it "sounds right" or "looks right" or "makes sense." That's the essence of what we do with Google results, many of which don't give us clear data to tell us whether or not they are academic. But in the land of Academia, our gut feeling about information doesn't come near to helping us determine whether or not a professor will accept it. Many results are at a lay level, far below academic requirements. While academic library catalogs and databases are not perfect, they are much more likely to take us to genuine Academic Information.

So we need a change in mindset. Google and Wikipedia can be helpful, but they need to take third or fourth stage when we are in Academia. There are better tools for Academic Information, tools that will much more reliably get us the resources that a professor thinks are worthy.

1.7 Warning - Not all information is informative

We live in a world of many words. The sheer number of words we encounter every day is far greater than it ever has been in all human history. Some of those words come together into information that we can use. Others come together into nonsense. ***Not all information is equal.*** As you enter the information fog, there are signposts that can help you to discern genuine information from everything else that passes for the real thing. Ask yourself:

> ➢ What are the qualifications of the author of this informa-
> tion? (usually your best measure of quality)
> ➢ Who else believes this?
> ➢ Has this information been subjected to some kind of peer
> review or other form of gatekeeping?
> ➢ Are there vested interests at stake? For example, is that
> glowing description of the latest gadget actually authored

by the company that wants to sell it to you and knows that you have money?

> ➢ What are some good reasons for ***not*** believing it?

Get ready. We are about to enter the information fog. I hope you enjoy the journey.

1.8 For further study

Study guide

1. How do traditional societies handle information?
2. How did the invention of writing change the pre-writing methods by which a society handled information?
3. Name several significant changes to the world of information brought about by the printing press.
4. In the process of publishing information, what is "gatekeeping" and why is it significant?
5. In what ways is the creation of the World Wide Web a "revolution" for information?
6. Name some advantages of e-books. Can you think of drawbacks?
7. What is peer review in journal article publishing?
8. What is the open access movement, and why was it seen as necessary?
9. Where is the best place to find government documents?
10. What are the advantages and limitations of Web 2.0 for information?
11. Why is not all "information" actually informative?

2
Taking Charge

You may be saying to yourself, "I've never been good at this research thing. In fact, I don't think I have a good research project in me."

My response is, "Of course you don't. A good research project is *out there*, not inside you. What you have to do is get out there, find the data, work with it, and use it to make a difference."

At this point, be aware that we are talking about a certain kind of research here, not the social scientific or scientific research that involves experiments, but informational research such as you will find in the humanities or in literature reviews in the social sciences and sciences. This kind of research is all about verbal data and information, its discovery and use.

Now, before you run off to a dark alley frequented by black market sellers of data, let me offer you a safer alte[...] follows is a list of basic things that you need to have w[...] in order to turn your anxiety into a brilliant project, leading to an excellent product.

1. You need an intense desire to do a brilliant project, not just an average one. By definition, most people can do an average project.
2. You need to take your time and plan your research as a *strategy* rather than as a mad dash through libraries and databases. Google can provide you with a lot of resources, but Google results have a nasty tendency to be academically uneven. Even libraries know when you have reached the panic stage. The books close ranks and refuse to be found. Titles in the catalog trade places so that you can't locate them. The smell of musty books renders you numb and silly. Databases can do even worse things to you (don't ask).

Don't panic. Take it easy. Work out a plan and show that data who's in charge here.

3. You need to become a friend to structure. If you're the kind of person who might follow your schedule if you could remember where you put it, or someone who views a library fine as a reasonable price to pay for never having to think about a due date, research is going to be a battle for you. Structure and organization, from the beginning of the process all the way to its triumphant end, is crucial, no matter how much pain it will cost you to adapt.
4. You need to develop *lateral thinking*. Lateral thinking is akin to what happens in a football game: The quarterback has no openings at all. If he runs with the ball, he'll be flattened. So, instead of moving forward, he throws the ball sideways to another player who can move it forward. These are the steps:

> ➢ Recognize that your advance along one line is blocked.
> ➢ Abandon your approach and look for another.
> ➢ Run with your new approach and make it work (or try yet another).

It's like the old story of the truck that got stuck in a highway underpass. No towing vehicle of any kind could get it out, and so the workers were left with the option of dismantling an expensive truck or tearing down an even more expensive underpass until…

…until the light bulb went on and some bright lateral thinker suggested letting the air out of the truck's tires to *lower* it. Lateral thinking works beyond the obvious, in the realm of the creative.

Nurture this gift of lateral thinking within you. It will help greatly in that moment when all your cherished strategies have failed you and you still don't have the information you need.

Here's an example: Suppose you are doing research on the legal trial of Galileo and discover that every book with the texts of the verdicts against him is already signed out (something that actually happened to one of our students). Rather than thinking that the library has let you down, and you are doomed to wander the streets as a pathetic warning to others, think beyond the library (a lateral) and check to see if someone has posted the verdict transcripts on the Internet (they have: **http://www.law.umkc.edu/faculty/projects/ftrials/galileo/galileo.html**). That sort of thinking can save you from the disaster which often lurks, ready to bite the unsuspecting. (The student got a B+ on his project).

2.1 Wrestling with a topic

"I have to write a research paper on Climate Change. Right now I don't know much about it, so I better get into Wikipedia, then find two or three books. I'm hoping it's not a lot of work to pull everything together, but do I have enough for ten pages? Seems to me that it shouldn't take that many words to explain that the climate is messed up because of greedy human beings."

My response? *Oh, if I could only take the speaker of these words aside and explain a few things myself…*

Do you know how many glaring problems I found in that one brief comment? The most serious one is that our Climate Change, research-paper-writin' student is not going to end up with a research paper, because reading up on a topic and explaining it is not research.

"What?" you say. "Not research? The student has a topic – Climate Change – finds some stuff on it, and writes it up. If that's not a research paper, what is? Don't tell me it's not research."

All right, I won't. If I were a member of the tough-love school of thought, I would say something like this to you: "Go ahead and write your paper explaining everything you can find out about Climate Change (something your prof has read a thousand times in a thousand papers just like yours). Turn it in and wait for your professor to read the thing and give you the usual dreary mark. Obviously, you don't like your prof anyway, and that's why you keep doing this too him/ her. Professors are no strangers to the kinds of boredom you inflict on them. In fact they're quite used to the tedious task of marking your essays. You bore the professor, and the professor pays you back by giving you a C. Any illusion that you actually did research will be dead by the time you get the essay back."

Not *ever* wanting to be as harsh as that, at least without providing some help, let me ask instead: "What is good and useful research if it's not what you've been doing?" To answer, let's begin by looking at what it is not.

2.2 Elements of inadequate research

➤ Inadequate research assumes that the task is merely to gather data and synthesize it (the data-as-goal philosophy). Thus the typical student "research" project involves amassing data, reading and absorbing it, then regurgitating it back onto a fresh piece of paper (sorry for the disgusting image). The purpose of the project is simply to study up on something and then explain it, using other people's writings as a guide.
➤ Inadequate research deals in generalities and surveys. It loves a superficial look at a big topic, and it abhors depth and analysis.

25

> ➤ Inadequate research asks no analytical questions and makes no pretense of advancing knowledge. It's happy just to report on what has already been done, to summarize the past.

> ➤ Inadequate research is so boring that you should be surprised that it ever gets completed, let alone foisted on your longsuffering professor.

2.3 The key to great research

What's the point of doing research, then? A flip response might be that a professor or employer told you to do a research project, and you're just following orders. But that's not the answer I'm looking for.

You should recognize first that there is a big difference between seeing data as a goal and data as a tool. What do I mean? Consider these two models:

Data as goal: Find out everything you can about a topic → Explain what you've learned.

Data as tool: Gather basic information about your topic → Identify a problem or issue related to that topic → Use the data you collect as a *tool* (a means) to try to solve that problem or issue.

Let's consider the Climate Change (CC) as an example:

Data as goal: Find out what you can about CC and its causes → Explain all this in a paper.

Data as tool: Read some basic data on the CC → Discover an issue (e.g. the persistent counter-argument that current climate change is a natural phenomenon rather than something caused by greedy human beings) → Ask a question like this one, "How convincing is the scientific support for climate change as a natural phenomenon as opposed to being primarily the result of human activity?"

You may find this approach a bit strange. Not only does "data as tool" ask you not to cover the whole topic (aren't you supposed to cover the whole topic?) but it focuses on an issue or controversy rather than merely explaining what you can find out about the topic in general. Its purpose is analysis and problem-solving.

But consider the alternative. You set a goal of retelling the CC story, then go through the horror of finding a bunch of sources, reading them, deciding what details to synthesize, snagging some good quotes, and making sure you cite your sources properly. After all that, you know you'll only get a mediocre grade unless you do something brilliant. But you don't have the time, and what is "brilliant" in a research paper anyway? There seems to be no clear path to going from mediocre to an A when you are only reporting on what you read. No wonder students seem to hate research papers so much.

Have you ever had a professor tell you that he/she expects critical thinking in your paper? If so, you have probably wondered how critical thinking works in research. So here is the answer - It involves grappling with a problem, issue or controversy. The approach I'm suggesting in this book should take you a long way in the direction of genuine critical thinking, but first we need to address a couple of questions:

1. Does the professor actually expect you to write on the *whole* topic? – In a very few cases, the answer will be "yes," and you'll have to do what the prof requires. But in most situations, professors expect you to narrow down by choosing only one aspect of the larger topic.
2. Does the professor want description (data as goal) or analysis (data as tool)? – Once again, a few profs may merely want a summary of what you studied, but most (especially those who refer to "critical thinking") want you to address a problem, using data as a means to analyze the issues and come up with some kind of solution.

If you are at all in doubt, contact your professor and explain to him/her what you want to do. Get advice. Not checking in advance may have you getting one of those fated comments: "This fails to meet the goals of the assignment," along with a low grade. If you check before you start your research, chances are the professor will give you a green light and maybe even a "well done" at the end.

The key to genuine research is a *good question* that addresses a problem calling for analysis. Without posing a question, nothing you are doing can be called research.

What, then, constitutes a good question? Here the situation becomes more complex, because you need to begin rethinking the whole research process. Later in this chapter, we will consider the actual strategies involved in getting a topic ready for research, but for now let's interface with some basic principles.

The first of these is that most any research topic presented to you needs some work before it is viable enough to use. Assume, unless you know otherwise, that the topic is too broad to be workable short of writing a book on it. A topic like the Climate Change or Theology of Suffering or Economic Conditions in Russia today is not likely to inspire depth of analysis because you don't have space in ten or twenty pages to be anything but superficial. You are going to have to focus on a more narrow aspect of the topic so that you can deal with it in depth.

Consider a bathtub with a gallon of water in it as opposed to a bathroom sink with a gallon of water in it. Which is deeper? The sink, because its borders are narrower. The same principle works in a research project—the narrower your focus, the more chance you have of getting some depth into your project.

Assume, second, that you are going to have to develop a sound working knowledge of the topic before you're going to know what to do with it. I see a lot of students floundering for hours at the beginning of a project because they really don't understand the basics of the subject matter they are dealing with.

Third, and I repeat this for a reason, assume that you may have to negotiate with the professor who gave you the project. You need to know that what you propose is actually going to fly with the person ultimately responsible for your fate. But cheer up—professors are generally thrilled by any tiny evidence of creativity in their students. Go to your professor and ask politely, "Would you mind if I pursued *this* issue raised by Climate Change? It looks really interesting." Your professor's heart will turn to mush and he or she will say quietly, "Yes, all right," while inside he or she is shouting, "A new approach! I'm getting a new approach!"

Caution: Don't ever say, "May I write on Water Pollution instead?" This signals to the professor that you don't like the topic you were offered, and you most certainly will end up having to write on it anyway.

2.4 A model for research

What, then, is research all about? Here's a model:

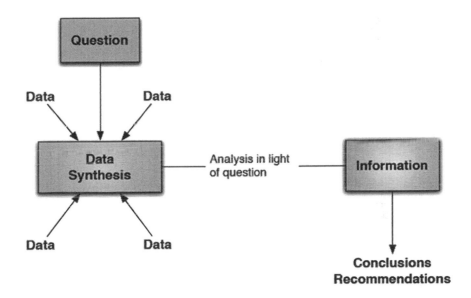

Explanation?

> ➤ You begin with a question.
> ➤ You collect data.
> ➤ You synthesize it (put it together in some coherent form).
> ➤ You analyze the data in light of the question (figuring out how each piece of data could be used to answer the question). This analysis turns data into information

(processed data that is ready to be used to answer the question).

➤ You come up with conclusions and recommendations.

The key to the whole thing is that *you need to move beyond merely gathering data, reorganizing it (data synthesis) and reporting on what you read.* When a question is injected into the mix, the data becomes more than an end in itself and turns into the raw material needed to answer the question. The result is analysis that turns data into information that can then be used to reach an answer. This may still seem a bit "foggy" to you, but we are about to embark on a journey that will make things much clearer.

For a tutorial on the research process, go to: **http://www.twu. ca/library/Flash_Tutorials/informational_research/index.html.**

2.5 Getting started in research

2.5.1 Getting a working knowledge through reference sources

Before you go off in all directions at once (like a draw-and-quarter execution in merry old England), get a grip on yourself. As a librarian, I see the same awkward experience repeated day after day—students walking uneasily through the front door of the library, then stopping, frozen to the ground.

I know what's buzzing through their battered minds: "I'm here, I'm actually here in the library, about to start researching my topic, and I don't have a *clue* what to do. Time has stopped, and people are staring at me. Why can't I move my limbs? Why is my head so numb? Maybe I'll die here, rooted to the floor, and they'll bronze me as a monument to the unknown student."

Take heart - it doesn't have to be like this. Let me give you the first step you need to take so that you break free from bondage. It's simple. *Get a working knowledge of your topic.*

Right, so what's a working knowledge? Here's a basic definition:

You have a working knowledge of a topic when you can talk about it for one minute without repeating yourself.

To start your research, all you need to do is acquire one minute's knowledge.

"One minute?" you say. "I've been told I have to present a fifteen page research paper with a dozen footnotes including appropriate journal references (whatever they are). Why talk to me about one minute of working knowledge?" I do so for the same reason that you take a flashlight with you to avoid stumbling around in the dark. A working knowledge gives you the basics of a topic and enough light so that you won't hurt yourself as you move on into more complicated territory. It isn't complete knowledge, but it's enough to tell you what the topic entails, what its boundaries are, even what some of its controversies, mysteries and dangers might be.

So where do you get a working knowledge? You could simply go on the Internet, where virtually anything is explained by some site or other. But, if you don't know much about the topic to begin with, the Net may not be the best source, because it's not easy to judge the reliability of information on a new topic. (We'll deal with that issue more fully in Chapter Six).

You would do better to investigate authoritative *reference sources* first. All academic libraries have recognized reference tools that provide concise and authoritative information on virtually any topic you might think of. Reference books will generally appear in the form of dictionaries or encyclopedias on general or specific topics. As well, handbooks, atlases—in fact, any tool that involves looking up brief information—may be found in a reference collection. You would be amazed at how many topic areas have dictionaries or encyclopedias devoted to them. From broader disciplines like psychology or chemistry to narrower ones (as, for example, the *Encyclopedia of Christmas*) you will find good, brief information on virtually anything you want, unless it is a very recent topic.

Many references sources are available in electronic form, but you (or your library) need to subscribe with real money to the best of these. The higher quality reference sources are not available without cost on the Internet, though some older or lite versions of reference tools are appearing there for free. Your most useful venue for good reference information is still a library, either in print form or electronically through the library catalog or some other database.

So you're working in a library context and wondering how to find a reference book that will give you information on marriage customs of the Kurdish people. You could do some sort of keyword search or wander the physical shelves of the reference collection, but there's an easier way to find what you want. *Think of the broad subject within which you topic lies.* In this case, you are looking at customs of a particular culture. Thus you could look up a subject heading in your library's catalog like MANNERS AND CUSTOMS - ENCYCLOPEDIAS to find a reference source like *Worldmark Encyclopedia of Cultures and Daily Life.* Then just look up "Kurds." Alternatively, you might find this reference source with a keyword search on cultures AND (encyclopedia or dictionary).

Let's try another example of the sort of material you're looking for in a working knowledge. Suppose you were taking a History of the Middle Ages course and one of the topics was the Lollards. The *what?* Let me give you a clue: They were a group of religious people who flourished in the late Medieval and early Reformation period. What sort of a reference source would you use for Lollards? How about a dictionary of medieval history or of church history? If you check into a reference source or two, following the famous Five Ws of inquiry, you might discover the following:

Who?

The Lollards were followers of John Wycliffe; more generally, the term was used of any serious critic of the English church in the late Middle Ages. Key figures in the movement were Nicholas of Hereford, William Swinderby, and John Purvey.

What?

Their teachings, summed up by the Twelve Conclusions of 1395, included personal faith, divine election, and the Bible as the sole authority in religion. They asserted that every person had the individual right to read and interpret the Bible.

Where?

The movement existed primarily in England and Scotland.

When?

It began in the 1380s (AD) and went underground after 1431, due to persecution. The movement declined in the mid-1400s but revived about 1490. It figured prominently in the congregational dissent of the seventeenth century and in the rise of the Hussites in Bohemia.

Why?

The Lollards claimed to be a reaction to the control over human life and spirituality that was exercised by the Church of the time.

My two reference sources were: *Dictionary of the Middle Ages* and *Oxford Dictionary of the Christian Church*.

Have I convinced you of the need for a working knowledge? If not, you're going to end up spinning your wheels and wasting time. Unless you start with a working knowledge you will inevitably find yourself sinking the moment you reach deeper waters.

2.5.2 Excursus: Wikipedia, the professor's dilemma

A lot of students use Wikipedia, the free online encyclopedia with an awesome range of articles on every conceivable topic (**http://en.wikipedia.org/wiki/Main_Page**).

Technically speaking, the Wikipedia phenomenon should have been a disaster from the beginning. Normally encyclopedias are created by an editor who assigns known experts in their fields to write articles that are then then carefully studied for accuracy and clarity before publication. Wikipedia's articles are written by the "hoi polloi" – the public, you and me, any Jane or Joe Blow who wants to add an entry. Sure, there are safeguards to help maintain a measure of objectivity and preserve a structure for what is included in a good article. But not only can anyone write an article, most anyone can edit an article too, though changes to certain entries may need to be verified by other users. In fact, the edits that actually stick (without being changed back by one of the volunteer watchdogs who guard articles from being vandalized) are those for which a large number of people agree that the change is needed.

Stephen Colbert, the TV satirist, has coined the term "wikiality." According to Wikipedia: "Colbert defined wikiality as 'truth by consensus' (rather than fact), modeled after the approval-by-consensus format of Wikipedia." (For more fun criticism see the Wikipedia article "Wikipedia in culture.") Colbert, on one of his shows, called on all his viewers to test his "truth by consensus" theory by changing the entry on African Elephants to say that the population of elephants had tripled in the past six months (it hadn't). Wikipedia ended up having to restrict editing on African elephant material due to the large numbers of changes that were made.

All kidding aside, is Wikipedia good or bad? That's a tough question to answer. The information in it is often amazingly reliable, but there are also errors. Many professors have simply opted for the safest road and told their students not to use it. Wikipedia itself tells its readers not to include its articles in research bibliographies. On the other hand, the journal *Nature* did a study that found the mistakes in Wikipedia to be only a few more in number than those in *Encyclopedia Britannica*. *Britannica* answered with an angry rebuttal claiming poor methodology, but *Nature* has stuck to its original findings. [*Nature* 438, no. 7070 (December 15, 2005): 900-901; **http://corporate.britannica.com/britannica_ nature_response.pdf; http://www.nature.com/press_releases/ Britannica_response.pdf**].

So, to use or not to use Wikipedia? I'm more on the side of "use with reasonable caution." Since it is an encyclopedia, you would not in most cases even consider including it in a research bibliography. Research papers normally don't contain reference book information, which is just background for your own development in a topic, unless the reference article is several pages long. You likely will use the Great W to develop your working knowledge or to plunder the often useful bibliographies at the ends of article. But be careful. Don't rely *just* on Wikipedia. What you read there at any one moment might be a sabotage of an article (to be corrected in a couple of hours) or something that is just wrong and hasn't yet been noticed. Compare what you read in Wikipedia with other, traditionally published, reference sources.

[For further discussion, see Badke, W. (2008). What to do with Wikipedia. *Online, 32(2)*, 48-50. Available: **http://www.infotoday. com/online/mar08/Badke.shtml**].

2.5.3 Full text reference tools

There is a growing number of reference works that are available in either print or online format. Each academic library will have its own collection of such tools, often available through your library home page or catalog. These resources are different from Google search results or Wikipedia (see Chapter Two) in that they have come through the more traditional publishing process of editors and expert writers (gatekeeping). Your profs will thus find them reliable, even in electronic form. Remember, though, that reference articles don't normally appear in your research bibliographies unless the articles are of substantial size

On the World Wide Web, the availability of reference sources that use traditional production and editing procedures is pretty limited. Here's a wildly eclectic list of high quality openly available online reference sources chosen at a whim for reasons I no longer recall except that I liked them:

> ➢ *Cambridge History of English and American Literature* (1907-1921, searchable by keyword and thesaurus): **http://www.bartleby.com/cambridge/**
> ➢ *Encyclopedia Smithsonian*: **http://www.si.edu/ Encyclopedia_SI/**
> ➢ *Stanford Encyclopedia of Philosophy*: **http://plato. stanford.edu/**
> ➢ *The Canadian Encyclopedia (Historica Canada)*: **http://www.thecanadianencyclopedia.com**

> *Baker's Evangelical Dictionary of Biblical Theology*: **http://www.biblestudytools.com/dictionaries/bakers-evangelical-dictionary/**

> *WolframMathWorld* (a mathematics encyclopedia): **http://mathworld.wolfram.com/**

> *Computer Desktop Encyclopedia* (definitions of terms in technology and computing): **http://www.computerlanguage.com/**

2.6 Finding a good question

An investigation of a topic is not research until you have focused it around a solid question that addresses a problem or issue. But how do you come up with a research question that is going to work?

2.6.1 *Narrow your topic to one aspect.* One big reason why research can fail is that the researcher is trying to conquer the world with one project. You simply cannot cover everything about teen suicide or abortion or the causes of World War One or why the moon *isn't* made of green cheese. You have to choose an aspect that is distinct enough that you can really work with it. Otherwise you end up with a superficial survey, because you are trying to cover too much.

The broader your focus, the more shallow your paper. You want depth. Avoid questions that survey and then compile large amounts of data. The resulting projects will never dwell on any one thing for more than a few lines, and they will have bibliographies that cover a wide variety of issues. Instead of looking at the life of Napoleon, analyze why he lost the Battle of Waterloo. Narrow is good; big sweeping topics breed ugliness and despair (or at least boredom).

2.6.2 *Identify controversies or questions related to your narrowed approach.* There's no point in re-describing what has already been described, since research is not merely the gathering of information but the use of information to solve a problem. Information is not an end in itself, but a means to help solve a problem. To tell me the life story of Napoleon or explain the problem of teenage drinking is to do what every reference source on the subject has already done. You are simply re-packaging existing information into a summary of the topic. This is where those excruciatingly boring and superficial "research" papers come from. You must vow never to write another one. Find something worth investigating and investigate it.

In the case of teenage drinking you might want to evaluate various kinds of public service advertising to determine which is most effective in reaching problem drinkers. (This could lead to the research question: Which form of public advertising is best able to reach teenage problem drinkers?)

2.6.3 Thesis statements

What if, instead of a research question, you have been asked to provide a *thesis statement?* Is there a difference? Yes. Research questions and thesis statements are actually two sides of the same coin. A research question introduces a problem to be solved. A thesis statement is *a tentative answer* to a research question. It is tentative in that your written research project is going to have to test your thesis and hopefully show it to be correct. Thus, if your research question were:

To what extent should the U.S. government have known of the risk of the New York 9/11 disaster before it happened?

Your thesis statement could be:

There was sufficient warning of a New York 9/11-type disaster before it happened, so the U.S. government should have been well prepared for its occurrence.

Or your thesis might be:

Despite the signs of a potential terrorist attack, the U.S. government did not have sufficient information to be prepared for the New York 9/11 disaster.

For either of these possible thesis statements the onus would be on you to provide convincing evidence to support your thesis (as well as giving due consideration to contradicting evidence).

The thesis statement route does have a tendency to create a bias, giving you the temptation to overlook or minimize evidence that does not support your case. Thus, unless you have been told to provide a thesis statement, using a research question is more likely to have you entering the investigation with an open mind.

2.6.4 Research questions - The bad and the ugly

Some research questions simply won't work. They are doomed to failure and will produce research projects that are walking disasters, if they can walk at all. One way to recognize a good question is to know what the bad and ugly ones look like, so here are some examples. [APPENDIX ONE will give you more examples and deeper explanations, so go there next]:

1. **The question that isn't there.** Imagine the horror of someone reading your "research" paper and looking desperately but in vain for a question or even the suggestion of an issue or problem to be addressed, only to discover that there is none. "What's the purpose of your paper?" the professor muses. "To tell me something I could have read in any reference book? To tell me once again what everyone knows already? To put me to sleep with your knowledge of trivia? To punish me for not being your favorite professor?"

2. **The fuzzy question.** Sure, there's a question, but it isn't clear enough to make it possible to answer. Asking something like, "Why was Saddam Hussein the way he was?" is no help at all. What way *was* he? Are you talking about his role as dictator of Iraq, his use of chemical weapons, his oil strategy, or just what? Until you clarify your focus, you will find no way to answer your question without simply surveying everything the world knows about him (which would likely depress the life out of you, not to mention your poor professor).

3. **The multi-part question.** *You must never let more than one research question intrude into a research project.* The shotgun approach is out. Research identifies *one* question, deals with that question through analytical use of data, and ***then quits.*** Never *ever* get stuck in the kind of proposal that says, "Why did the financial meltdown of 2008 happen? Should people have foreseen it? Were the governmental measures to solve it the right ones to use? How can we prevent future meltdowns?" Your second, third and fourth questions are loose torpedoes on your own ship. They will sink you because they'll kill your focus or at least broaden it into something too big to deal with. *One question per research project is all you need or want.*

4. **The open-ended question**. This is often expressed as, "What are the implications of…" or "What were the results of…," thus encouraging you to produce a list of possible outcomes. Open-ended questions tend to be troublesome simply because they fragment your conclusion into many possible answers and thus destroy any hope of the paper having a single-minded goal. The way to cure this kind of question is to close the end. For example, instead of asking, "What were the implications of the end of WWII?" you could ask, "To what extent was the defiance of the French *Ministry of Industrial Production* by the automotive company, Renault, the reason for its success following WWII?" You have set out only one possible area to study instead of many and thus closed up the end or goal for your project. The focus of the implications is now much narrower than it was.

5. **The question that will not fly.** Some questions are amazingly inventive, but they try to answer problems that the data simply will not answer. Asking, "Is today's generation smarter than the previous one because it knows how to text message?" (a real question asked by an undergraduate in one of my classes) may look cool, but exactly how would you gather relevant data to answer it? If your question is ambitious, ask yourself whether it's even possible to find an answer. If not, curb your enthusiasm.

Summary comment:

In my experience, the best research questions are *simple* ones that still require a good deal of analysis to answer. If you start with a highly complex question, your analysis is going to have to be that much more complex. The ideal is to have a question so simple and clear that you can actually see the goal before you, in your mind's eye, as well as the path you need to take to get there. Yet the path must require some struggles before you get to the answer. And it must be capable of leading you to concrete evidence that supports your answer. You use the evidence you gather as a means to discover the solution rather than as the solution itself.

[For more on research questions, including many more examples of both the good and the bad, see APPENDIX ONE. Yes, really. See APPENDIX ONE. You'll thank yourself later.]

Clearing the Fog – Research is a conversation, not a soliloquy

To be, or not to be, that is the question:
Whether 'tis Nobler in the mind to suffer
The Slings and Arrows of outrageous Fortune,
Or to take Arms against a Sea of troubles... (Shakespeare,
Soliloquy from *Hamlet*)

A soliloquy is a revelation of a character's inner thoughts, sometimes reflecting on events of the past but always remaining personal. It is one person speaking his/her own mind in isolation from others. Research is not that.

When you do research, you enter into a conversation. Imagine that you are sitting in a room with several great scholars, each of whom has a perspective on the research question you're addressing. You listen to them and enjoy the way they debate with one another. Then you join in by evaluating their positions and perhaps coming to some conclusions about your own. It's all very civilized but it can get intense.

RESEARCH IS A CONVERSATION

Smith says...

Jones has found that...

Blackstone thinks Smith is out to lunch and has his own findings

Dickson agrees with Jones

Corban finds some value in Smith but also sees merit in Blackstone

You make sense of it all, and offer evidence for your judgment of who is most to be believed

Research is a conversation. In too much of what is called "research" these days, the views of other scholars are just filler built around what you, the writer, want to say (your soliloquy). With such a misguided approach, the only reason to include material from other sources is that your professor said you needed 5 books and 3 articles. You assume they all pretty much say the same thing, and you wonder why you need all this stuff to explain something that maybe needs only two sources.

But that's not "research." Research is a conversation, even a debate. Each of the voices who are speaking through the information you've found has something to contribute, and your task is to make sense of what they are saying, critique it, and come out with your own conclusion on the matter. You pay attention to the differences in positions and you take seriously the contribution each source is making. In the end, it's your own conclusion that matters most, but you haven't really succeeded at research until you've let the conversation happen.

2.7 The preliminary outline

Chances are that, if you're like most people, you're not in any mood early in a research project to be thinking about an outline for your final product. People who start working on their outline before they've done their first catalog search are either sick or lost souls, because any sensible person knows that you compose your outline AFTER you write your paper.

Wrong.

If you want to spare yourself a ton of grief, start on a preliminary outline now. Why? Simply because you need to build yourself as clear a road map as possible in order to get your research done efficiently (by "efficiently," I mean that you will save time). A research question may be crucial to giving your search a goal, but an outline is crucial to tracing the path you need to follow in order to reach that goal.

What's a preliminary outline? It is simply three to five points that you think you'll need to cover if you want to answer the research question. Don't worry - you won't necessarily be bound to the outline, like the albatross around the neck of the Ancient Mariner. It's preliminary and open to modification. Yet, though it may change over time, you need to start on an outline now. It's your roadmap for your research project. Without a roadmap, you'll soon be on some dead end trail with no place to turn around and the search and rescue people looking for you.

How do you develop a preliminary outline? Begin with your research question and dig your outline out of terminology in your question. Suppose you have the following question: *Was the American belief that Saddam Hussein had weapons of mass destruction before the beginning of the Iraq War of 2003 based on plausible evidence?* The question itself gives clues for a preliminary outline. You need to look at evidence that he possibly did have such weapons, evidence that he didn't, and the reasons why the US found the evidence that he did so compelling.

Once you have a few basic elements, try to organize them into a rough order. For example:

> ➤ Introduction to the history of belief in Saddam's weapons of mass destruction
> ➤ The Evidence available at the time that Saddam had weapons of mass destruction
> ➤ Evaluation of the plausibility of the evidence available
> ➤ Conclusion

Essentially, the outline is drawn right out of the research question, like this:

Was the American belief that Saddam Hussein had weapons of mass destruction when the Iraq War of 2003 began based on plausible evidence?

- Introduction to the history of belief in Saddam's weapons of mass destruction

- The evidence available at the time that Saddam had weapons of mass destruction

- Evaluation of the plausibility of the information available

- Conclusion

Take note that your preliminary outline is just that—preliminary. You can change it and develop it at will, or even scrap it and create a new one. Your professor only needs to see the final version, so initial blips and failures will stay private. But you do need to get some sort of outline going as soon as you have a research question, because the outline tells you what you need to cover in order to write the paper that answers your research question.

2.8 How about a few good examples?

2.8.1 "The thought of Erasmus of Rotterdam"

Your much beloved philosophy professor has assigned you "The Thought of Erasmus of Rotterdam." Having studied a few philosophy dictionaries (and taken a peek at Wikipedia), you narrow your topic to "The Humanism of Erasmus of Rotterdam." You *could*, at this point, decide to begin your paper with "Erasmus of Rotterdam was born in the year…" You *could* go on to explain what he taught about humanism, and then conclude, "It is clear that Erasmus was an important thinker in the realm of humanism, who deserves more attention."

This method is called "regurgitating your sources." It establishes a conduit between your books and your typing hand without ever really engaging your brain. It also makes for a very dull paper. Professors fall asleep over dull papers.

On the other hand, you could be analytical. Having read your sources and affixed your working knowledge firmly in your mind, you could engage your brain in finding a research question. How about asking this: *Why did Erasmus become increasingly pessimistic about human nature in his later years?* This would certainly demand study of Erasmus' humanism, but it would go further. Now you have the makings of an approach that could contribute something fresh and exciting to the topic.

2.8.2 "Teenage Alcoholism"

You are taking a sociology class and are supposed to write a paper on "Teenage Alcoholism." I suppose you could regurgitate some statistics, recite a few case studies, and then conclude, "This is a serious problem for which we need to find answers." Or you might narrow your topic and ask a genuine research question like this one: *Of the most common school-based models used to address Teenage Alcoholism, which shows the most promise?*

2.8.3 "Climate Change"

For a course on environmental issues, you have been assigned, "Climate Change." You could write up a true horror story about the loss of Arctic ice, along with a warning at the end that "somebody" needs to do something. A descriptive paper like this one would string together quotations from current leaders in the debate who are decrying the way our leaders studiously ignore the problem. Your conclusion could read, "Thus it is clear that governments must change their attitudes." You have narrowed your topic, but you've failed to apply an analytical, problem-solving research question to it. An analytical research paper would go further, perhaps looking at the cost to the world economy that comes from saving a few bucks by ignoring climate change. Your question could be: *Is it ultimately good for the economy in times of economic downturn to devote less money to addressing climate change?*

2.8.4 "Behaviorism as a model for social engineering"

You have been given a topic which is fairly narrow but still covers a lot of territory. Behaviorism as a social engineering model entails a lot of ins and outs. Why not narrow it down to the Behaviorism model put forward by B.F. Skinner? You might now take the easy way and summarize his book *Walden Two*, which is Skinner's model for social engineering (but easy is the way that leads to destruction). Or you could ask: *How would B.F. Skinner revise his model of human living in Walden Two if darker basic human traits like selfishness, aggressiveness, and deceit were taken into account?* (things which Skinner blissfully ignored).

One final note of caution: **Always clear your narrowed-down topic and brilliant research question with your professor or supervisor**. Disaster could be awaiting you if you don't. Of course, some of us like to flirt with disaster. Do you feel lucky?

2.9 For further study

Study guide

1. What three things do you need to seek if you want to do research well?
2. Name four elements of "inadequate research." Why is each an enemy of "great" research?

3. Define a "working knowledge" of your topic and explain why it's important to have one.
4. What is a "reference source?"
5. What should we do with Wikipedia?
6. What are the steps to finding a good research question?
7. Formulate a definition of genuine research.
8. Describe the difference between a research question and a thesis statement. Why is the former often a safer approach?
9. Describe the following types of bad research questions: The fuzzy question, the multi-part question, the open-ended question, the question that will not fly.
10. Why do you need a preliminary outline early in the research process?

Practice with research questions

Go to APPENDIX One and try *A1.2 Practice with Research Questions*

Assignment for a research project of your own

1. Choose a topic of interest to you.

2. Get basic information for a working knowledge of your topic from at least one specialized reference source from the library (not a general encyclopedia but a subject specialized reference source like *Dictionary of Developmental & Educational Psychology*) and from Wikipedia. Compare and contrast the ways in which the library reference source and Wikipedia deal with the topic.

3. Summarize in about half a page what you've learned (your working knowledge), *listing the reference sources you used.*

4. Present three or four possible research questions related to the topic, in question form, which might be suitable for a research essay. These questions should deal with one aspect of the topic, as narrowly as possible. They should not be easy to answer, nor should they be intended to describe what is already known. Try to make them as analytical as you can (seeing them as problem-solving questions rather than as an attempt to compile existing data). Try turning each of them into a thesis statement.

5. Choose the one question or thesis statement you think is best.

6. Create a preliminary outline based on your question.

Teaching tool

For a short animated tutorial on the research model presented here, go to:
http://www.twu.ca/library/Flash_Tutorials/informational_research/index.html.

3

Database Searching with Keywords and Hierarchies

It's time to begin traveling into the realm of e-searching, a land much more complex and (frankly) more exciting than you ever imagined when you first Googled something and actually got what you were looking for. So pack your bags. We're going to be out there in the land of search for at least two chapters. On the plus side, by the end of our exploration you're sure to be a better and wiser searcher.

3.1 What's a database?

Chances are that you fancy yourself as a tech genius and the word "database" doesn't sound like "root canal." But this doesn't mean you have a full perception of what a database does or have learned how to *search* a database quickly and effectively, coming up with the results you need most of the time.

Then again, you may not yet have warmed to the possibility of search tools beyond Google, nor do you think of journal databases as friendly creatures ever ready to help you, like big Saint Bernards in avalanche territory. For you, "database" may well be a bad word, a frightening word. If that's your situation, let me give you a soothing message: "Fear not."

Actually, databases are everywhere, and I guarantee you've already searched one or more though not necessarily with all the skill you needed. When was the last time you looked up a phone number with one of those 411 sites on the Web or used an online library catalog? These are databases. Here's a definition:

A database is any collection of data that can be retrieved using organized search procedures.

Many people today are hotshots on various devices. They can make the keys sing, the app activate and the pages scroll. They think that, because they know their way around the technology, they are also expert searchers. Not so. In fact, few of us understand database searching well enough to do it effectively, let alone efficiently.

Case in point—I once found the dregs of a search on an electronic journal database. The database itself had over 1,000,000 article citations listed in it, and this searcher had typed in the keyword *Johnson*, resulting in 4,386 hits. That is, 4,386 descriptive records of journal articles related to the name *Johnson* had become available to him/her. What was worse, the searcher had actually started pulling up each of those 4,386 entries in turn, looking for the right one. Ten hours later, red-eyed, fingers like angry claws…one can only imagine the *angst* that this session created.

You may know how to make technology work for you, but disaster will befall you if you are limited in your ability to search databases. It's a whole lot more than throwing a few words into a search box. Fear not, however. I'm about to show you things you probably never knew you didn't know.

3.2 Keyword searching

The keyword has become the main tool of research in today's electronic database environment, and many people assume that keywords are their friends.

That's not exactly the case. Have you ever had "friends" you trusted only to a certain point, because you had to tell yourself to watch your back when you were around them? You knew they appeared decent and could be helpful, but they could just as easily betray you or do you harm. That's the keyword - useful, handy, but potentially a backstabber. Keywords represent the Wild West of database searching - bold and exciting, but risky and just as likely to mess up your life.

In the next chapter we'll look at a more civilized and sophisticated way to search many databases (with controlled vocabularies), but for now, let's do what we can to tame the fickle keyword.

3.2.1 Database basics for keyword searching

We start with the principle that every database is made up of words. The search tools we use, though inherently unintelligent when it comes to real thinking, are experts at recognizing words. To understand how keyword searching works, you need to know that most academic databases contain descriptive *records* that stand in the place of actual content when you search. That is, you are not actually searching the content but descriptions of the content. For example, every time a new book is added to a library, it is processed by creating a descriptive *catalog record*, which might look something like this:

LC control no.: 2012371524
Type of material: Book (Print, Microform, Electronic, etc.)
Personal name: Gleick, James.

Main title: The information : a history, a theory, a flood / James Gleick.
Published/Created: New York : Vintage Books, c2011.
Description: 526 p. : ill. ; 21 cm.
ISBN: 9781400096237
Subjects: Information theory —History.
           Information technology —History.
Notes: Includes bibliographical references (p. 477-503) and index.
Call number: Q355 .G55 2011

    This is, in essence, a description of the main details that the database needs to have available in order for you to identify and find the book. When you search the database by keyword, you will be looking for *significant words* in this record. You are actually searching descriptive records, not the book content itself, at this stage. Now, imagine that there are thousands of records, and you're interested in finding a list of books about interactive aspects of the Internet. You should be able to think of important words (= *keywords*) and input them into a search box. The database search program will then look for those words in each of the **records** in the database and will download to your screen any records that have the words you've asked for.

    To find books on interactive aspects of Internet use, you might search book titles in the database like this:

Interact* and Internet (Don't worry about the search form yet. We'll get to the details below).

    You will get records for books with titles like:

* *Interaction and collective intelligence in Internet computing*
* *Digital borderlands : cultural studies of identity and interactivity on the Internet*
* *Murder on the Net : a guide to logging on and using the Internet via an interactive murder mystery adventure*

(All of the above are real book titles.)

Insight #1: *With keyword searching, what you type is what you get. The search program you use cannot do much to interpret your request or give you the next best solution (though some may search on a few synonyms). All it can do is identify the words you ask for and give you the relevant data. Garbage in, garbage out.*

Notice one little trick I performed above - *truncation* (sometimes inaccurately called *wildcard*). With many keyword searches, you can type part of a word, then add an asterisk (*) or sometimes a question mark (?) or dollar sign ($), depending on what symbol the database uses, and the search software will look for every word that begins with the letters you typed. E.g., **interact*** will ask create a search for search for **interact**, **interactive**, **interaction**, even **interactivity**. (Most search engines on the Net do not use truncation.)

You can also sometimes do **middle truncation** (the real meaning of "wildcards"), in which truncation is done within a word (e.g., Wom*n for Woman or Women).

Even given the variations allowed through truncation, keyword searching demands a whole lot of precision. The search function in the database will only find the exact thing you want it to find. If you mistakenly type **intract*** instead of **interact***, the search function will give you data with words like **intractable**, thus spoiling your whole day and making you grouchy in social environments. So your mother was right: Spell it correctly the first time.

3.2.2 Boolean searching

Many years before computers, a man named George Boole invented a mathematical system that enabled people to visualize combinations of various classes of things. Tech people have taken his system into the world of database searching in order to formulate searches where two or more terms are used. Let's look at some of the basic commands used in Boolean searching:

The OR Command

Suppose that you're looking in a database for information about cars. You realize that a keyword search will pull out all information that has the word "cars" in it, but some people use the term "automobiles." How can you tell the database search program to look for *both* words at the same time and give you data whether that data uses the word "cars" *or* the word "automobiles?"

In a situation in which you are searching for synonyms— different words that mean the same thing—use the OR command. Let's visualize it this way:

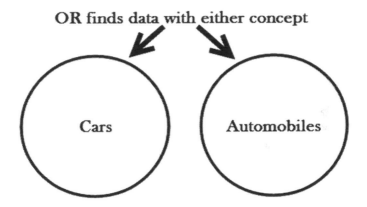

That is, you are saying, "Database Search Program, please give me everything on cars or on automobiles. I don't care which." So you will get all the data with "cars" in it, plus all the data with "automobiles" in it. Both words don't have to be in each of your results. Any one word will do.

In a keyword search in a library catalog or some other database, your search may look like this:

Cars OR Automobilcs

Another situation calling for an **OR** search might be that in which two concepts are closely related, and you suspect that finding data on either of them will further your overall goal. For example, in doing a search for "Gestalt Therapy" you might also want to search for the father of Gestalt Therapy—Fritz Perls. You can formulate a search like this:

(Gestalt Therapy) OR (Fritz Perls)

Notice that I've identified phrases with parentheses. Some databases, and most Internet search engines, use quotation marks instead. Check out the help screen in the database to see what it uses. With an **OR** search, you typically get a lot of "hits", that is, citations to relevant data in the database.

Insight #2: *An OR search is usually for synonyms or for keywords that are already closely related. You use it to anticipate the various ways something might be described or approached so that you don't have to do multiple individual searches.*

The only alternative to doing an OR search is to do separate searches on each of your search terms and then compile the various sets of results. OR lets you avoid the pain of such an experience.

The AND Command

One of the most profitable ways to use keywords is to combine them so that you can narrow down a search. For example, if you wanted to look at the problem of educating homeless youth, a keyword search could be formulated to produce very precise results.

Let's visualize it with a diagram first. If you're searching for the relationship between homeless youth and education, you don't want every piece of data about homeless youth, nor do you want every piece of data about education. You want the data that comes when homeless youth and education intersect. Thus:

AND finds only data with both concepts

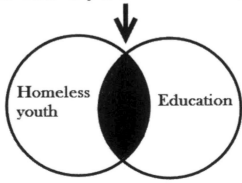

Your formulated keyword search will look like this:

(Homeless youth) AND Education

A tip: Be very careful not to add unnecessary words to AND searches. Suppose that you were searching for material in a database on Osama bin Laden's influence before and during the Iraq War of 2003 (including his supposed alliance with Saddam Hussein). The temptation might be to load up your search with terminology, along the lines of:

(Osama bin Laden) AND (Iraq War) AND 2003 AND influence

But stop and think - You are searching for *keywords*, probably in a title. Are all these words likely to appear in a title, along the lines of "The Influence of Osama bin Laden on the Iraq War of 2003?" What if the database had an article whose was, "Bin Laden and the Iraq War?" It's on target as far as your search goals are concerned, but your multiword search above is going to eliminate this article from the result list. Why? Because the article doesn't have the words **Osama** and **influence**, nor the date **2003**, in its title. In other words, you eliminated a good article from your results by using too much terminology.

How do you solve a problem like this? You do it by becoming a minimalist.

Insight #3: *With an AND search, always look for the fewest number of terms required to get data that is on target with your search goals. The more unnecessary terms you add, the more you risk screening good data (that does not use those terms) out of your results.*

For the search above, all you really need is:

(Bin Laden) AND (Iraq War)

You might even be able to get rid of **Bin**. The "**2003**" isn't needed either, because Bin Laden had little involvement in the 1990 Iraq war (other than wanting his fellow Saudis to handle Saddam themselves instead of having the Americans do it).

Insight #4: *A keyword AND search is used to search for data that relates two or more topics or concepts together. The data found will show the effect of the relationship between or among these topics.*

An **AND** search is a limiting kind of search. It asks the search program to provide data only when that data contains *all* the keywords linked by **AND**. Thus, you should expect that an **AND** search will give you fewer hits than if you had searched each keyword on its own. This can be a difficult concept to grasp. If you're having trouble with it, go back up to the **AND** search diagram. Or consider the example above: you don't want every piece of data about Bin Laden plus every piece of data about the Iraq War. You want only the data that *relates* Bin Laden to the Iraq War. Thus the **AND** search has set limits for your search. It has narrowed down the data that you want to receive.

Insight #5: *AND searches will narrow or limit your topic. Thus you can expect that you will not get as many "hits" with an AND search as with an OR search.*

Nesting ANDs and ORs

There are times when, within your AND search, several synonyms of key terms are possible. Unless you enjoy doing multiple searches, you can combine synonyms into your search by "nesting" ORs within an AND search:

Homeless AND (youth OR adolescen*) AND (education OR school*)

This might look like it's contradicting the caution I just gave about avoiding over-complicated searches, but there are actually only three words that are linked with AND. The rest are alternate terminology using OR, which will not eliminate relevant articles.

You can see that I put parentheses around (i.e., "nested") the OR terms that belong together, because search programs can get confused easily. The parentheses make it clear to the search engine how to treat this search. Notice as well that I truncated adolescen* so I could include, in one search, "adolescent," "adolescence," and "adolescents." I also truncated "school" to cover "schools" and "schooling" as well.

The NOT Command

If I'm back to looking for information about cars, but I'm *not* interested in any car made in Europe, a NOT search is what I need (Please don't send me e-mails and messages asking why I have a problem with European cars - it's a long story). With this search, I want to tell the search engine to give me everything about cars but no data about European cars. Here's how to do a NOT search:

*(cars OR automobiles) NOT Europe**

Notice what I've done. First, I took note of the fact that "automobiles" is a synonym for "cars." Thus I included both terms, nesting them with parentheses so as not to confuse the search engine as to what I meant by my **NOT** command. Then I added the **NOT** and did a truncation on Europe (using an asterisk) so the search engine could look for "Europe" and "European" with a single search. What I'm saying with my search terms is that I want data about either cars or automobiles as long I don't have to deal with European cars or automobiles.

Exceptions to the Above

Exceptions? Why are there always exceptions? Probably because every database likes to do its own thing. Here are some variations that you may find to the standard Boolean **OR, AND, NOT** searches:

> In many databases, you can do an **AND** search simply by leaving a space between words. Instead of:

homeless youth AND education

you can type: **homeless youth education**

> But note that some other databases will see **homeless youth education** as a phrase, thus requiring you to put the AND back in between "youth" and "education.
> In some databases, **NOT** has to be expressed as **AND NOT**. In Internet search engines, **NOT** is generally expressed with a hyphen before a word, with no spaces:

-European

> Many databases ask you to put quotation marks around words that need to appear together, e.g.:

"apple trees"

Others call for parentheses: (**apple trees**).

> There are some databases that actually search for synonyms of the term(s) you input so that they can bring up material you might not have found through a simple keyword search.
> Some databases provide a choice of search boxes with which to build searches, like the first example below (AND, phrase, OR, and NOT searches). Others will use a search grid with drop-down boxes like the second example:

Search for results that:

Have all these words

Form this phrase

Have any of these words

Do not have these words

Search

		Keyword ▼
AND ▼		Title ▼
OR ▼		Author ▼

Search

Clearing the Fog – What's the best way to choose keywords?

It's all very well to know how to use keywords, but experience shows that many people struggle with what words to choose in the first place. Here's a common misunderstanding I regularly observe: We want to talk to the database like it's a person. We want to *explain* our goal. This generally results in using too many words. It also produces monstrosities.

For example, you are researching the question, "How well has the government done in tightening bank regulations since the recession that began in 2008?" So you try to explain to your database what you want, and it comes out like this – *Government control of banking so we won't have another recession like 2008*. Nasty business, that. First, you have lots of words that the database won't even look at: "of," "so we won't have," "another," "like." Second, nothing in your search terminology says you are looking at banking regulations since 2008 in light of the recession. Trying to explain stuff to a database doesn't work, because databases don't think like human beings. They search for words.

So how do you fix your search? As much as possible, use actual words from your research question, or at least synonyms of these words. And keep it simple. Try this out: *"Bank regulations" recession.* If you need to get more precise results, try *"Bank regulations" "since the recession."*

Rule of thumb – If you want results that reflect what you are seeking in your research question, then use search terminology that comes directly out of your research question. And never try to explain to a database. That's usually about as successful as asking your dog where she buried your cell phone.

3.3 Keyword searching with hierarchies

Keywords are flat. What do I mean? Keyword search engines scan across the broad surface of databases looking for matches. I type in "Iraq" and the search engine finds the word "Iraq." In some results, Iraq is the main topic. In others it is incidental to whatever the data is actually about. Sometimes the results are about the culture of Iraq, sometimes the people of Iraq, sometimes the history of Iraq. Because keywords are flat - simply appearing where they appear without revealing the depths of context and meaning - the keyword search engines bring up all occurrences of a word, regardless of what surrounding meaning or definition is present. This can be a problem, because real knowledge is not flat but hierarchical.

3.3.1 Hierarchies

I know this is starting to look like hard going, but it shouldn't be all that threatening. Let's start with a brief look at how knowledge is organized. Put quite simply (because I'm only really capable of simplicity), every bit of knowledge has a context within which it fits. Most knowledge can be organized from broad categories (at the top) to narrow categories (at the bottom). The broad categories help to determine the meaning and boundaries of the narrow ones. Let me illustrate:

Can you define the following word?

ROCK

"Sure," you say. "It's a hard object that comes out of the ground."

To which I answer, "How wrong you are! Don't you know that 'rock' is a verb?" My definition, a symptom of my growing age, is that the only rock worth anything is the rock I do in my rocking chair.

"I'm not wrong," you retort. "You're wrong."

To which your friend standing next to us says with a smirk, "You're both wrong. It's music. Classic Rock is real music, and I'd rather be listening to it than wasting time hearing you argue about definitions."

What's the problem here? Why can't we agree on the meaning for one word with only four letters in it? The reason is simple: If I say, "I'm planning to take a whole evening to rock in my rocking chair," you know that my definition of 'rock' is something like 'a back and forth motion.' If, on the other hand, I say, "The rock that went through my window was two inches across," you know that 'rock' is now a noun meaning 'a hard substance taken from the earth.'

Words by themselves don't really mean anything for certain. They only have a definite meaning when you put them in a context. Words get their meaning from the sentences surrounding them. In turn, sentences become understandable within their paragraphs, and paragraphs make sense within the larger context of the complete document. The important word here is "context." Meaning is derived from context, and without context we have only confusion.

So what? How do meaning and context relate to research? Exactly like this: All data exists within one or more information hierarchies (contexts). Let me illustrate with the word "rock."

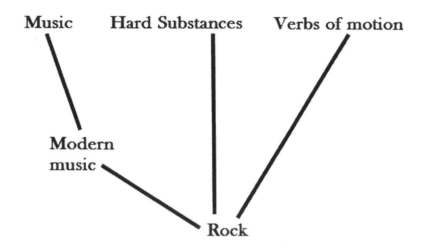

"Rock' is a sub-class of more comprehensive categories. For example, "rock" may be a sub-class of modern music, right alongside other sub-classes like "adult contemporary," "elevator music," and the compositions of John Cage. "Modern music" in turn is a sub-class of the larger category of "music" along with other sub-classes like "classical," "baroque," etc. What we end up with is a hierarchy. Each higher grouping is broader than the one below it.

But notice that "rock" is capable of having several different hierarchies attached to it, depending on the meaning we give to the word. It can also be a sub-class of "hard substances in the earth" or of "verbs indicating motion."

All data comes within a context. Without context the data cannot tell us what we need to know.

Let's now move into an area that better resembles a research topic. Take something like the Roman emperor Constantine. Depending on how you approach him, he can exist within a number of contexts (= hierarchies):

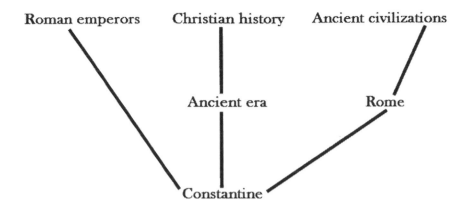

You can deal with him as a sub-class of "Roman emperors" alongside other sub-classes like Julius Caesar and Nero. "Roman emperors" in turn are a subclass of "Roman history", which in turn is a sub-class of "Ancient History." Alternatively, you can deal with him as an important figure within the larger subject of "Early Christian History," since he was the first emperor who affirmed Christianity so that it could eventually become the official Roman religion. Or you can discuss him within the higher class of "Ancient Civilizations," since he ruled one of them. Each of these hierarchies leads to a different approach to the same topic.

Information is hierarchical. The key to making use of this fact is simply this:

Insight #6: *In research, you must always know where you are in the hierarchy. What higher class does your topic belong to? Are there other hierarchies your topic could belong to? Are there sub-classes of your topic that could become factors to consider?*

We live in a time of "sight-bites." Information comes to us in tiny chunks, and Twitter is king. But sight-bites can leave us confused, like a tweet without the thread it belongs to. The more our data is disconnected from its setting (context) the more likely we are not to grasp its full meaning or to misinterpret it. Every time we encounter any kind of search result, we need to be thinking about what it is a part of, what its context is, where it belongs in the larger scheme of things. When you are doing research, you really don't want to be as scattered as snowflakes in a blizzard. You want your data to come together into something that makes sense.

3.3.2 Clustering search tools

Most traditional search engines on the World Wide Web (including Google and Yahoo) do a flat search for keywords thus separating results from their possible hierarchies. For example, if I search for "William Badke" in Google, I get a bunch of website links to all aspects of me (frightening, isn't it?). But those results don't distinguish between Badke the author, Badke the librarian, Badke the faculty member, Badke the semi-successful fiction writer, and so on. Badke is always only Badke (sigh).

A few tools are attempting to do something about this. Let's look at some of them:

3.3.2.1 Carrot2 (http://search.carrot2.org/stable/search)

Carrot2 is an example of a clustering search engine. It does a metasearch of a number of standalone search engines and then gathers main topic links in a list. When I search on my name, it includes the expected citations of various websites, and it lists the following linked terms in a side column:

All Topics(66)
- Research Strategies(15)
- Associate Librarian at Trinity Western University(12)
- Information Literacy(7)
- William B. Badke(12)
- Finding your Way through the Information Fog(10)
- Associate Librarian for Associated Canadian Theological Schools(4)
- Hitchhiker's Guide to the Meaning(4)
- Witty Manner(4)
- Internet(3)
- more | show all

Mercifully, unlike what actually happens with some search engines, Carrot2 doesn't ask me if I mean William Blake, or William Badge (both of which are blows to my ego). Instead, it gives me a way to focus my search on one *aspect*, for example, information literacy (not to mention my "witty manner.")

This tool has pulled key subject language out of my initially flat search, subject language that can group my results by the context (hierarchy) within which it exists. Thus websites related to my book *Research Strategies* (15 of them) are grouped together in that context. Websites about my work in "information literacy" are grouped together as well. Then comes my "witty manner," and so on. All are aspects of my WWW persona arranged hierarchically from my initial search on my name.

3.3.2.2 Yippy (http://www.yippy.com/)

Yippy is similar in its clustering function to Carrot2, but has a cooler name. This alone makes it worth checking out.

3.3.2.3 [Google Wonder Wheel, described in the 4th edition of Research Strategies, no longer exists. Google killed it without mercy in 2011. Rest in peace, Wonder Wheel, wherever old search functions are buried.]

Insight #7: *It is important to think hierarchically. What you are searching for belongs to a higher and broader category and may well have several narrower aspects that come below it. Knowing where you are in the hierarchy is important to enable you to broaden or narrow your searching intelligently.*

3.4 Keyword searching – The good, bad, and ugly

The good part of keyword searching is that it is quick and flexible, as well as giving you the opportunity to narrow down to specific topic areas or combine concepts from more than one subject discipline.

The bad part is that you are controlled by the *treachery of words*. What do I mean? Simply that different words can mean much the same thing or a single word (e.g., rock) can be capable of a lot of possible meanings. Keywords as search tools can easily betray you.

The ugly part is that keywords are flat. They aren't capable of telling you whether your result is broad or narrow in relation to your topic, nor can they spell out the hierarchical contexts within which your keyword might be found. Clustering search engines try to overcome this problem by suggesting contexts that form hierarchies within which your keyword results can live.

So use keywords, but be aware that they are not superheroes. In fact, that designation may well go to controlled vocabularies, our next topic.

3.5 For further study

Study guide

1. What is a "database?" Name a few examples of familiar databases.
2. What is a "database record?"
3. In keyword searching, what strong ability of computers is used?
4. What is a "truncation" or "wildcard?" Give an example along with the appropriate symbol.
5. Explain the "OR command" in Boolean searching and indicate in what types of searches it works best.
6. Explain the "AND command" in Boolean searching and indicate in what types of searches it works best.
7. Explain the "NOT command" in Boolean searching and indicate in what types of searches it works best.
8. Some databases will allow you to leave out the Boolean AND, and just input keywords with spaces between them. In other databases, if you do this the computer program will understand that you are constructing a _____.
9. Why do words by themselves have no definite meaning? How do they get a meaning?

10. All data comes within a _____.

11. Explain an "information hierarchy." Choose two or three topics and illustrate how each fits into one or more hierarchies (a diagram works best for this).

12. Regarding hierarchies, in research you must know where you are _____ _____ _____.

13. What does it mean to say that keywords are "flat?"

14. How do clustering search tools like Yippy help to resolve the problem of the flatness of keywords?

Practice with keywords and hierarchies

1. How would you formulate a keyword search to get results in a database on the following?

   a. The causes of World War One.
   b. Destruction of the museums in Iraq during the 2003 war.
   c. The role of crime in the novel, *The Great Gatsby*
   d. The problem of fear in patients with the psychological disorder "paranoia."
   e. Teen violence.
   f. The movie, *Vanilla Sky* (as opposed to the painting, *Vanilla Sky*).
   g. Kidney stones in Schnauzers.
   h. Racial conflict in London.
   i. Relationship between unemployment and homelessness in Cleveland.
   j. Stravinsky's musical composition, *The Rite of Spring.*

2. Try a search on Carrot 2 (**http://search.carrot2.org/stable/ search**), starting with the keyword **Napoleon** and finding sites on his role as Emperor of France (Hint: Use left column).

3. Create some hierarchical diagrams for the following: *Microsoft, Iraq, Arnold Schwarzenegger,* and *Anorexia.* Indicate three possible higher contexts and three lower.

Suggested key to practice with keywords

1. Keyword Search Terms (My Suggestions)

 a. *The causes of World War One*: This is actually a tough one because you can call this war World War One, World War I, WWI, and even The Great War. Most of these descriptors are actually phrases, and it may be hard to combine them in a search in a database while maintaining their identity as phrases. You may have to search each possibility in turn, e.g., World War One AND Cause* (notice the truncation), World War I AND Cause*, and so on. **Note that Internet search engines don't use truncation well (*), so save truncated searches for library catalogs and journal databases.**

 b. *Destruction of the museums in Iraq during the 2003 war*: Likely you can get by here with as little as Museum* AND Iraq AND War. Don't worry about the 2003, since the 1990 Iraq war did not raise the issue of museums, so the database will have no problem distinguishing the two wars.

 c. *The role of crime in the novel,* The Great Gatsby: The name Gatsby is rare. In this case, you don't need to fill the search with terms. Simply try Gatsby AND Crime.

 d. *The problem of fear in patients with the psychological disorder paranoia*: You have a challenge with the term Paranoia, since it is widely used in contexts other than psychology. Thus, a search like Paranoia AND Fear could create a lot of irrelevant hits, among which will be a few that deal with the psychological disorder variety of paranoia. But don't think that adding terminology like Psychological Disorder will help the situation. It won't, simply because keyword searches look for *words*. It's unlikely that the writers of an article on fear issues in the psychological disorder of paranoia will use the title, "Fear Issues in the Psychological Disorder of Paranoia." The title will much more likely be "Fear in Paranoia," or something similar. Our discussion of controlled vocabularies in the next chapter will offer an alternative to solve this problem.

e. *Teen violence*: Try (Teen* OR Adolescen* OR Youth) AND violence. Note the use of truncation and the choice of synonyms in an OR search.

f. *The movie,* Vanilla Sky *(as opposed to the painting,* Vanilla Sky*)*: Try Vanilla Sky AND Movie, or even Vanilla Sky AND Cruise [because the movie starred Tom Cruise.]

g. *Kidney stones in Schnauzers*: Try Kidney Stones AND Schnauzers. With AND searches, always try to make it as simple a process as possible.

h. *Racial conflict in London*: Try Race AND London, but there is a potential that "race" may bring up material on racing. Perhaps Racial AND London would work more effectively. Avoid adding terminology like Problems, Issues, and so on, since title terminology of your data rarely uses such terms.

i. *Relationship between unemployment and homelessness in Cleveland*: Try Unemploy* AND Homeless* AND Cleveland. [Remember, if you are trying this in an Internet search engine, most don't use truncation (*), so you will need to spell out the whole word.]

j. *Stravinsky's musical composition,* The Rite of Spring: For this one, continue the principle that short and simple is better than filling a search with terminology. Since this composition is distinctive, Rite of Spring should be enough. If it's not, add **AND Stravinsky**.

2. To the right of your search results for **Napoleon**, you will find a link to sites for Napoleon as Emperor of France.

3. The following are merely suggestions. Other options are possible:

Microsoft—higher categories: computer software, competition laws, successful companies. Lower categories: Office, court cases seeking to break up Microsoft, Microsoft's emphasis change from computers to devices.

Iraq—higher categories: Archaeology, Arab Nations, History of War. Lower categories: Destruction of museums in Iraq in 2003, Iraq's relations with Iran, the Iraq war of 2003.

Arnold Schwarzenegger—higher categories: Body building, movie actors, politicians. Lower categories: Arnold as actor, the 2003 California recall election, Arnold's movies after his governorship.

Anorexia—higher categories: Weight loss, psychological conditions, eating disorders. Lower categories: The medical consequences of anorexia, the role of self-esteem in Anorexia, the role of "thin culture" in the increase of anorexia cases.

Assignment for a research project of your own

1. State a research question on a topic of your choice. Have a good look at it and determine exactly what you want to search for.

2. Do a *keyword* search for books in a library catalog by:
a. Choosing important words related to your topic, and doing searches by these words either individually or in Boolean combinations. ***Indicate the actual searches you tried, e.g., (Skinner OR behaviorism) AND Walden.***
b. Listing 8-10 books, **relevant** to your topic, which you identified through your keyword search. Keep as narrowly focused on your research question goal as possible.

4

Metadata and the Power of Controlled Vocabularies

The terminology of this chapter title may have you quivering, but you're about to learn some cool words to impress your friends and some cooler concepts to make you a better searcher than you ever could have been with keywords alone. I do have to lay a bit of theory on you, though. Sorry about that. Theory seems too often like joining a club with a tough initiation. The task of getting in might be more frightening than the potential membership benefits.

In this case, however, understanding a few basics will help the rest of the chapter make sense.

4.1 It's all about the metadata

Research is a quest that can have you trekking into mighty strange territory to harvest the information you need. This is the task of "search." If you are devoted Googler (or Bing-er, or whatever) you already know about the joys and sorrows of search. One disturbing fact emerges – search is a messy thing, often leaving us with far more results that we *don't* need than the few we do. So you find yourself saying to your search box, "No, no, no, I want *this*, not *that*, you blockhead search engine."

And it is exactly that – a blockhead, I mean. Search engines are not intelligent creatures. They recognize letters and words, and they can find exactly what you type into the box. But they don't know when the actual results are irrelevant, even though those results contain your search words. In fact, they don't even know what your words mean.

Now imagine that you're trying to discover why Google personalizes search results (more on this later, including a Clearing the Fog vignette from me). So you go to the Google search engine and type in **Google personalization.** A lot of the results are from the Google site, and none of them specifically seem to be addressing the "why" question.

So now you search **Google personalization "why do they do it"** (using quotation marks to search it as a phrase). Disaster. Nothing in the result set is remotely what you are looking for. What went wrong? Well, part of the problem is that you are trying to ask Google a question with your **"why do they do it"** phrase. Your question requires Google to work through a complex cognitive task, something it is trying to learn how to do but hasn't quite pulled off yet. Google doesn't reason at all well yet, despite its claims that it does. A better search term would be **"rationale"** (results will be closer to what you are looking for). A more significant reason for your bad results is that Google isn't functioning with any serious metadata.

In this chapter I want to take you into the heart of the machine to understand why some searches succeed and others fail. I want you to get a grasp of why some databases work better than others and why this has everything to do with the way those databases and their data are constructed. So here goes.

4.2 Understanding metadata

It might seem better for me to avoid throwing complicated terminology at you, because you get enough of that in the normal course of your life, but "metadata" is a cool concept, and knowing what it means can make you a winner at social gatherings. To understand metadata, you need to grasp how databases are constructed.

Any database is only as useful as its retrieval capability. If you can't retrieve specifically what you need, when you need it, then what you have is a data dump, not a database. For some databases, and for much of the WWW, retrieval is done solely through keywords that are found within the data itself. This, as we will see, is a pretty ineffective way to locate specific pieces of information.

Enter metadata. If a database constructor wants to be successful in setting up data for retrieval, good metadata will do the trick. Consider this fictional listing from an online telephone directory:

Smith, Harley Q.
2947 Olivier Ave.,
Anytown, WA.
699-555-4023

This is a name, address and phone number for one listing in a phone directory. Now, suppose that you're doing what many people who still use land lines do these days - looking up the number of a friend. Imagine for a moment that the directory you're using only searches on keywords, that is, it searches on the full text of entries like the one above, making no distinctions in categories within the results. Your search is: **Harley Smith,** and it finds:

Boyton, **Harley**, 7690 **Smith** St., Clumpers, MN. 908-555-2956
Harley, John, 2187 Jones St., **Smith**, ND 867-555-4289
Smith, Amos, 2798 **Harley** Rd., Johnstown, AR 223-555-1972

Smith, Douglas, 1197 Samuels Ave., **Harley**, CN. 256-555-6843
Smith, **Harley** Q. 2947 Olivier Ave., Anytown, WA. 699-555-4023

You can see that this database isn't very concerned about word order or word proximity, and that it doesn't know a personal name from a street name. It doesn't even know if Harley is the first name of a person, last name of a person or the name of a town. The keywords are all there, but you got 5 results instead of one, and all but one are not what you were looking for.

So what was the problem? A lack of metadata. The database search engine simply looked for your search words in a sea of undifferentiated text. It had no way of identifying the name of a person.

Now let me show you how a good phone number database sets itself up:

First Name: Harley
Last Name: Smith
Street: 2947 Olivier Ave.
City: Anytown
State: WA
Phone: 699-555-4023

Each shaded part (or "field") of the above entry serves as an identifier (e.g., Name, Street, City) that distinguishes something you might want to look up. The encoding is metadata – that is, a system of field terms that come along with the data. The database is constructed so that, when you enter a search in an online version of this phone listing, your search box might look like this:

Find a Person

First name   Last name
[   ]   [   ]

Street Address
[   ]

City   State
[   ]   [   ]   (Search)

Searching first name Harley and last name Smith will get you:

Smith, Harley Q. 2947 Olivier Ave., Anytown, WA. 699-555-4023

You get only one (correct) result. Why? Because the database creators inserted *metadata* [descriptive labels] into the data to distinguish names from street addresses from cities. Now the database knows the difference between a personal name and a city name, so you get results much closer to what you are actually looking for.

4.3 Metadata in practice – The database record

Let's see how metadata works in the research process. For most databases, but not the searchable part of the WWW, the database search engine doesn't really look for the data itself but searches the metadata. The metadata comes in the form of a data "record," that is, *a short description of the data*. If the data were books in a library, the metadata would be the "records" that describe each book, and the records would be what the catalog's search engine would look through, not the books themselves. The same would be true of an electronic database that searches for journal articles, though these days, because so many journal articles are in electronic form, it is possible to search the full text of articles as well as the metadata records.

Back in 2003 I published a book entitled *Beyond the Answer Sheet: Academic Success for International Students* (great book by the way; you owe it to yourself to get a copy and make me rich). Shortly after publication, a library catalog record (metadata) was produced for the book. It looked like this:

LDR: 00793nam 2200265Ia 45x0
005: 20030610113341.0
008: 030610s2003 nyua 001 0 eng d
020: $a 0595271960
035: $a ocm52399619
090: $a LB2375 $b .B33 2003
100: 1 $a Badke, William B., $d 1949-

245: 10 $a Beyond the answer sheet : $b academic success for
international students / $c William B. Badke.
260: $a New York : $b iUniverse, $c c2003.
300: $a v, 152 p. : $b ill. ; $c 24 cm.
500: $a Includes index.
650: 0 $a Academic achievement.
650: 0 $a Foreign study.
650: 0 $a College student orientation.
650: 0 $a Student adjustment.
650: 0 $a College students.
650: 0 $a Students, Foreign $x Education (Higher)

A lot of this record looks like meaningless code, but some of it is fairly easy to understand. The number 100, for example, designates the author of the book, and the number 245 designates the title. Thus, if we had a library catalog search engine that could be set to search only within 100 fields for authors, it should be able to pick up a list of all the books I've written that are located in the particular library I am searching. The search engine doesn't search through the whole record but knows to go directly to the 100 (author) field and searches only that field in every record in the database, looking for my name. Thus the database truly knows the difference between an author and a title, because the metadata is set up to distinguish these things. Here is the same thing as you would see it in a library catalog.

LC call number: LB2375 .B33 2003
Personal Author: Badke, William B., 1949-
Title: Beyond the answer sheet : academic success for international students / William B. Badke.
Publication info: New York : iUniverse, c2003.
Physical description: v, 152 p. : ill. ; 24 cm.
General Note: Includes index.
Subject term: Students, Foreign—Education (Higher)
Subject term: College students
Subject term: Foreign study
Subject term: Academic achievement
Subject term: College student orientation
Subject term: Student adjustment

Metadata, unfortunately, is pretty much non-existent on the WWW, so Google, Bing, etc. are forced to search only on keywords. If you do a search on the WWW, it becomes obvious right away that there is no search box to look for authors of websites or for types of websites (e.g., reviews of Toyota cars as opposed to Toyota's corporate website). This isn't the search engine's fault. Most websites just don't have the encoded metadata to enable such a search to be done. The best you can usually do (e.g. with a Google advanced search) is select a search of title words from websites or set a few other limiters.

Without metadata, you usually get tons of search results, but you have to do a large amount sifting to find a match with what you were actually searching for. If you search a library catalog, on the other hand, you will find that there is an available author search, a title search, a subject heading search, etc. that can help you nail down what you are looking for. Why? Because the library catalog is made up of metadata records.

Even with adequate metadata, the big problem with electronic databases is not getting information into them, but *retrieving* the information you need. For this purpose, there are two basic search tools available to you: **keywords** and **controlled vocabularies**. We looked at keywords in the previous chapter, so now we'll turn to the controlled vocabularies, which depend totally on metadata.

4.4 Controlled vocabularies

A few years ago, as people started sharing things on the WWW (photos, favorite bookmarks, etc.), *folksonomies* began to develop. A folksonomy is simply a user-created method of labeling items (tagging) so that you or anyone else in your circle of friends of colleagues can use these labels to find your items. A couple of examples are Flickr (**http://www.flickr.com/**) for photos and del.icio.us (**http://del.icio.us/**) for website bookmarks. The labels or "tags" used in these sites can be displayed as "clouds" of links to actual data. Here is what a "tag cloud" might look like for the City of New York (text size indicating relative popularity of the various tags).

ny newyork nyc newyorkcity

Simply click on the tag you want, and you will get a display of items that have had that tag attached to them. With these clusters tags (which together form a folksonomy), users can search across one another's collections, pulling out, for example, favorite pictures from Japan or bookmarks to sites on ballroom dancing.

One big problem, though: The tags are user generated. This means that consistency goes out the window. One user tags her photos of New York with the term "newyork." Another uses "nyc," or "newyorkcity" or "ny" (most tagging systems demand that you tag with only one word, or close up the spaces if you use more than word). This means that if you search across the collection for pictures of New York, you need to know all the relevant tags that are being used for the subject. You'll most certainly miss a lot of items just because you didn't use obvious tags.

In some ways, it would be great if some dictator webmaster actually issued a set of standardized tags and insisted that everyone use them instead of making up their own. Hmmm…Actually that's the answer. A set of tags that is uniform so that all the pictures of Japan have to be tagged "JapanPictures," not "JapaneseVacationPictures," nor "PicturesOfJapan." That way, you would find all the Japan-related pictures that are in the collection.

Too bad I can't claim credit for the idea. The Library of Congress in the late 1800s was faced with the prospect of creating a new method of cataloging its large collection. As part of the process, the librarians determined that the only way to be sure all books on a particular topic could be identified was to standardize a system of subject headings (tags?) that would be used in the descriptive record (metadata) related to each book. They created records containing these subject headings along with other metadata (authors, titles, etc.). Today, most academic libraries in North America simply use the subject headings created originally by the Library of Congress (why re-invent the wheel?).

4.5 Library of Congress Subject Headings

Earlier I showed you a copy of a database record to one of my books. Now I dare to show it again:

LC call number: LB2375 .B33 2003
Personal Author: Badke, William B., 1949-
Title: Beyond the answer sheet : academic success for international students / William B. Badke.
Publication info: New York : iUniverse, c2003.
Physical description: v, 152 p. : ill. ; 24 cm.
General Note: Includes index.
Subject term: Students, Foreign—Education (Higher)
Subject term: College students
Subject term: Foreign study
Subject term: Academic achievement
Subject term: College student orientation
Subject term: Student adjustment

If you look at the Subjects fields just above, you will see terminology like:

> Students, Foreign — Education (Higher).
> College students.
> Foreign study.
> Academic achievement.
> College student orientation.
> Student adjustment.

Each of these is a Library of Congress subject heading related to some aspect of the book's subject matter.

How did these subject headings originate? Quite simply, the Library of Congress (LC) in Washington, DC created an extensive list of the terminology by which most topics in the world of information would be identified and then it organized these terms in alphabetical lists. Some subject headings were easy: dogs are **DOGS**, sunflowers are **SUNFLOWERS**, and so on. Some were more difficult: What do you call senior citizens? LC chose **AGED,** much to the outrage of senior citizens. Television faith healers are **HEALERS IN MASS MEDIA**. Why? *Because LC said so.* That's the point with controlled vocabularies. These vocabularies are created by people "out there" who then ***control*** them and don't let you change them.

The fact is that you can't have it both ways. You can either choose your own search terminology (as in keywords or tagging), in which case you can't be sure you'll find everything, or you can let someone (in this case, Library of Congress) standardize your terminology, meaning that someone other than you chooses what we are going to call everything. If you use standardized terminology, you have less flexibility than with keyword searching, but you are more likely to find most of what the database has to offer about the topic you are seeking. Thus:

Insight #1: *Controlled vocabularies, unlike keywords, get at what the data is actually about, rather than seeking out the words the data uses to describe itself (keywords). Thus, with a controlled vocabulary search, you are more likely to get nearly everything on a topic in the database you're searching, regardless of what words are in titles, etc. The tradeoff is that, with controlled vocabularies, you have to use the subject terms provided by the system. You might not like these terms, but they are what you've got. No variations are allowed.*

How does a controlled vocabulary work? Armed with a set of predetermined subject headings, catalogers (creators of metadata records) decide which subject heading (or headings) to assign to a particular chunk of data. In the case of LC, every time they get a book to catalog, they write a description of the book (i.e., the catalog record), which then becomes metadata, and one or more controlled subject headings is added to the record.

So a book entitled *Them Television Preachers* may have the subject heading **HEALERS IN MASS MEDIA** assigned to it. A book called *Active Seniors in Today's World* may be labeled with the subject heading **AGED**.

Note something very important here. The book *Them Television Preachers* did not have any of the actual words of the subject heading in its title. The title told you the book was about TV preachers. It said nothing about healers or about mass media. The same was true for the second title—*Active Seniors in Today's World*—the term "aged" is not to be seen anywhere in the title. Why, then, were they given the subject headings they received? *Because some intelligent librarian sat down with these books, determined **what they were about**, and then assigned the closest subject headings from the already existing controlled vocabulary list.* Thus:

Insight #2: *The actual wording in the title of whatever you are searching for is not important for controlled vocabularies. Subject headings are assigned on the basis of somebody's judgment as to what the item is actually about. The title words can be the same as words in the subject heading or they can be radically different.*

Consider the advantages. I have 5 books with the following titles:

Terminal Choices
Choosing Life or Death
Euthanasia
The Practice of Death
The Right to Die

All of them are about mercy killing or euthanasia. You might not have guessed that fact by looking at the titles, but the intelligent LC librarian determined that they are all about the same topic and assigned the same subject heading to all of them: **EUTHANASIA**. Euthanasia describes what these books are actually about regardless of the words used in their titles. One term pulls together all five books, even though you would need several keyword searches to find all of them.

Controlled vocabularies are a good solution to the problem of *retrieval*. It is a real challenge (and sometimes impossible) to input all the right terminology so that the database will deliver to us in a single search the information we need. If we wanted a list of books about euthanasia, it would be nice to have a predetermined word for the *concept* of euthanasia so we could type it into the search engine and get back a list of all the euthanasia books regardless of the wordings of the actual book titles. This is what a controlled vocabulary is

81

designed for. Most of the books **on** euthanasia in a library will be retrieved just by typing in the subject term **EUTHANASIA,** no matter what their titles are.

Insight #3: *Use a controlled vocabulary as a search tool when you want most or all of the data on the same topic regardless of what the data actually says about itself in titles, etc.*

But let's be clear about one thing—controlled vocabularies are "controlled" in the sense that someone other than you has determined what they will be. You as the user can't mess with them by changing their words or rearranging their structure the way you can with keywords. You *use* controlled vocabularies; you don't create them, and you can't fool with their form.

Insight #4: *Messing with controlled vocabulary wording or form defeats the purpose of controlled vocabularies. Subject headings are created by someone other than you, and they can't, in most cases, be manipulated or turned into keywords.*

Let's see how the *LC Subject Headings* controlled vocabulary system works in practice. The Library of Congress provides subject headings for the books in its own library collection, but it has also conveniently issued its list of approved headings so that all of us can use their system. Most libraries in North America have chosen to do just that, so that your library's subject headings are likely derived from the Library of Congress.

Your library may have a print edition of *Library of Congress Subject Headings* as a set of large red volumes. Below is a mock-up of what you might see on typical page from the guide. On the right are the subject headings or alternative headings. On the left is a description of what you are seeing on the right:

The Library of Congress has enhanced its subject heading system online in recent years (**http://id.loc.gov/authorities/subjects.html**). If you happen to search for a heading that is not authorized, it will list one or more authorized subject headings. If you find an authorized heading, like **Peanuts,** you will get further information (illustrated below but condensed to save space):

▦ Peanuts

Variants
> ▦ Arachides
> ▦ Arachis hypogea
> ▦ Earth nuts
> ▦ Goobers
> ▦ Grass nuts
> ▦ Ground-nuts
> ▦ Groundnuts
> ▦ Monkey nuts
> ▦ Pindars
> ▦ Pindas
> ▦ Pinders

Broader Terms
> ▦ Arachis
> ▦ Oilseed plants

NOTE—*This index is not a library catalog in itself.* It is simply an online guide to subject headings that you can then take to your local college or university catalog and use to find the books you need.

Clearing the Fog – Subject headings are not keywords, no they're not.

One of the most difficult concepts in academic research is that of the subject heading. Blame it on Google. Most readers of this book have long been avid keyword searchers on the WWW, where subject headings are as scarce as coconut trees in the Alaskan wilds.

Keywords are words that actually exist within the data you are searching (for example, a website on basket weaving in which the words "basket weaving" are actually found). This means that search engines can be as dumb as a bag of hammers and still seek out a string of letters and bring up the data when it finds the string of letters. It has no clue what the letters mean or even if the word it brought up means the same as the word that is in your mind.

Subject headings require human intervention and thus are smarter than keywords. They are tags, descriptors, and thus ways of explaining what the data is actually about. Subject headings are not words in the data. In fact, their form might be quite different from the words in your data (or possibly the same if the chosen subject heading is common terminology for your topic). They are, instead, preset terminology that *explains what the data is actually about.* They are not words *in* your data but words *above and beyond* your data that describe its subject matter.

Here's an example:

I was researching the ongoing crisis of Arctic Ocean ice melt due to climate change, so I did a *keyword* search in a library catalog on **artic ice**. Here are some of the things I found:

➢ Under **ice:** Waldo Lyon and the development of the **Arctic** submarine
➢ Art in the **ice** age : Spanish Levant art, **Arctic** art
➢ After the **ice** : life, death, and geopolitics in the new **Arctic**

The third one may be on the topic I'm working on. The first two are definitely not. Keyword searches can't read anyone's mind. They just find the words you input.

The subject heading for Arctic Ocean ice is **Sea ice—Arctic regions**. When I search on this librarian-created tag, I get results that are firmly on the concept in my mind:

- ➤ IceBridge airborne survey data support Arctic sea ice predictions
- ➤ Fever at the poles
- ➤ Transition in the fractal geometry of Arctic melt ponds
- ➤ Arctic report card 2011

The first result from our subject heading search uses our original keywords: arctic ice. The second one uses neither word but deals with global warming and arctic ice. The third and fourth lack the word ice. Yet all four are on sea ice in the Arctic. The subject heading found all four because it was focusing on what the books were actually about rather than on their title wording. That's smart. Keywords proved dumber than subject headings in this case.

Keywords and subject headings are not the same, no they are not. They do completely different types of searches.

4.6 Working the angles—Identifying controlled vocabularies

Controlled vocabularies can involve more than subject headings. Names can be tricky in databases – Am I "Badke, William" or "Badke, Bill?" Thus many databases also have controlled vocabularies of names, by which they standardize the form of an author's name so you can find everything by that author in the database. Titles of books or articles have their own controlled vocabulary built in – A title takes a unique form in its choice and order of words so that titles tend to be standardized automatically.

But subject headings, whether in a library catalog or some other database, are challenging to identify. Let's look at types of databases that have controlled vocabularies and try to understand how they are organized to provide you information.

4.6.1 Library catalogs

Some library catalogs may not have guides to subject headings embedded in them, which is why you might need to identify relevant subject headings by using the *Library of Congress Subject Headings* volumes or the online version, described above. Some catalogs do have built in cross reference systems, so you can simply try out a word in a subject search (e.g. "Goobers") and it will link you to the right subject term ("Peanuts").

There is another way to identify subject headings. Being a bit of a purist, I hesitate to share this, because it's not foolproof, and you may end up missing headings you could have used. But here it is:

First, perform a keyword search in the library catalog, choosing words you think might appear in titles of relevant books on the topic you are dealing with. Find a book that is directly on your chosen topic and click on the title of the citation to it to open up the full catalog record. For example, you might be writing on **Pacific Island societies**, so you use these terms in a keyword search. You discover in your result list the ideal book and open up the full record:

The growth and collapse of Pacific island societies : archaeological and demographic perspectives /
Author: Kirch, Patrick Vinton
      Rallu, Jean-Louis
Publisher: Honolulu : University of Hawaii Press, ©2007.
ISBN: 9780824831349
Subjects: Ethnology — Oceania.
      Ethnology — Hawaii.

Look at the line that says "Subjects." There are a couple of official, authorized forms of the Library of Congress subject heading for this concept **Ethnology—Oceania** and **Ethnology—Hawaii**. They might not be the subject headings you would have chosen if you were setting up this system, but that doesn't matter. What you have with these subject headings is the means to find all the other books on the topic, usually just by clicking on the hyperlinked subject headings in the catalog record. So, click on **Ethnology—Oceania,** and you will get a list of all the rest of the library's books on Oceania's ethnology (cultures, societies), even if words in titles would not have led you to them in a keyword search, e.g.

> *The growth and collapse of Pacific island societies: archaeological and demographic perspectives*

> *Oceania : an introduction to the cultures and identities of Pacific Islanders*

> *The archaeology of difference: negotiating cross-cultural engagements in Oceania*

Once again, your keyword search would have missed the second and third result above because they lack one or more of the keywords, "Pacific Island societies". The subject heading search grouped the books on the subject, even when their title words did not reveal their true nature. This method of finding subject headings is relatively simple: Use a keyword search to identify one book on your topic. Open up the citation to get the full catalog record. Go to the LC subject heading(s) used for this book in the catalog record, and click on its (their) link(s) to discover similar books.

4.6.2 Other databases

There are a many databases out there that use controlled vocabularies, including journal databases and institutional repositories. Here are some clues to finding their subject headings systems:

> ➢ A term commonly used is "Thesaurus," that is, a guide to subject headings that not only identifies authorized subjects but also can lead you to broader, narrower or related terms that are also authorized. Sometimes there

is also a "scope note," that is a definition of what is meant by a certain subject heading.

➢ At other times in a database you may see a link to "Subjects" or "Descriptors," which mean the same thing.

➢ In connection with the options above, or sometimes separate from them, you may find a "browse" function. "Browse" generally involves working with controlled vocabulary terms (subjects, authors, titles, etc.) from alphabetized lists of headings.

➢ You can also discover subject links in the full records for articles initially identified through a keyword search.

4.7 Getting more creative—combining controlled vocabulary and keyword searching

Let me begin this section by re-emphasizing something: *Keywords and controlled vocabularies are **not the same***. Keywords are constructed by you as best guesses. They are intended to find *actual word*s in your data or data record with the hope that those words will guide you to the resources you want. Controlled vocabularies are constructed by someone else, and they exist outside of the data you are searching. They are intended to bring you all the resources on a topic regardless of what terminology is used in the titles, and so on. But, to ensure that controlled vocabularies provide this service, their form/order/terminology is preset and cannot be changed.

That said, there is a way to construct searches in which a subject heading gets you to the right subject matter, and keywords help you to narrow within that subject area. It's called *faceted searching*. Let's try an example. Consider the following from one of the EBSCOhost journal databases, PsycINFO:

I am interested in psychotherapy with autistic children. Thus my three terms "psychotherapy," autis* (truncation for autism, autistic, etc.) and child*. The initial 1248 results are more than most searchers want to deal with. This database allows (even encourages) you to do the search in stages. [Note that other types of databases will do this in other ways. The EBSCO example is just that – an example. For other databases, root around in them until you find similar functions.]

In PsycINFO on the EBSCOhost platform, you can go down the column to the left of your results and identify subject headings that move beyond words in titles to identify the central subject matter that you want. This gets you fewer results that are much more focused on what you are looking for:

I chose the subject headings "autism" and "child psychotherapy," bringing my results down to 581 from 1248. I can be sure that the remaining articles are more centrally on the topic, because I used subject headings that didn't depend on words in titles. If I wanted to (and I probably do), I could go back to the subject headings in the left column and choose one or two more that would drop the total number of results even further.

4.8 Keeping on track with controlled vocabularies

Some databases today, including most of what is found in Google or Bing, can be searched only by keyword. Keywords have advantages, but the lack of controlled vocabulary search options can be a definite drawback when all you want is a set of data on one subject regardless of what the data says about itself. Thinking of all possible keywords that might give you relevant data can really give you a headache.

Some people have a lot of trouble grasping the essential difference between keywords and controlled vocabularies, especially when the same words can sometimes be used for both. For example, there is a subject heading **Tax evasion,** but that could just as easily be a keyword expression. What's the difference? Well, the keyword search **tax evasion** could bring you up a book like *The Detection of Tax Evasion in the Bronx.* A subject heading search would bring up this title, but it would also find *The Psychology of Escaping the Taxman*, something your keyword search on "tax evasion" would miss completely. Essentially the difference is in the way the database search engine searches for the words. **Tax evasion** as a keyword search will find only those actual words in a title. **Tax evasion** as a subject heading will search for all the database records that have been tagged with the subject "tax evasion," even if their titles don't contain the words "tax evasion." With subject headings, good results will come up even if the title words aren't right.

Keywords are best used if you don't know a subject heading, if your topic is narrow or crosses disciplines (like "The education of homeless children"), or if the database you are using has no metadata. Controlled vocabulary subject headings are best when you want to find most of what a database has on a topic, and you are concerned that a keyword search will only reveal some of what is there.

In some situations you can combine the two, but use great care so that the results you get are close to what you wanted.

4.9 For further study

Study guide

1. What is "metadata"?
2. What is a "record," and how does it relate to metadata?
3. Why doesn't the actual title of the book matter a great deal when a cataloger attaches a controlled vocabulary term to it?
4. What are the advantages of controlled vocabularies?
5. In Library of Congress Subject Headings, what do the following abbreviations mean?
   UF
   BT
   NT
6. Explain the method of starting with a keyword search in order to identify controlled vocabulary subject headings.
7. Define the following:
   Thesaurus
   Descriptor
   Browse function
8. Is it possible to search controlled vocabularies and keywords at the same time? When would you want to do so, if it is possible?

Practice with controlled vocabularies

1. Use Library of Congress Subject Headings (**http://id.loc.gov/authorities/subjects.html** - click on "Search Authorities") to find the authorized subject heading for each of the following:
   a. LASH ships
   b. Arts, Zen
   c. Clothes hangers
   d. Prevention of Crime
   e. Canadian Religious Poetry
   f. Rookies (Baseball)
   g. Literacy and computers
   h. Pencilflowers
   i. Ancient philosophy

> j. The Roman influences on law in the United States [a tough one to end with. Try various combinations of words.]

2. In the following catalog record, which are controlled vocabulary terms?

> Title: The hitchhiker's guide to the meaning of everything / William Badke.
> Author: Badke, William B., 1949-
> Publisher: Grand Rapids, MI : Kregel Publications, 2005.
> Description: 176 p. ; 22 cm.
> ISBN: 0825420695
> Subjects: Bible — Criticism, interpretation, etc.
>   Meaning (Philosophy) — Religious aspects — Christianity
>   Life — Religious aspects — Christianity

Suggested key to practice with controlled vocabularies

1. Library of Congress Subject Headings—Correct Headings

   a. *LASH ships*: See: Barge-carrying ships
   b. *Arts, Zen*: See: Zen arts
   c. *Clothes hangers*: See: Coat hangers
   d. *Prevention of Crime*: See: Crime prevention
   e. *Canadian Religious Poetry*: See: Religious poetry, Canadian
   f. *Rookies (Baseball)*: See: Rookie baseball players
   g. *Literacy and computers*: See: Computers and literacy
   h. *Pencilflowers*: See: Stylosanthes
   i. *Ancient philosophy*: See: Philosophy, Ancient
   j. *The Roman influences on law in the United States*: See: Law—United States—Roman influences [Did you find it?]

2. Clearly the three subject headings are controlled vocabularies: Bible—Criticism, interpretation, etc.; Meaning (Philosophy)—Religious aspects—Christianity; Life—Religious aspects—Christianity. But so is the author's name (because it is pre-formatted for standardization). So is even the title, which comes in a specific, formal order.

Assignment for a research project of your own

Do a *Library of Congress Subject Heading* search on a topic of your choice in a library catalog by:

1. Identifying the best subject heading either through the Library of Congress Subject Headings resource (print or online) or by starting with a keyword search to find a book on the topic and then locating the subject heading you want through that book's catalog record.
2. Doing the search by using the appropriate search box for subject headings or by clicking on the relevant link in a catalog record.
3. Carefully evaluating your results to identify those books most relevant to your topic area.
4. Making a list of 8 to 10 relevant books identified through your controlled vocabulary search.

5

Discovery Searches, Library Catalogs and Journal Databases

Now we move into the area where the rubber meets the road. This chapter is intended to guide you into the major database resources available to you through a library, using the keyword and controlled vocabulary methods described in the previous two chapters.

5.1 Discovery Searches

An increasing number of libraries today have discovery search tools, such as Primo (from Ex Libris), Summon™ (from ProQuest) and EBSCO Discovery Service. It may not be easy for you to determine if your library has such a beast, but look for a single search box on your library's home page that enables you to search for books, journal articles and other resources all at the same time. A discovery search tool is essentially one-stop shopping, like a "Google of the Library," bringing you a ton of results of every type with a single search.

Sounds great, doesn't it? Well, depending on what happens next, it can be great or simply more of the information fog you're already used to. Generally, you get a list of results that are either broken out into books, articles, and so on, and/or you are given a means to choose a particular kind of resource and narrow your results to that. See these options from example of a search on "climate change" in EBSCO Discovery Search:

Quite a number of discovery tools as used in libraries actually let you start with a choice of the type of resource you are looking for, thus getting the narrowing out of the way early (something that is usually a good thing in our era of information glut).

Articles & More	Books & Videos	Course Reserves	Journals (A-Z)	Reference

Search for articles, books, videos, images and more. **↖ Click on a tab before searching**

Find: [   ] [Go] [advanced search] [help]

The best way to know if your library is using a discovery tool is to see what is covered in the search you are about to do. You may see labels like, "Search library collections," "Search for articles, books, and more," "Search everything." Or you may be given the opportunity to specify a type of resource from several possible, as in the illustration above. These are solid clues that you have a discovery search in place. If you are still unsure, you can ask a librarian.

As a researcher, I'm not terribly big on discovery searching. Maybe that's because I'm too old and set in my ways. But more likely it's because I know that you absolutely don't need, in most cases, a glut of information. A few results that are dead on target usually trumps a great host of results, only some of which are helpful. Discovery tries to be an academic Google, but it often fails to help users enough with getting directly to the few relevant results they need.

Here are some distinctions. Summon™ in its results provides you with a selection of links to articles, books and other resources, each resource type in its own section on the page. You can't refine your search from the results page, and links to articles or books take you to the database or catalog they came from. Primo mixes result types but allows you to select out books, articles, and so on from the left column. It also allows you to narrow by date and keywords. EBSCO Discovery Service, now the discovery tool with the largest client base, mixes result types but allows you to select out books, articles, etc., set date ranges, and so on. A unique feature with EBCO's tool is its commitment to subject headings as a means to narrow your results.

If your library doesn't use a discovery service, then you can take a breather and get a soda before moving to 5.2. If your library does have a Summon™, Primo, or EBSCO Discovery Service, read on anyway while we look at more specific search tools. You can still generally, even when there is a discovery tool, specify whether you want to use the library catalog or journal databases.

5.2 Library catalogs

Books tend to create fogs of misunderstanding, because they're blunt instruments. In order to write a book, you need a topic broad enough to be covered in a couple of hundred or more pages, but you also need enough focus to avoid it becoming multi-volume or becoming superficial. Thus finding a book on a narrowed down topic that is driven by a research question may well be a challenge. Here information hierarchies can help. If you can't find a book on Bulimia, you might find one on the broader topic Eating Disorders (higher in the hierarchy). If you can't find a book on Constantine, you might find a book on the broader topic of Roman Emperors or Roman History of his era. Generally, you need to assume that few books will be exactly on your topic. That is why strategies are needed.

Library catalogs are electronic search engines for books in physical or electronic format. When you search a library catalog, you are searching the metadata record created for each book, a record that includes the following, among other things: Author, title, publisher information, description, subject heading(s), and call number. This is where things can get tricky: Library catalog search interfaces differ widely from one another, so you need to "read" them in order to navigate them well. Common interfaces:

1. A discovery search tool that allows you to narrow your searching to only books if you wish. Here the basic option is a fairly broad keyword search, so you might want to dig around for tabs or an advanced search that can help you develop a more focused search plan.
2. A catalog offering a single search box yet allowing you to specify (through a drop-down) what type of search you want to do (e.g., keyword, title, subject heading, etc.).
3. A catalog that opens in an advanced search with several boxes that enable you to specify type of search and to format it with Boolean operators.

Here's a collage of the three types:

5.1.1 Making the catalog work for you

If your topic is a reasonably standard one, you will probably do best with a controlled vocabulary subject heading search. It's safer in that you know you will find most books that are available on the topic. The only problem is that you may need only a portion of the information found in each book. For example, if your research question is, "How close to attainability is B.F. Skinner's utopian vision found in his book *Walden Two?*" you might well find that there are few books available specifically on *Walden Two*, and you are going to have to do a controlled vocabulary subject search on **Skinner, B.F. (Burrhus Frederic), 1904–** and then find material on *Walden Two* within books describing his thought. Of course, you'll also need to look at the actual book, *Walden Two*, itself.

(For information on how to identify Library of Congress Subject Headings for your search, see Chapter 4, above.)

If your topic is not a standard one or if it combines a couple of subject disciplines (such as the influence of *Walden Two* on the 1960's hippy movement), you may want to go for a keyword approach. Here are a few warnings, however:

> ➢ Keywords tend to function best when targeting specific and/or non-traditional approaches to topics. The library you are using may not have enough diversity to meet your particular narrow and quirky need.
> ➢ Always remember that keyword searching, while it may focus down your quest to exactly what you want, is a very inexact science. You have to input the right word(s) configured in the right way, and you are highly dependent on the actual terminology of titles in the collection.
> ➢ Be sure you don't use too many keywords at once. Start with one or two, and if that doesn't give you what you want, try one more. Rarely will you need more than three.
> ➢ Never forget that, in an AND search, every time you add a term you eliminate data from your results. This may be good if you have too many hits, but make sure that the data you are eliminating is not crucial. It's better to get more results that you need to sift through to find what you need, than to have a smaller set of results that doesn't meet your requirements.

Some catalogs will let you combine controlled vocabulary and keyword searching. If you do this, you'll need to keep your wits about you. In general, the subject heading gets you into the right territory, the broad subject area. Then you add keywords to specify, within this subject area, the narrower concept you are looking for. For example, your subject heading might be **Homelessness**. You could then add the keyword, **Canad*** (for **Canada**, **Canada's**, **Canadian**, etc.).

Why not, then, simply make them both keywords? Because "homelessness" can be expressed in a variety of ways. In the catalog you might have titles such as:

Canada's Homeless: An Inquiry
Street Life in a Canadian City
Ain't Got No Place to Call My Own: A Canadian's Story

Two of them don't even use the term **homeless**. Thus, searching with a subject heading that is not dependent on title terminology can get you all the books generally on the subject, and additional keywords will specify which books you want from that broader pool (those dealing with the Canadian setting).

Alternatively, you can combine two or more subject headings, looking for where they overlap, though this method is less likely to get you solid results than a subject heading and keyword combination.

Above all, when catalog searching, keep your wits in place. Thinking hierarchically can also be a help. Ask yourself one or more of the following questions:

> ➤ What broader subject could this topic be a part of?
> ➤ If one approach is not working, what are other ways that I might look at the topic? (i.e., what other hierarchies could potentially contain the topic? How could I narrow to only one aspect?)

5.2.2 E-Books

Electronic books are catching on as consumer-friendly products. While many people have little desire to sit in front of a LED screen and read 300 pages of text, portable e-readers and tablets are making e-books a lot more practical.

Within library catalogs you will find an increasing number of your results to be e-books with web links instead of call numbers. Major suppliers of e-books to libraries are EBSCO and ebrary, though you will find any variety of platforms. Here begin the challenges. Each e-book platform functions in a different way. But an even bigger difficulty is that library-based e-books tend to be slow to load (I tell my students to think of how long it would have taken them to get the same book in print by visiting the physical library). It may also be a challenge to know how much of any book you can download as, for example, a PDF, as opposed to simply having to navigate through the whole book in its native reader.

In most cases you will find links to e-books in the same library catalog you use to find print-based books. If there is not an easy way in your catalog to search for e-books separately, try a keyword search focused on book titles and add the term: **electronic**. Or use an advanced search, which may let you specify e-books as a search parameter.

Navigating library e-books can be a challenging business. The left-right arrow type of interface for page turning is slow to load and tedious to spend time with. If you want to do more than click arrows, look for:

➢ Tables of contents with links
➢ Full text search boxes to enable a search within the book
➢ The ability to download a portion of the book as an easier-to-navigate PDF. The portion you can download may be as small as 20-60 pages, but it could be the whole book. Clues include a download link or even a "print" link which actually prints to PDF.

The Google Books project (**http://books.google.com/**) has become a mainstay for many researchers, though its limitations abound, the most challenging being the fact that only portions are available for many of the titles, due to copyright restrictions. Its companion, Google Play (**https://play.google.com/store/books**) is the commercial side, which does give you much more access but often at a cost. Google Books itself is searchable by keyword, so the results can be the same sort of mixed bag you find with any other Google search. If you want to discover a particular title, you can get a host of books with the same title words in various word orders, and the one you want may or may not be high in the results.

Google Books has an advanced search, if you can find it (check the link at the bottom of your first results page, though it will likely have moved by the time you read this). Or go to **http://books.google.com/advanced_book_search,** which is the URL for the advanced search. If you want an exact title, you can use the option in the advanced search – "with this exact phrase." Google Books' advanced search now also has a subject search linked to catalog records supplied from various sources. It works fairly well. A better option for searching by subject may be to identify one book, click on the "About this book" link, and find a catalog record near the bottom of the linked page.

If there is one, it will have subject links that will direct you to other books on the subject. All of this, of course, is as useful as painting your toenails and putting on sneakers if you don't get access to the full text of the books you were seeking. The "Find in a library" links may help you discover a readable copy locally.

Amazon.com, the bookseller, has a "Look inside" feature that provides access to portions of a lot of books they sell and also offers a keyword search for content. Copyright restrictions prevent full content from being viewable or searchable in most cases.

There are free e-book collections out there, viewable full text, but they are limited in number. Some examples are Directory of Open Access Books (**http://www.doabooks.org/**), ACLS Humanities E-Book Collection (**http://quod.lib.umich.edu/a/acls/browse.html**), and National Academies Press (**http://www.nap.edu/**).

One advantage of electronic format is the ability to search across a book, or even across a whole collection of books, using keywords to find the most relevant passages. While this may be a neat feature, there is always the need for caution to avoid using chunks of information out of context.

An alternative, of course, to using the library for e-books is to buy your own. I only wish I was rich enough to do the masses of e-book buying some people make a regular habit. For more on e-books and specialized e-book readers, go back to section 1.5.1 in chapter one.

Clearing the Fog – How to create in-text citations from e-readers when page numbers are missing

When you want to include e-books from specialized readers in notes or a bibliography you can run into a challenge, depending on what e-reader you are using: the original page numbers of the print document may have disappeared. Kindle has a "location number" system for such situations, but many other readers do not. So how do you cite a page number from something you are reading on an e-device that has lost the original pagination?

Here is the consensus as it currently stands for the three most common formats:

APA – Use the pattern of citing the section(s) rather than page number(s). Thus an in-text citation might look like this if you are referring to a particular part: (Johnson, 2013, Chapter 3, para. 34). It's a bit nasty, since you might lose track while counting to paragraph 34 of chapter 3, but at least you can explain clearly what part you are citing.

Your Reference List citation will look like this:

> Badke, W. B. (2003). *Beyond the answer sheet:*
> *academic success for international students.*
> Bloomington, IN: iUniverse. Kindle version. [or Nook
> version or EPUB version, whatever type it is]

See **http://www.noodletools.com/helpdesk/kb/index.php?action =article&id=207&relid=2.**

MLA – MLA cuts you a break. In the absence of page numbers, you just need to cite the chapter, rather than including the paragraph number. Thus the in-text citation will look like this: (Johnson, ch. 4). A citation in your Works Cited will look like this:

> Badke, W. B. (2003). *Beyond the answer sheet:*
> *academic success for international students.*
> Bloomington, IN: iUniverse. Kindle file. [or Nook file
> or EPUB file, whatever type it is]

See **http://www.mla.org/style/handbook_faq/cite_an_ebook**.

Chicago/Turabian – This style, while it has an in-text citation variant, tends to prefer footnotes or endnotes. Create the standard footnote according to this style, then cite chapter and paragraph, when there are no page numbers: John Jackson, *Finding the Right Word* (New York: Wordfinder Press, 2014), chap. 14, para. 23.

The bibliography citation will look like this:

> Jackson, John. *Finding the Right Word.* New York:
> Wordfinder Press, 2014. Kindle edition. [or Nook
> edition or EPUB edition, whatever type it is]

See: **http://www.chicagomanualofstyle.org/tools_citationguide. html**.

5.3 Journal databases

Just when you thought that finding books was trouble enough, someone is sure to suggest to you that there's another world of research materials crying out for attention - *journals*. Actually, the whole category of this type of resource is broader than you might think, and journals are only a portion. Librarians, ever the stuffy folks we are, call the whole field "periodicals," that is, materials that arrive in the library periodically, as opposed to a book that arrives only once. Included in the category is everything from newspapers to popular magazines (or e-zines) to trade magazines to scholarly journals. But I'm going to call them journals anyway, because this term is more familiar to the vast host of people who aren't librarians (and who, strangely, seem thankful for that fact).

Clearing the Fog – Do you know the difference between an article and a journal?

This is a common trick question that I love to ask undergraduates, who almost never know the answer, though their creativity in trying to come up with one is both amazing and (I have to admit it) sometimes a bit amusing. They tell me that an article is general and a journal is more specific, or a journal is general and an article is more specific, or a journal is more personal than an article. Nice tries, but no.

The problem comes from the fact that we encounter most articles as citations in database result lists. We're aware that there are details that describe the article as part of something bigger, such as 43(2):12-32, but the digital world has killed our consciousness of the analog origin of this stuff.

Here's the answer: *Articles are the individual pieces. Journals are the packages within which articles are found.*

Let's think analog for a moment. Back in 1984, if you subscribed to *Journal of Chemical Ecology*, you paid your money, and several times a year a paperback book-like item would be delivered to your (analog) mailbox. When you opened the pages of this issue of the journal, you would see within it individual articles, like chapters in a book. At the end of the year if you were particularly nerd-like, you would bind all your journal issues into a *journal volume*. Thus the journal is the package that you hardly ever see these days in the electronic environment. The article is one of the chapters in the journal, a piece in the package.

In the illustration below, you will see a mashup of the actual cover of an issue of a print journal, an article you can find within this issue of the journal, and the form in which you would find that article in an electronic database.

Article as you would find it in a database

Periodical

Questia.com: implications of the new McLibrary

By: **Badke**, William B. *Internet Reference Services Quarterly*, 2001, Vol. 5 Issue 3, p61-71

Subjects: COLLECTION development (Libraries); VENDORS & purchasers; ELECTRONIC pul

Database: Library, Information Science & Technology Abstracts

5.3.1 Some background on the journal scene

Before we get to journal databases, let's clarify what makes journals different from books. The most significant difference is that you can't catalog a journal like you catalog a book. When a librarian gets a new book for the collection, the book is cataloged (i.e. has an electronic metadata record created for it) and is put on the shelf. After that, there is nothing to do but sign the book out and check it back in until it falls apart. The cataloger's job is done.

But journal issues *keep on arriving* every week or month or quarter or year. By definition, they are *periodical.* You can't catalog them once and for all like you can a book, because they keep morphing as more issues are added to the growing collection. While it might be possible for a librarian to assign a subject heading to each article in each journal as it arrives and then to create a database to enable you to find articles on any given topic, it just wouldn't be practical. No librarian has the time to create a separate database of all the library's journal articles. This is where commercial journal databases come in as alternative catalogs just for journal articles.

Before we get to these databases, let's recognize that the field of what we are calling "journals" is governed by some significant categories:

Popular vs. trade vs. scholarly

Popular magazines generally come out of a different mindset than do scholarly journals. Both are supposed to inform, but popular magazines also need to entertain (for example, *Time Magazine*). They may be intelligent, but they do not pass the tests that scholars demand in scholarly journals. *Scholarly journals* are usually the territory of academics and students in higher education rather than the general public who read magazines. They tend to have notes and bibliographies, with a reading level that is advanced (for example, *Journal of Ambulatory Care Management*). In the middle are *trade magazines* that specialize in some particular industry or technology where information is shared. They are less "popular" in tone (and are, indeed, often highly technical), but they generally look like popular magazines and do not major on footnotes or bibliographies (e.g. *Online Searcher*, a magazine for information professionals).

Scholarly journals use a system of **peer review**, by which manuscripts submitted for possible publication are read by other scholars in the field (peers). This gatekeeping process is intended to weed out inferior work. Peer review itself has come under attack as preserving the status quo and preventing younger scholars with fresh ideas from publishing, but it is still the best system we've got for keeping journal article quality as high as possible. (For an alternate view and very perceptive assessment of peer review, see Brian Martin, "The Politics of Research," **http://www.uow.edu.au/~bmartin/pubs/98il/il07.pdf.**)

Print vs. electronic

Journals, now that they have substantially left behind the analog days, live primarily in the electronic world. Most published journals have electronic versions available, even if they continue also to publish in print. In fact, the print format for journals is becoming a rarity, saving thousands of trees and the squirrels that inhabit them. Why? Simply because people really like what e-journals can do for them. E-journals are instantly accessible from anywhere that has an Internet connection, you can print or save only what articles you want to keep, and they are much more searchable for key concepts than are print journals.

But there are challenges:

- ➢ Electronic back-runs are generally short, going back into the 1990s but rarely earlier. An exception to this is JSTOR, a storage database for the most significant academic journals, going back decades in many cases.
- ➢ There are dreaded embargoes everywhere. An embargo limits the release date of the electronic version for a period of time. For example "12 months embargo" means that you won't see the electronic version of the article until 12+ months after the print version has been released.

> ➤ Format can be a challenge—HTML loads faster in your device but sometimes doesn't contain original graphics or loses the original page numbers. PDF has graphics and the original page numbers but loads more slowly and creates a larger file than does HTML. PDF is now the format of choice for most online journals.
> ➤ Not every journal you want electronically is available through your institutional databases.

Many students are tempted to pay attention only to journal articles that are available in electronic full text, bypassing citations to articles the library may have in print or microform. That can be a mistake if the best article on a topic is only available in some hardcopy format. It's wise to avoid taking the easy road in a misguided quest to finish your research early. (Why do I sense that you're not liking what I'm telling you? Really. It's true. Good, thorough research might demand using the occasional print journal or even microfiche, but this is far more satisfying than simply getting the job done fast and missing the best resources).

Free journals – Partially an academic myth

What's the point of doing all this database searching from library web pages when there are tons of good journals right on the Internet? Ah, the ever-hoped-for, ever-elusive dream of being able to access the full text of every article you need, right on your screen via Google! Sadly, reality is rarely what we hope it will be.

It's simply not true that every article from every journal in the world is offered in digital form on the open Net for minimal or no cost. Why not? Let me share a brief primer on economics. Our world turns on the ability of people to manufacture things and sell them to other people. If we all worked really hard to produce things and then simply gave away what we produced, the world would stop spinning on its axis and life as we know it would disappear. Economics makes the world go around.

Thus journal publishers, before they make their material available to vendors of full text indexes, demand to be paid and paid handsomely (too handsomely, I would suggest). If a journal publisher cannot (or will not) come to an agreement with the database vendor, the full text for that journal will not be available except for a fee through the journal publisher's website. Full text is rarely free – it is either paid for by your library's expensive subscriptions to journal databases or you have to pay for your own journal subscriptions online.

The production of journal and popular magazine articles is big business in our world. While lots of people put up websites at no charge to you, few publishers of journals are even remotely as generous (except for those who are part of the open access movement described in Chapter One). The vast majority of journal articles, even those that are electronic, can only be accessed after someone (you or your library) pays a hefty price. Sure, you can find some really good articles for free, but that's not true for most of them. The databases you use through your library are password-protected for a reason—your library has paid big money to give you "free" access to them. And it's in those databases where most of the articles are.

Clearing the Fog – Some tips on journal article citations

A journal article citation is the description of an article needed to help you find it. While the format of a citation may vary, here is what is usually provided in an article's metadata:

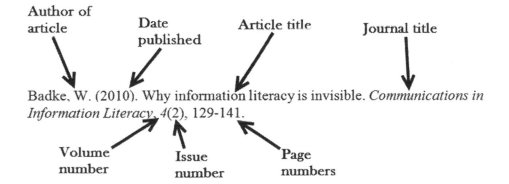

Citation error alert: Some students record the ISSN within database records of articles, thinking that the ISSN is like a call number for a book and thus can work as a citation. The ISSN looks like this: 4562-8793. It is a code number to identify the journal the article came from but is *useless* to help you find any particular article. For the most part ignore it. Instead, record these features:

- author
- date
- article title
- journal name
- volume number
- issue number
- and page numbers

(I should turn this list into a song for all of us to learn. In fact, I actually did).

Author - date - article title - journal name - volume number - issue number and page numbers

5.3.2 Introduction to journal databases

Even thinking of using journal articles in a research project may give you a shudder of horror. You imagine sitting down in front of piles of printed journals, thumbing through each one in an anguished quest for something (anything!) on the "The Implications for Generation Y of Max Weber's Approach to the Sociology of Cities." Hours later, in bitterness of heart and soul, you will emerge, red-eyed, with one article that is only vaguely relevant.

Journal research used to be done that way when your grandfather was a wee lad in school. Now things are very different, due to the development of journal databases.

These databases are created this way: Indexers sit down in front of piles of articles or, more likely, their electronic equivalents (often related to a specific subject discipline, such as psychology or history or religion) and create a metadata record for each article. The metadata is loaded into the database, thus making it searchable. By doing a search, you can generate a list of article citations from various journals that are relevant to the subject you are studying. Often the whole article is right there as a PDF. You can also, if you want, search within the full text of the electronic articles themselves in many databases.

Approaching a journal database means first being able to "read" its *interface.* The interface is what you actually see on your screen when you search for the data. It includes the screen display, search methods, and so on. Interfaces change constantly. Data doesn't. What this means is that the screen may look different the next time you use the database. The instructions on use may be different. Even the methods you need to follow to search the database may be different. The data inside it is the same, so *do not panic.*

How to read an interface

> *Go over the features visible on the screen.* There is likely a basic search available, but is there also an advanced search? Are there ways to limit your results by date, audience, type of resource, and so on? Can you search within a single journal? Is there a subject heading search available (sometimes described as a "thesaurus" or a "browse" function)?

> *Look for anything that says "search tips," "help," or "how to use this index."* Most people generally skip instructions, which is why their new lawnmower blows up or their software freezes on the screen. If you are one of those people, at least keep my suggestion in mind when you (inevitably) lose your way at some point. There really are times when it is a good idea to use the help screen

> *Start with a keyword search and identify two or three results that look like they are relevant to your research question/thesis.*

> *Click on the titles of these relevant articles, one by one, to open the full record.* Is the author's name hyperlinked (allowing you to find other articles by the same author)? Are there subject heading links within the record that you can click on? Do these headings seem specific or are they very broad in their coverage (and thus less useful)?

> *Can you locate subject heading links somewhere else on the results page, in a column to the left or right of the results or somewhere above the list of result citations?* If so, they may help you to take your keyword search results into a more focused subject area. For example, if you've done an initial keyword search on "globalization" and one of the suggested subject headings next to the results is "social justice," you can use it to focus your emphasis down to social justice issues in globalization.

Insight: *Be careful about subject links. Some will take you to results that combine your original keyword search in an AND with the subject heading. Others ignore your original keyword(s) and take you directly to everything on that subject. In this case, you may have to add your keyword(s) to the subject heading later by doing a further AND search.*

> *Look for a "Thesaurus," "Subjects," "Browse Subjects," or "Indexes" link.* Any of these can take you to authorized subject headings for your database. In this case, you can start with a subject area, then either link it to another subject area or add one or more keywords in an AND search.

> *Find out through a help screen how keyword searching is done in the database.* What sorts of Boolean operators are in use? Is phrase searching allowed?

> *Try a search on a broad basis first, perhaps inputting a subject heading or only one keyword.* If you get more than about 500 "hits" (citations to individual articles), look for a means to refine or narrow your search by adding more words or a relevant subject heading. But be careful, in doing so, that you don't eliminate good data—it's better to have to wade through more hits than to miss crucial articles because you narrowed with too much vigor. Avoid using narrowing words that you don't really need.

Let's see an example

If you want to learn to swim in the sometimes risky waters of journal database searching, you have to arm yourself and just jump in. Let's look at a sample search using *EBSCO Academic Search Premier*, a user-friendly database with considerable full text content. By the time you read this, the interface may have changed, but the image below gives you a good idea of ways in which sophisticated databases can do a good job of leading you to relevant journals.

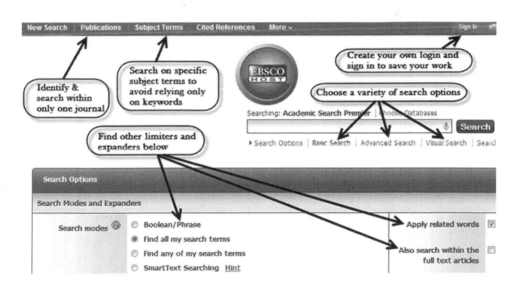

Notice some of the features of this first screen:

> ➤ The name of this database is "Academic Search Premier."
> ➤ While there is a basic search box, you can also choose an "advanced search" that allows you to build your investigation using Boolean terms.
> ➤ You can opt to search within one journal (publication) only. This is generally not recommended unless a professor has told you to do so.
> ➤ There is also a "Subject Terms" button, indicating that this index has a controlled subject vocabulary. In some databases, this will be called a "Thesaurus."
> ➤ There is a sign-in feature that gives you space in which to save your work.
> ➤ You can preset search options to specify the kind of keyword searches and the sorts of results you want.

Clearing the Fog - Please stop treating academic databases like Google – You're hurting their feelings

Most of us have keyword fever. Throw some words into a search box and harvest results as quick as you can. But academic databases for books and journals have a distinct advantage over your average Google or Bing – they have metadata that enables you to be very specific about what you are looking for. The better academic databases also have options to search within results, thus letting you facet (or stage) your search. With features like this, you could do an initial keyword search, get hundreds or thousands of results, and then drill down by searching within results until you have a much smaller but much more specific and relevant set of results. Here's an example from the EBSCO Database, PsycINFO, in 4 stages:

If you want an animated tutorial on how to stage (facet) your searches in this database, go to **http://acts.twu.ca/Library/ PsycINFOBasic.swf**.

You need to do the stages. Academic databases are much more sophisticated than Google. Don't treat them like Google. Academic databases have feelings too.

5.3.3 RSS feeds from journal databases

RSS (Really Simple Syndication) feeds enable you to be updated when new material appears in a database. Many databases allow you to identify search terminology you want to track. Every time new articles, related to a specified set of search terms, appear in the selected database, you are notified and given links to find these new articles. Look for the RSS icon (an orange square with 3 half circles in the lower left corner), or a link to "RSS" or "Search Alert."

5.3.4 Table of contents alerts

If you are a real keener, you might want to keep up with what's being published in a favorite journal or two. A great way to do this is with a journal table of contents alert service like JOURNAL TOCs (**http://www.journaltocs.hw.ac.uk/**). Just register and choose your journal(s). You will get a contents notification (though not the full text of articles) every time a new issue comes out. It's free.

5.4 Approaching journal databases – Tips and hints

5.4.1 Be prepared for challenges.

The journal scene is not nearly as tidy as are books. Journals provide a never-ending supply of issues year after year, and they can exist in a variety of formats (PDFs, HTML, open-access on the Net, and even paper and various microforms), but even then you may discover that the very article you need is nowhere to be found in your metropolitan area.

Here's a psychological trick that might help you—*prepare yourself for challenges.* An illustration: If you are aware from long experience that you will face a traffic jam at a certain place every day on the way to work or school, you are ready for it. Only when a traffic jam happens unexpectedly, in a spot you didn't expect it, do you get frustrated. In the same way, if you prepare yourself for journal database challenges, you're less likely the mutter to yourself when they happen.

Before you start using a database, say to yourself, "I know this search is going to tax the last fragments of my patience, but it's good for me, it really is, it really, really is, and *I will succeed!*"

5.4.2 Read the interface.

Every journal database is different in the way it searches and the search options it offers, even two databases produced by the same company. Before you simply throw some words at a database and demand articles in return, check out what's available to you. Is there an advanced search? Is there a thesaurus or a subject heading search? In what ways can you limit or expand your search? Is there a tutorial available? (You can find quite a number of short animated tutorials for using various databases from the ANTS project at **http://www.screencast.com/users/ants/folders/Database%20 Tutorials** or **http://www.youtube.com/user/1LIONTV.**)

5.4.3 Be aware that databases tend to be something of a black hole.

You send in a request, and the database tells you what it found (not what it didn't find). The database search program will rarely let you know what you did wrong or what might actually be available if you did a better search. It won't give you three 6.5's and an 8 like Olympic judges do. The data you want could well be in there, but you won't know that unless you vary your search strategies to draw it out.

5.4.4 Resist the urge to fill the search box with words.

Most keyword searches can be done with two words or, at the most, three. Remember this simple insight—the more you input into a search box the more strain you're putting on your search. If it's an AND search, you are telling the database that you want *only* those articles that have *every* word you've entered (which often results in few or zero hits). If it's an OR search, each and every article that has any one of your words will appear (sometimes resulting in thousands of hits). Get focused. *Use as few words as you need to define your topic, no more.*

5.4.5 Think about staging (faceting) your search.

Unlike Google, where you do a search and then pull in your results like you're fishing with a net, a journal database allows you the option of starting broadly and then narrowing in stages. "Stages?" you ask, bewildered that I would even suggest that you might not get great results on the first try. Yes, stages. Like a video game requires stages or like most any activity in life requires steps to be taken. In our example of a real search below, I'll show you how to stage (or facet) a search.

5.4.6 Look for controlled vocabularies and advanced searches.

Tools like controlled vocabularies and advanced searches can help you to specify what you want, especially when keywords could be ambiguous. For example, if I searched EBSCO's *Academic Search Premier* for "paranoia," I would get a host of articles on all kinds of paranoia—political, social, spouses who hire detectives, people claiming to have been kidnapped by aliens, folks suspicious of luncheon meats, and so on. If I could find a subject heading within *Premier* for the psychological disorder of paranoia (and I could), I would limit the scope of possible results considerably. Now, if I tried an advanced search—SUBJECT Paranoia and KEYWORD Fear, I would find articles on the issue of fear among people with the psychological disorder of paranoia. It is that kind of fiddling with features that gets you the *best* results instead of merely a bunch of results.

5.4.7 Think before you search.

Even when you figure out how a journal database actually works, you need to think deeply about the terms you input. What will uniquely identify your topic in the minimum number of words? If your results show hit rates of 1,000 to 100,000 articles, you're aiming too broadly in your search, and you need to narrow down your terminology. If

you are getting only one or two hits, you're probably too narrow –
you've been inputting too many search terms or asking for something
so minute that there's only one scholar in the whole world who's
remotely interested in the topic, and she's on vacation. A tip - as often
as possible, use actual terminology from your research question, or
synonyms of that terminology.

5.4.8 Retrace your steps.

Be prepared to go back and figure out what you did wrong or how you
could get better results. Look for "Refine Search" or "Search Again"
options. Journal database searching often demands experimentation
to find just the right combination of terms that will nail down what
you are looking for.

5.4.9 When in doubt, use the instructions.

Every journal database worth its salt has instructions to guide you
through the process of searching. After you've exhausted your
own common sense, use the instructions. Different databases have
different capabilities and search techniques. You may find that the
reason you get 354,000 hits one time and zero the next is that you are
abusing the database by trying to make it do things it's not prepared
even to contemplate.

5.4.10 Remain calm and get help if you need it.

What's the most terrible thing that could happen if you blew a search?
You might have to try again or (worst case scenario) one of your
friends will have watched you fail. Rarely will you have done any
permanent harm to the database itself (unless you got violent, which
is not recommended), so the only damage is to your time and your
ego. If you find yourself hopelessly lost, there is usually a reference
librarian to help you out, either personally or via some remote means
like e-mail or messaging. Swallow your pride and ask for help. Having
a bad day in front of a database isn't the end of the world. Above all,
resist those evil thoughts that take up residence in your mind, such as,
"I will never ever get this" or, "For people like me, ignorant would be

a step up," "I must be a few pepperoni short of a pizza," or, "I want to break something." Cool your heart and try again.

5.4.11 Sometimes problems arise because you're using the wrong database.

A database for agriculture won't help you with a psychology project. A history database won't be much good if you're researching cockroaches. The right database for the right job is a rule not to be forgotten. If you can't find one for the subject area you're working on, try a larger, broadly based database that covers a number of different topics. These types of databases, however, have their own problem in that their coverage of any one subject area is limited.

Insight: *For specialized topics, start with specialized databases (e.g. for mental illnesses use a psychology database) and resort to more broadly based all-topic databases only if the specialized ones don't deliver enough of what you need or if you need an interdisciplinary emphasis.*

5.4.12 Check out the possibilities of interlibrary loan.

A database may provide a citation to an article you really want, but the electronic full text is not available, nor does the library have the article in any other format. Fret not. While not all academic libraries offer interlibrary loans (the ability to get the article from somewhere else), yours very well may. Have a look at your library web page for information about interlibrary loans or ask a librarian. Do you feel better now?

5.5 Citation searches, related articles and reference lists – Alternative ways of searching

5.5.1 Citation searches

In the sciences and to some extent the social sciences, the relative importance of journal articles (and their authors) is measured by the number of citations to them found in other articles. If an article is cited often, it is viewed as being more important than if it is seldom or never cited.

What is more, citations to a key earlier article within several later articles can form a history of how the earlier article has been used by other scholars since it was published. Finding out who have cited a key early article can be a good way to add to your own resources.

The major tool used in citation searching is Web of Knowledge's three part citation index system – *Science Citation Index*, *Social Sciences Citation Index*, and *Arts and Humanities Citation Index*. While fairly complex to use, you can start with a keyword search, get a list of results, and then sort the list by "Times Cited." When you find an oft-cited (sounds Shakespearean, doesn't it?) article, you can click on the "Times Cited" link to get a list of all the literature that has cited it. Not only does this tool help you determine the relative importance of articles, but it can get you a lot of resources that have cited an important one, thus building up your own bibliography.

Google Scholar (**http://scholar.google.com**) offers a "cited by" link below many of the scholarly works in its results list. It seems to work quite well to track citations and is becoming a serious challenge to Web of Science, though many argue that the actual citation numbers in Google Scholar are inflated. Google Scholar is freely available on the Net while libraries have to subscribe to Web of Science.

5.5.2 Related articles

For quite a number of journal databases, when you open the full record of one of the results of your search, you will find a link to "related articles," or "find more like this one." A feature like this can be of great help when you really want to add to resources. Google Scholar also has this feature.

5.5.3 Reference lists

Once you have a relevant article in hand, a great way to find others like it is simply to look over the notes, bibliography or reference list in that article. What one writer cites tends to be relevant to the topic or issue overall. Advanced researchers often use this method more often than even the searching of databases. But be aware of a couple of things. First, a reference list will always have resources that are older than the original article. Second, what any author cites may not be all that is actually out there. Reference lists can be quite selective and limited in scope. Still, they can be an effective source to mine for additional resources.

A number of databases provide, right in their citations, a list of all the sources a particular article used in its notes or bibliography. Thus, even if you can't get the article itself, you can discover the books, articles, etc. to which that article referred.

Clearing the Fog – What's a doi?

Journals in the sciences and social sciences, with the humanities coming along too, have embraced the doi (digital object identifier) system which, in essence, stamps a barcode-like number on each article a journal publishes. That doi then remains attached to that article, no matter in what format the article is found. Here is an example of an article citation with a doi:

Badke, W. B. (2005). Can't Get No Respect: Helping Faculty to Understand the Educational Power of Information Literacy. *Reference Librarian, 43*(89/90), 63-80. doi:10.1300/J120v43n8905

How can you find the doi for an article from a database when you want to cite the article properly?

> You can click on the citation's title in your result list and look through the full record for that article to locate the doi.
> If your database has a citing feature, the citations it creates will have the doi in them.

Here is an example of the open record and citing feature from an EBSCO database:

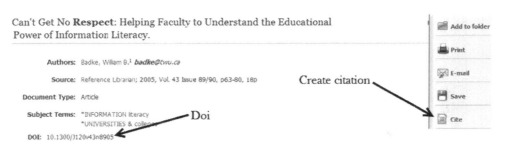

The doi is especially important for citations in APA format. An interesting but challenging style note is that APA format *demands* that you include the doi, rather than providing the name of the database you got the article from.

So what if an article has no doi? APA requires you to Google the journal title (not the title of the article, but the journal it came from). Find the journal home page URL and add it to the basic citation, as in this example:

Badke, W. (2001). Questia.com: implications of the new McLibrary. *Internet Reference Services Quarterly*, *5*(3), 61-71. Retrieved from http://www.tandfonline.com/loi/wirs.

5.6 Trying out a live journal database

Let's test-drive a real journal database, remembering that interfaces and features vary, depending on which one you use. In our case, you will be taking EBSCO's broad-based *Academic Search Premier* for a spin around the block, because the topic you will be approaching is quite interdisciplinary rather than limited to one subject discipline.

You begin with the question, "How effective was the cleanup of the Gulf oil spill of 2010 in restoring the previous environment?"

You can start with a simple keyword search, just to see what's out there. In this case, the terms ***Gulf oil spill*** should do the trick. You end up with 3756 results. Too many, but there are ways to narrow your search and cut down the result numbers:

Let's have a look at some clues in the image above:

> ➤ 3756 results are too much to handle. Having used keywords, it may well be that some of the results have the right words but refer to the wrong oil spill.
> ➤ You can limit to peer reviewed (scholarly) articles only.

> There is a subject heading toolbar to the left of the results. Clicking on it opens a number of subject heading options, including one for the 2010 BP spill, and two others for cleanup and environmental aspects of oil spills. Checking off these boxes (but not checking off everything in a wild dash for the best article) will focus the results to the 2010 oil spill, cleanup and the environment.

Once you have checked off the relevant limiters, you have only 340, but they'll be more relevant:

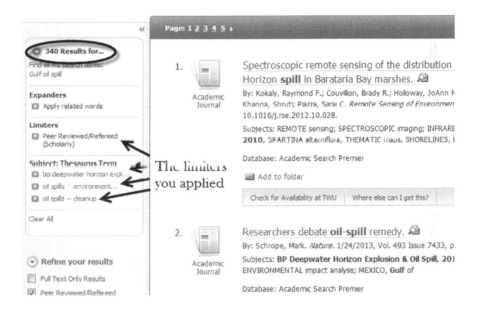

Additional strategy:

Another way to find subject headings to help narrow your search is to open the citation to one of the articles in the results (by clicking on its title). Subject headings will be hyperlinked in the full record. For example:

Another Tragedy on the *Gulf* Coast.
Authors:
> Kennedy, Maureen Shawn

Source:

> American Journal of Nursing; Sep2010, Vol. 110 Issue 9, p7-7,
> 1p, 1 Color Photograph

Document Type:

> Editorial

Subject Terms:

> *EDITORIALS
> *OIL spills
> *BP Deepwater Horizon Explosion & Oil Spill, 2010
> *OIL spills — Environmental aspects
> *HEALTH

Clicking on BP Deepwater Horizon Explosion & Oil Spill, 2010 will get you everything in the database on the 2010 major oil spill. You can then narrow even further by adding a keyword to the search box (e.g. AND cleanup)

5.7 Varieties of the journal database

It's now virtually impossible to keep up with the number and types of journal databases available, or with their ever changing interfaces. Staying in touch with research libraries and librarians seems to be the only way to remain up to date. Of course, for many people even the thought of keeping in touch with a librarian may seem unusual, despite the fact that we're the kindest (and coolest) people in the world.

Most library home pages now have links to their journal databases, using wording like "Find articles," "Find journals," and so on. In most cases, you can look up journal databases by the title of the database (e.g. PsycARTICLES) or by the subject area you are interested in (e.g. Psychology).

If you expect constant change in the area of electronic research, you won't be disappointed. Despite the fact that it's hard for anyone to keep up, the capabilities of these newer databases are amazing, and you can benefit greatly from them as long as you keep your wits about you. Just don't treat them like Google. They'll remember what you did and not be so kind to you the next time you use them.

5.8 Final pep talk

Don't be afraid of journal databases and articles. They want to be strong and effective resources for you, if you'll let them. Scholarly articles in journals and magazines will provide you with a wealth of current and specific information that you dare not ignore. Most journal databases have sophisticated ways for you to focus search results on what you need rather than leaving you floundering in a sea of less than relevant articles.

More and more libraries are providing short guides to their individual databases. Spending 5 minutes or less watching an explanatory animation is probably worth it, especially if you fear you are going to muddle for a couple of hours, saying things to yourself that would make even your dog blush if he could understand you. For a great site to find short tutorials on a number of databases, go to ANTS project at Screencast.com: **http://www.screencast.com/users/ANTS/folders/Database%20Tutorials** or **http://www.youtube.com/user/1LIONTV.**

Just heed the following pieces of advice, and you will survive the journal maze:

➤ Stay calm.
➤ Stay focused.
➤ Read the directions.
➤ Plan your searches well.
➤ Ask for help when you need it.

5.9 For further study

Study guide

1. What is discovery search? What are its advantages and disadvantages?
2. In a library catalog, when would you use controlled vocabulary subject headings, and when would you use keywords?
3. How can hierarchies help you when you are searching a library catalog for a topic?

4. Why is it futile to believe that the electronic full text of every book you want will be available to you for free?
5. How are journal databases created, and what are they intended to do?
6. Explain the difference between "data" and "interface."
7. Identify each part of the following journal citation:

Badke, William. (2010). Why information literacy is invisible. *Communications in Information Literacy 4(2)*, 129-141.

8. In journal database searching you should be prepared for _____. How does such preparation help you?
9. Why should you resist the urge to fill the search box with words?
10. What are the advantages of thinking before you search?
11. Why is it often better to stage (facet) your search with keywords as well as subject headings and other limiters rather than simply to do a one-stage keyword search?
12. Many journal articles are available in electronic "full text" format. What are some of the advantages and difficulties with accessing full text?

Practice with journal databases

Go to one of your institution's databases and "read" the interface, trying to figure out what search features it provides. Try searches on the same topic using different features. What did you learn about the value of enhanced search features to get you the results you need?

Assignment for a project of your own

1. Choose a topic of interest to you.
2. Choose two journal databases. If you do not have access to university databases like those produced by EBSCO, ProQuest, and so on, choose from the following free Internet-based databases: **http://www.ingentaconnect.com/** or **http://magportal.com/** (but note that their interfaces are not nearly as sophisticated as commercial products available through your library).

3. Do a search for journal articles on your topic with each database.
4. Indicate what subject terms or keywords you used in your searches.
5. List 6 articles from each database that are relevant to your topic - author, date, article title, title of journal, volume number, page numbers.

Note: Be sure the databases you use are relevant to your topic.

6

Internet Research

The early 1990s saw the beginning of an information revolution as dramatic as the introduction of the printing press in Europe in 1440 (though we dare not miss the fact that the Chinese people had a printing press 400 years earlier). The printing press made it possible to replace the normal copying of documents by hand with a process that produced multiple copies at the same time. All of a sudden, the availability of written information increased dramatically.

The creation of the World Wide Web in the 1990s led to the same kind of revolution, but on a larger scale. An information delivery system primarily concerned with paper and print (libraries, bookstores, hard copy journal subscriptions and so on) became an electronic universe available to anyone with a device and a service provider. Today, the average student gets well over two-thirds of his/her information from search engines like Google or Bing.

Please supply your own answer to the following question: **The World Wide Web is an environment where:** _____

_____.

Stumped? Let me supply some possibilities:

The World Wide Web is an environment where:
- ➤ you can freely interact with the rest of humanity
- ➤ you can find information on virtually any topic
- ➤ almost everyone is trying to sell you something
- ➤ you can surf until your eyes fall out
- ➤ anything that's worth anything costs *money* to retrieve (or else you're told that access is "forbidden!")
- ➤ you can meet new friends or pick up predators
- ➤ you can't absolutely trust anyone or any piece of information
- ➤ you can get your questions answered
- ➤ you can spend a lot of time you don't really have to spare

Maybe your response should be "all of the above." The WWW is wonderful and frustrating, helpful and potentially deceptive, beneficial and a real time-sink. And it has become the common denominator of our daily lives. As the phenomenon of doing things electronically grows, the only common medium that can meet its needs is the WWW. It has become the basis for the things we need to get done. It is the number one vehicle for all informational research, whether through a search engine or a specialized subscription database.

True, some people are calling for us to start over with this thing, using what we have learned to create a new World Wide Web that works more efficiently (see, for example, the Named Data Networking Project - **http://www.named-data.net/**). But no one is advocating that we abandon it.

6.1 A brief introduction to the Net

I hesitate to recite history, but there are a lot of people who grew up with the Net and really don't appreciate its back story. Back in the late 1960s, the US military developed a worldwide computer network in order to remain in communication with everybody involved in the space program and defense research. This network (really a network of networks) eventually came into the hands of non-military people - scientists, computer buffs, and so on. It lacked a common communication language that was easy to use, so only specialists could profit from it. In the early 1990s, a common communication language (html) and a common communication protocol (http) were created and made public so that anyone who had access to this network could move around it with ease. This resulted in the formation of the World Wide Web (WWW). Essentially, the WWW is a subset of the larger Internet, though in common language the two terms are often used interchangeably.

The following sites on the Internet will provide you with good information about using it for research purposes:

http://www.learnthenet.com/english/index.html
This one, called *Learn the Net*, is very informative and user friendly. It also has a lot of links to other information about the Net.

http://www.lib.berkeley.edu/TeachingLib/Guides/Internet/FindInfo.html
This is a tutorial with links from the University of California, Berkeley.

Disclaimer: In the pages that follow, several URLs will be provided. Addresses change rapidly on the WWW, so I make no guarantee that you will find what you're seeking by inputting the URLs given. Sorry, but that's life, raw and nasty, though still interesting. Keep these URLs up to date with my live links page: **https://sites.google.com/site/researchstrategiesweb/home/livelinks**

6.2 Google Scholar and other free academic search engines on the Net

6.2.1 Why start with academic search engines?

We have Google. Why get all stuffy and start our discussion with academic search engines like Google Scholar? Well, my motive is partly based on the fact that this book is about academic research. Another part is the fact that most readers are already familiar with Google (though I'll happily reveal a few things later in this chapter that you possibly did not know).

The other part of my purpose comes from a lingering concern that a lot of students are using general search engines without much regard for evaluation of the websites they find. Academic search engines at least get you to information that has often gone through some sort of gatekeeping process, or so we hope.

But fear not, we'll deal with more broadly based search engines soon. For now, we'll look at academic research tools, whose result lists are most often academic journal articles, books and conference proceedings rather than websites.

6.2.2 Google Scholar (http://scholar.google.com)

Google Scholar, though an increasingly significant player in the academic world, isn't really a subset of the Google search engine. It is for the most part a separate resource devoted to scholarly literature - books, journal articles, conference proceedings and academic websites found on the WWW. Think of it as a type of academic one-stop shopping center. Yet, before you come to believe that you've found paradise, be aware that GS does have its challenges:

➤ It is limited to the standard basic search box and some rather elementary advanced search features. Thus any sophisticated search techniques using controlled vocabularies or clustering are out of the question.

> ➤ Not all publishers of academic information are included, though GS is getting more comprehensive all the time.

> ➤ The definition of "academic" is fairly broad. I've found second year undergraduate student papers through GS as well as works by scholars with a Ph.D.

> ➤ It's unclear how the results are ranked. What qualifies your results to be on the first page as opposed to being on the fifth or twentieth? In GS, you can rearrange your results by date (though the results only go back a year), or you can set a date range for results. But you can't organize your results by type of material (articles, books, conference proceedings and academic websites). Citations of every type are jumbled together.

> ➤ The quest for actual full text is a frustrating one. Increasingly, there are links to full text posted by authors, but more often than not, following a link to a journal article will get you only to an abstract of it. The full text will cost you significant coin. This can be offset in a couple of ways: first, check to see if your academic library has linked its journal holdings to GS through the "library links" process (ask your librarian about this or go to **http://scholar.google.com/intl/en/scholar/ librarylinks.html**), and second, check your own library's journal list to see if it subscribes to the journal named in a citation you found in Scholar. A number of database providers like EBSCO and JSTOR have begun including links to full text articles if the searcher is logged in to GS through his/her library and if the library subscribes to those EBSO databases.

All of that said, Google Scholar can be a very useful resource, especially for helping to identify something about which you have only partial information, for finding other articles by an important author on your topic (use the "cited by" and "related articles" links under each citation), or simply as one more place to search for resources. It will not, however, usually serve as first choice ahead of the journal databases available through your library.

Google Scholar's help system (**http://scholar.google.com/intl/ en/scholar/help.html**) is very good, so I won't take time to explain all of its functions. I would urge you, however, to make use of the advanced search feature, which has some useful limiters. (If you can find the advanced search, that is – when last seen it was that little upside down triangle in the right end of the basic search box). You should also know that, under Scholar Settings (the wheel in the top right of the first Google Scholar screen), you can set yourself up to be able to download citations from GS to a bibliographic manager like RefWorks or EndNote (more on bibliographic managers in chapter 7).

Here are some of the common types of citations you can expect to find in Google Scholar:

➤ Journal articles – Look for the journal name just under the title link in the citation. There is no specific descriptor (like [Journal]) used to identify journal articles.

➤ Books – Not the full text in most cases; designated by [Book]

➤ Citations – This is a bit tricky – a citation is a reference to a scholarly article or book found within one of the articles or books in the GS database. So it's a reference to a reference. As such, *it has no link* to take you to a place where you can obtain it, though you can link to the source that referred to it, as well as do a search on Google to see if it's available on the open Net. This type of result is designated as [Citation].

➤ Conference proceedings – Conference proceedings have no special designation to tell them apart from journal articles, so you have to look at how they are described under the title link in the citation. Here's an example:

> Time division duplex for preventing reflection interference in visible light communication
> YF Liu, CW Chow, CH Yeh - … **Conference** (WOCC), 2012 21st …, 2012 - ieeexplore.ieee.org**… Conference Proceeding** 2012 21st Annual Wireless and Optical

> Communications **Conference** (WOCC)-April 19-21, Kaohsiung, Taiwan
> Related articles Import into RefWorks More

Note that the name of the conference is stated. As long as we are looking at this entry, you can see that it is also possible to identify related (= similar) articles, and you can import the citation into a bibliographic manager (if you set this up in Scholar Settings).

➢ Academic and government websites – These will have URLs instead of journal names or descriptions like [Book] or [Citation].

Google Scholar appears to be going up against two large commercial databases – Web of Science and LexisNexis. The former lets scholars see how many times and in what publications a particular article has been cited (referred to) by others. This helps determine the relative importance of that original article. Google Scholar has a fairly sophisticated "Cited by" feature that, in many cases, pulls up more citations than Web of Science does. This is probably because GS has a broader definition what is academic literature than does Web of Science. Google Scholar has also geared itself up to search for legal opinions and legal cases, something that was once the major turf of the database LexisNexis.

Google Scholar is no longer one of the tabs on the Google products bar. This has led some to question whether or not Google is planning to merge Scholar into Google itself (see **http://www. maxkemman.nl/2013/09/what-if-google-killed-scholar/**). If this were to happen, much of what makes Google Scholar function for academic searching (see: "Clearing the fog," below) might vanish. What is more, struggling students would have even more trouble discerning what is academic/scholarly and what is not. As usual, I have no crystal ball, so let's wait and see what happens.

While we might assume that few people would want to compete with Google Scholar in Google's turf, a number of other academic open access search tools are attempting to do just that. Before we get into them, let me mention one new initiative, just in its fledgling stages – the Knowledge for All Project (**http://library.upei.ca/k4all**)

- which is attempting to enlist higher educators worldwide to develop an open access tool like Google Scholar that is non-commercial and uses the more powerful search tools of the subscription-only databases. Will it succeed? Time will tell.

Clearing the Fog – Google Scholar may be more valuable for what surrounds a citation than for what is in it.

A few features on the Google Scholar results page, beyond merely the citations, are worth checking out:

> **Can't get no respect**: helping faculty to   **PDF]** from twu.ca
> understand the educational power of information literacy
> WB **Badke** - The Reference Librarian, 2005 - Taylor & Francis
> SUMMARY While there is much discussion today about information literacy, proper implementation of it within university campuses is still a struggle, often due to the fact that librarians and teaching faculty have different "cultures" that create different priorities. ...
> Cited by 49 Related articles All 6 versions Import into RefWorks Cite

> ➢ **Cited by** (under result citations): This will tell you how many times a resource has been cited (referred to) by other sources, and it will give you a list of which sources have cited it. The more citations (in general), the more highly regarded a resource will be. But there are some cautions: a. you need to see how old the resource is (older resources have opportunity to be cited more often but may not be more important than an equally cited newer resource); b. you need to recognize that authors may overly cite themselves, thus inflating the number of citations for their works; and c. on rare occasions a source has been cited many times simply because everyone hates it.
> ➢ **Related articles** (under each search result citation): A link to resources that have similar words in them and thus may be on the same topic. Great for expanding your

bibliography (as long as you actually read the things you cite; not reading at least some of everything in your bibliography is an academic crime akin to mocking a professor on Facebook).

➢ **All _____ versions**: This might be helpful in locating a full text copy if it doesn't seem readily available.

➢ As the open access movement grows and more scholars post copies of their published work on their own websites, the availability of full text right in Google Scholar is growing. Watch for links to the right of citations that say "PDF."

➢ Ever evolving, Google Scholar in late 2013 introduced My Library. It is a feature you need to enable (**http:// googlescholar.blogspot.ca/2013/11/google-scholar-library.html**). Once you have enabled My Library, you will see a Save link under each citation and a My Library link to the left. Clicking "Save" puts the citation into My Library. You can also create labels that will let you group your citations. What is more, you can do a Google Scholar search of the full text within My Library.

6.2.3 BASE (http://www.base-search.net/)

BASE, produced by Bielefeld University Library, is a large search engine that covers academic open access web resources mainly found in university electronic repositories. Thus it focuses only on academic literature that is openly available on the Net. A couple of advantages of this tool over Google Scholar are that the academic sources are humanly selected (rather than computer selected) and that BASE offers a full list of the academic publishers from whom it selects (Google Scholar doesn't). The disadvantage is that it covers only open access (freely available) resources and does not index commercial/password-protected academic material as Google Scholar does.

6.2.4 Microsoft Academic Search (http://academic.research.microsoft.com/)

Following upon the failure of Windows Live Academic, Microsoft has a renewed academic search tool – Microsoft Academic Search. Its database is still smaller than Google's, and it produces fewer results than does Google Scholar, but it has a few unique features: Ability to search by a particular author, journal, conference, date and doi (Digital Object Identifier); ability for users to correct errors in the information; ability to graphically view relationships among scholars; and availability of larger records which are profile pages for content or authors. You also get a citation graph for each work that has been cited by others. (On the down side, a search on my name brought up "William Bake," with a query as to whether, for some reason, I actually wanted items by me - William Badke. Not the best way to get on the good side of a textbook author). For more information on features, see **http://academic.research.microsoft.com/About/Help. htm.**

6.2.5 CiteSeerX (http://citeseerx.ist.psu.edu/)

CiteSeerX is a search engine for academic scientific information that is open access (freely available) on the WWW. As such, it offers real full text of more than 2 million scholarly articles. But it does a lot more. In the scientific and social scientific worlds, the value of research papers is often determined by how many other papers refer to (cite) them. If your paper has a hundred citations to it in other people's papers, it will be considered to be more valuable to the scientific community than if it only had one citation. CiteSeer is able to break down the details of the articles it lists so that you can see what sources each article cited and which articles have cited that article. Helpful charts demonstrate citation history. There are also a number of sort features to reorganize search results.

Citations to an existing paper can also help scholars follow a trail of research on a topic: Paper A, published in 2001, was cited by paper B in 2003, paper C in 2004, paper D in 2013, and so on. The later papers demonstrate how the research in Paper A has been used in new ways to expand knowledge, thus creating a history trail related to the development of the topic.

6.2.6 Scirius (http://www.scirus.com/srsapp/)

This site bills itself as follows: "Scirius is the most comprehensive scientific research tool on the web. With over 545 million scientific items indexed at last count, it allows researchers to search for not only journal content but also scientists' homepages, courseware, pre-print server material, patents and institutional repository and website information." The content provided includes both journal articles and academic websites, though some of the journal material is citation only (not full text), since it comes from commercial databases like Elsevier's *Science Direct*. Thus, you may or may not have direct free access to electronic full text.

Scirius, in its advanced search, allows you to limit to articles, conferences, scientist home pages, theses, etc., or any combination of these. It offers searching of full text or titles, authors and other specific fields. You can sort results by relevance or date. Scirius also provides, on the results page, links to terminology you can use to narrow your search. You can export your results so that they can be put into a bibliographic manager.

6.2.7 getCITED (http://www.getcited.org/)

getCITED is an interesting experiment in the interactivity of Web 2.0. Academic users of this search engine submit their own material or citations to it and have the ability (if properly signed in) to revise anything in the database. Think of it like the Wikipedia of academic search engines. In this case, why don't we let it speak for itself? The following is from the getCITED home page:

> getCITED is an online, member-controlled academic database, directory and discussion forum. Its contents are entered and edited by members of the academic community. By putting its content in the hands of its members, getCITED makes it possible to enter in and search for publications of all types. This means that, in

addition to the books and articles accessible with other databases, book chapters, conference papers, working papers, reports, papers in conference proceedings, and other such research outlets can all be entered and then searched for within getCITED.

6.2.8 Others

Here are a few of the many other academic search engines giving access to freely available resources on the Net:

> **arXiv (http://arxiv.org/)** – a database of preprints (not yet published article manuscripts) in math and several of the sciences. Over 600,000 articles.
> **Directory of Open Access Journals (http://www.doaj. org/)** – database of thousands of open access (thus freely available) academic journals.
> **Directory of Open Access Books (http://www. doabooks.org/)**
> **OAIster (http://oaister.worldcat.org/)** – database of academic websites (also available within the larger **Worldcat.org** database)
> **Social Science Research Network (http://ssrn.com/)** – database that includes almost 250,000 articles in various branches of the social sciences.
> **Wolfram Alpha (http://www.wolframalpha.com/)** – OK, this one is not a journal search engine, but it's so cool that I had to include it. Billed as a "computational knowledge engine," this tool will do a wide variety of mathematical calculations, but much more. As the site itself tells us: "We aim to collect and curate all objective data; implement every known model, method, and algorithm; and make it possible to compute whatever can be computed about anything. Our goal is to build on the achievements of science and other systematizations of knowledge to provide a single source that can be relied on by everyone for definitive answers to factual queries." Try it out. For example, input your birth date and it will

tell you how many days you have lived upon this earth. Really quite amazing.

More of these types of free online academic search tools will emerge over time, fuelled in part by the growing open access movement that is making a lot of academic information available for free. But be warned – much of what you want is found within the journal databases your library pays for. The myth that most journal articles are freely available on the open Web is as believable as the alligators in New York City sewers.

Be aware, as well, that none of the free online academic databases above do searches nearly as well as do commercial academic databases available through your library. While they cost nothing and look cool, their level of sophistication is pretty low. It's like trying to compare a Timex with a Rolex. The Rolex wins.

6.3 Search engines for the rest of humanity – Google and friends

6.3.1 Searching by search engine, using keywords

In the most common Internet research situation, you want information on a topic, but you don't have a specific address (URL). This is where a search engine can help you by taking the keyword(s) you input and searching the WWW for data that is relevant. As you will soon discover, each search engine does the job a bit differently and with different results.

Some search engines are better for certain searches than for others. Most *rank* their results so that, by their algorithms, the most relevant, useful results will come first. But be careful with this. Some sites (often in a different script or with a colored background) are at the top of the results list because they have paid to be there. Ranking is done by complex software functions, but it is still ranking-by-computer. Not wanting to seem anti-tech or anything, humans are still smarter than our devices in evaluating the usefulness of data, so we should not simply trust the ranking assigned by a search engine.

In general, most students commit two great errors when using a search engine. First, they don't go deeper into results than one or two pages. A lot of searchers, in fact, don't look beyond the first five results. This means that they are relying on search engine ranking rather than using their superior brains to probe deeper and find the really good result that might be on the third page of results. Second, they fail to evaluate the websites they choose from their results, somehow assuming that search engine results are all pretty good and have probably been checked out by someone (they haven't).

Insight: *If you want to rise above basic level as a researcher, vow to spend more time after searches, especially Internet searches, looking over and carefully evaluating your results. You need to aim to check out 4 or more pages of results before you give up. And assume that your results are a mixed bag when it comes to both quality and relevance. Evaluation is a must. If you haven't found what you want, it's not that hard to modify search terms and try again.*

What options do we have available to us for creating effective searches? That depends. Each search engine has its own set of search paradigms. Most search engines have a **"tips"** or **"help"** or **"about"** link you can click on to be guided on the best ways to input keywords for that search engine.

> ➤ In most cases, search engines automatically create an AND search. Note that + signs are no longer used to create AND searches in most searches engines, as they once were. Use quotation marks if you want to include words that would normally be ignored like "the," or "of," (e.g. **"The" Office** for the popular TV series, which, like MASH and Seinfeld, will be forever in reruns.).
> ➤ OR is usually required for "or" searches, but make it OR in capital letters.
> ➤ NOT is often done with a dash in front of a word (**-trees** [no space]).

> Most search engines allow you to group words that normally belong together. To do this, use quotation marks (**"accountability groups"**). If you don't use the quotation marks, it's often OK, since most initial results will have the words in close proximity. But the search engine could also bring you sites that use the two words even though they are not related, as in: "The president is calling for more *accountability.* This has been rejected by several banking *groups* that insist …"

> Most search engines *do not use* truncation or wildcards (e.g. Freud* for Freud, Freudian, etc.)

As a skilled researcher, always check the search tips for a search engine and make sure you know what you're dealing with. Some of them want you to input names in certain ways. Others want you to use capitals for proper names and titles. Most will allow you to refine your search if you find you're not getting what you want or you have too many hits.

6.3.2 A basic introduction to the best search engines

Truth to tell (and I usually try to be truthful, because I'm not a convincing liar), you could likely get by with Google (**www.google. com**) and never use another search engine. But it's a good idea to keep a number of engines in your garage. Each engine creates its own index of the Internet, so that, while Google's is the biggest, it may not have included sites that are found in another search engine's index.

You need to be aware that, though the following search engines are currently the best around for the WWW, the quality of the actual websites they cover varies from the most scholarly to a page created by some guy who thinks he's a duck. *You* are the gatekeeper now, and evaluation is all important (more on this later in the chapter). Many professors simply won't accept websites in bibliographies unless you can prove that the material has been produced by reputable scholars or at least people who have advanced knowledge of the topic.

Virtually every search engine now uses personalization, especially if you log into them (more on this below). You will have to decide whether or not you want to be tracked.

Every time I bring out a new edition of this book, the list of best search engines is different. Inevitably some merge with others, some change their foci, and some just die. I remain hopeful that the list below will survive this edition, but by the time you read this, a great new search engine may well have arisen and the features of those described below may have changed. Yet, I dare to introduce them to you anyway, brave and foolhardy soul that I am. Here goes:

Google (http://www.google.com/)

Google has the biggest index of the Net and consistently does the best job of locating what you're searching for. Here are some key features:

- ➤ As you input keywords to use as search tools, Google automatically forms them into an AND search and seeks to bring you websites that contain those words in close proximity to one another.
- ➤ Google uses a technique called PageRank that prioritizes your results by giving you first those sites that are most often found as links on other websites. This "popularity" measure seems to work well in searches so that the most relevant sites often appear in the first 20 or so results (but not always). There are other things going on in Google's algorithm box, but Google isn't talking in public about most of them.
- ➤ Google offers simple techniques to create Boolean searches:

  - AND is automatic
  - You can create an OR by inputting OR. Google will nest searches with ( ) as in Freud (ego OR id), but if you are not sure it's working, use the advanced search, putting **Freud** into "with all of the words" and **ego id** into "with at least one of the words." (More on the advanced search below).
  - Phrases can be searched by putting quotation marks around them, e.g., "apple trees." Or you can use

Google's phrase search option - "this exact word or phrase" - among advanced search features.

- You can't truncate search words, e.g., educat* for education, educator, etc. This feature simply doesn't work in Google or most other search engines. Educat* will get you sites using the word Educat.

- Google used to allow you to put a plus sign before words that had to be included in a search, e.g. **+The Office**, for the television comedy The Office (normally Google would ignore "The"). That no longer does it. Now, Google uses quotation marks around words that must be included in the search or which must be searched as given. Thus you need to search **"The" Office**, so that Google will include **The** in the search. You can search **"Latina"** (with quotation marks) so that Google will find only **Latina**, not related words, such as **Latino**.

➢ Google has links on its search page to allow you to toggle among various formats for its results - Web, Images, Maps, and so on.

➢ Google has a "Search Tools" button above your search results that allows you to limit to a time range or specify only sites updated in the past hour, day, week, month or year. This button also lets you choose types of websites and provides (gulp) *your location* – how does it know where you are? See the "Clearing the Fog" section below for this dark and mysterious side of Google.

➢ Google has a pretty good "Advanced Search" feature that helps you do all sorts of things, *if you can find the advanced search*. For some unstated reason, Google is burying its advanced search function deeper and deeper all the time. You first have to do a basic search. On the results page, upper right, you will see a wheel. Click on it and the advanced search function will appear as a link. Here are some things you can do with it:

- The "Find pages with..." options let you build complex Boolean searches.
- You can specify the languages of the websites you want returned.
- You can ask for return of results only in specified formats (PDF, MS Word, PowerPoint, etc.).
- You can select only the most recently updated websites.
- You can specify where you want your search terms to appear in the documents you retrieve (e.g. anywhere, or in the title or URL).
- You can ask for only those sites belonging to a certain domain (registered Internet name, like .com or .edu).
- You can locate the websites that have links to a specified site.

➤ Google has a small inverted triangle next to the URL in each search result. Click on it, and you will find options to see a cache of the site (what it looked like the last time Google added it to its search index), similar sites, or an opportunity to share the site with others. Formerly, Google had an option to view a thumbnail picture of each site, but that choice is gone (as of Spring 2013).

➤ If you sign in, using the box on the upper right of results, you will be prompted to set up an account with your g-mail ID. This will give you a few other features, like the ability to share websites with others. Google also provides automatic enhancements to your searches to improve results if you are logged in. But be cautious: *Logging in gives Google more of an opportunity to retain information about what you are searching. If you have privacy concerns, go to the iGoogle privacy policy statement at* **http://www.google.com/policies/privacy/.**

➤ Google Instant is a feature that lists possible terminology under the search box while you are typing, so that you don't always have to type in the whole search – just select the search terms from the list below the search box. This feature may also give you clues to a better way to formulate your search terms. There is a demo located at **http://www.google.com/landing/instant/**.

Google offers separate search engines for books (Google Books - **http://books.google.com**), scholarly material (Google Scholar - **http://scholar.google.com**), blogs (Google Blog Search - **http:// blogsearch.google.com**), things to buy (Google Product Search - **http://www.google.com/prdhp?tab=wf&ie=UTF-8**), and so on. Each of these is either at the top of the Google home page or can be found under the "more" link.

In October 2013, Google search moved into the next phase of its development with a new algorithm (method of gathering and delivering search results) called Hummingbird (because it's "precise and fast"). The goal is to move away from mere keyword-matching and deliver what the user is really looking for. All of this is wrapped around a better ability for Google to handle real questions. Thus, instead of searching on <climate change arctic>, Google wants to be able to handle a question like, <What's happening in the arctic because of climate change?> At the time of publication of this edition of *Research Strategies*, the verdict is still out on how much Hummingbird will improve search.

All in all, Google remains the biggest and best Internet search engine. Try out some of its extra features to improve your searches.

Clearing the Fog – While you are searching Google, Google is searching you

Eli Pariser, in a celebrated TED Talk in 2011 (**http://www. youtube.com/watch?v=B8ofWFx525s**) pointed out the risks found in the "personalization" of search engines. He was describing the growing ability of search engines to track your preferences and provide you with personalized results. When you do a Google search and click on the top button "Search Tools," you see your location boldly stated. Google knows where you live. How scary is that? But knowing your location is only the beginning of the challenge.

Did you know that, if you and I use the same search terms in Google or several other search engines, our results will be different? Yes, different. Your results will reflect your location and also your "search history," which Google collects over time. That is, Google is compiling your preferences – the topics you are interested in – so that it can get a snapshot of you. Google's reason for personalizing, at least on the surface, is that the search engine is "helping" you by providing results that better meet your preferences. But it probably has a lot more to do with Google's ability to send you *personalized ads* which target your preferences.

Google helps make personalization easier by encouraging you along the way to "sign in." Once you do, Google has all the information you have provided to it, including your data in Google+.

Sure, you can turn off some aspects of personalization (see **http:// support.google.com/accounts/bin/answer.py?hl=en&answer =54048**), but not all. My own view is that personalization does more harm than good. Just because I searched for a topic yesterday does not mean that I will not take a different slant on that topic today or even search for a new topic. Limiting my options (e.g. to sites in my own region before farther away sites come up) is not something I want from a search engine. It makes me frustrated and sad that my beloved Google, along with Bing and most other search engines have chosen to go this route.

There, now I feel better.

Bing (http://www.bing.com/)

Microsoft's search engine, "Bing," is known for its changed-daily full screen photos. Bing is intent on taking market share from Google. But - hold on - in late 2013, Bing began rolling out a new version that integrates Internet Explorer 9 and Windows 7 to create what they are calling a work of "beauty." The new interface is indeed beautiful, more video- and app-like than the much more static Google (though by the time you read this, Google may have followed suit). At this point, Bing is definitely the leader in coolness if not in search results themselves, where Google still leads. Bing's significant features:

➢ The basic search uses conventions similar to Google's.

➢ In the new version of Bing, the advanced search is gone, something we've already seen as the likely sad future of most search engines. First they hide the advanced search, then they kill it altogether. This, in my estimation, is a very bad idea.

➢ From the bars at the top of the screen, you can track your search history, do related searches and narrow your results, as well as opening the same search to other media like images and video. There are also "related searches" links provided on the right.

➢ Bing's image and video search results are superior graphically and functionally to Google's. Bing promises a non-text image search similar to that already available through Google.

Yahoo! Search (http://search.yahoo.com/)

While Yahoo! Search uses Bing as its search engine, it does have some unique features:

➢ One of the coolest of these is that any keyword combination produces (below it) a strong list of suggested ways to narrow the search as well as providing preview links to the best websites for your search or for any of the suggestions. Thus, before you even hit the Search button, you have clues to improve your search and nail down more relevant websites.

➢ The advanced search is on the results page (the wheel image in the top right). Advanced searching is quite Google-like. You can also filter results on the left by how long it's been since sites were updated.

Ask.com (http://www.ask.com/)

Then we have Ask.com, formerly Ask Jeeves and built on the Teoma search engine. True, Ask has cool icons and a number of nice skins available (under the Themes link), but its look on the surface is like Google. Its advanced search features are quite Google-like though more limited than Google's.

A few features are noteworthy:

➤ Ask.com had an AskEraser feature (in the Settings link), which, when turned on, deleted your search history and prevented Ask from retaining your data. In keeping with the ever stronger march of personalization, Ask has now removed this feature. As with most search engines, using your data is vital to their economic health. Privacy, sadly, loses in the process.

➤ As a throwback to the days when Ask wanted users to pose actual questions in a natural language search, there is related site AskAnswers (http://answers.ask.com/), through which you can ask real questions. As with much of the WWW, it's up to you to determine how solid the answers are to the questions you ask.

➤ Ask is becoming more of a social networking tool and has a separate Q&A Community feature that may be worth checking out for crowd sourced answers to your questions (http://www.ask.com/answers/).

Blekko (http://blekko.com/)

Blekko, though little known, has real potential, mainly because it forms a kind of "best of the web" on your search terms, broken down into sub-categories. Here's how it works:

➤ Do a search on **"climate change" arctic**
➤ You will get results broken down by sub-category, such as, top results, environment, science, latest.
➤ Clicking on each sub-category will take you to relevant websites.

> ➤ A click on the right arrow within each category will open up another page of results.

Essentially, you have a search engine that pools the best results into various aspects of what you were originally searching for. All in all, this is a search engine to keep an eye on.

6.3.3 RSS feeds from search engines

If you are interested in staying up to date with recent results from a search you have done, many search engines allow you to set up RSS feeds that will notify you by e-mail when new sites with your search terms appear.

6.3.5 The coming semantic search engines

Semantic search is often promised as the future for search engines, though it is still in the early stages. It essentially means that a search engine discerns what you are actually looking for, thus going beyond the mere words in your searches. Most search engine providers are working very hard on semantic search development.

Google has a growing feature called the "Knowledge Graph" that will provide information related to a search you have done and put it to the right of your results. For example, a search on Leonardo Da Vinci creates a Knowledge Graph that provides pertinent facts about him, links to his paintings and links to other Renaissance paintings. For initial information about this feature see **http://googleblog.blogspot. co.uk/2012/05/introducing-knowledge-graph-things-not.html**.

Xerox has an in-house tool called FactSpotter (**http://www.xerox. com/innovation/news-stories/text-mining/enus.html**). It is billed as a search engine that digs deeper and identifies what the searcher is looking for by analyzing the semantics of the search. Essentially, the software considers words in their context (other words in the search) to determine what word meaning is wanted. For example, a search on Lincoln Vice President will connect the name Lincoln with Abraham Lincoln because of the reference to Vice President, and will bring back information on his first vice president, Hannibal Hamlin.

Public semantic engines include **Swoogle (http://swoogle.umbc. edu/)**, **SenseBot (http://www.sensebot.net/)**, and so on.

Many other semantic search engines are under development. These tools are pointing the way forward to new ways of searching, though none are earth-shattering yet. For more on semantic search engines, see **http://searchengineland.com/semantic-search-what-is-it-how-are-major-search-and-social-engines-use-it-part-1-133160.**

6.4 Searching by subject tree

All information exists within hierarchies. For example, cell phones are a subclass of telephones, which are a subclass of electronic communication devices, which are a subclass of all communication devices. (For a review, see section 3.3.1, above)

Information hierarchies form tree-like structures. There are certain sites on the Internet where you can search down various hierarchies or subject trees from more general categories to specific ones.

For example, Yahoo! has a Directory (**http://dir.yahoo.com/**) that leads you to a list of categories like Arts & Humanities, News, Science, and so on. Click on any one, and you can follow a hierarchy down to more specific information. Many of the portal-type sites provide similar hierarchies (see below).

6.5 Portals

A helpful research tool on the Internet is the "portal," which serves as an introduction to important sites on a subject. Typically, its main feature is a collection of links to sites that have been checked out for quality. What you end up with is a hierarchical way of searching the Net without a search engine. Its advantage is that someone has evaluated the sites, so you have a better chance of finding material that you can actually use (though your own critical thinking skills still need to be engaged).

Many portals are organized by subject. Here are a few examples:

➤ Psych Web (**http://www.psywww.com/**) is a psychology portal to websites categorized by type. Locate a category like Scholarly Issues, and it will lead you to a page that subcategorizes web links under headings like Cross-Cultural Psychology, Hypnosis, and etc.

➢ History Subject Guide (**http://guides.lib.washington. edu/history**)

➢ Voice of the Shuttle: Literature (In English): **http://vos. ucsb.edu/browse.asp?id=3**

➢ Biology Online (**http://biology-online.org/**)

➢ Wabash Center Internet Guide to Religion (**http://www. wabashcenter.wabash.edu/resources/guide_headings. aspx**)

But how do you locate such sites in the first place? Here's where a more general portal can help. A general portal is usually much larger, and often serves as a doorway to more specific subject portals. For example:

➢ Infomine (**http://infomine.ucr.edu/**). Subtitled, "Scholarly Internet Academic Collections," it boasts over 100,000 academically valuable sites, organized by broad subject categories or searchable by its own internal search engine. Many of the sites it lists are actually subject portals.

➢ Multimedia Educational Resource for Learning and Online Teaching (**http://www.merlot.org/**). This is a project of several universities and academic organizations to organize and peer review websites valuable for higher education. You can search it directly or hierarchically by subject categories.

➢ IPL2 (**http://www.ipl.org/**). The result of a merger of Internet Public Library and Librarians' Internet Index, this general portal is searchable directly or by means of hierarchies.

6.6 The Hidden Internet

You may have heard of the so-called "Hidden Internet," "Invisible Web" or "Deep Web." It's billed as that portion of the Net that only the chosen few can see. Before you start thinking in terms of nasty conspiracies, you should recognize that there could be legitimate reasons why certain Web information would not be easy to find.

6.6.1 What do we mean by "Hidden?"

A simple definition of "hidden" in this context would be: "Any information carried on the WWW that can't easily be found by a Web search engine." Considering the fact that all search engines must first "discover" information before they can index it, there is always a strong possibility that some sites will be hidden at any particular time. Beyond this are sites that search engines did find but that have deeper portions accessible only through a password or a search by a site's own search engine (for example, an online library catalog).

6.6.2 What's in the Hidden Internet?

The Hidden Internet includes the following:

➢ Sites that are password protected—corporate intranets, subscription databases, banking information, e-mail accounts, and so on. These are protected to maintain security and restrict access only to patrons who are entitled to be there.

➢ On the darker side, cybercrime, nastier forms of criminal activity (like child porn), terrorism and encrypted government information (think "spies.") are protected so that only their authorized users can get in.

➢ Information can be buried within non-restricted databases such as library catalogs. A search engine might find a library catalog or other database, but it won't get past the front door to identify/view individual records within that database. Why? Because the Internet search engine can't actually search the database, which has its own search engine. So you might find the catalog of a university

155

library with Google, but Google can't search that catalog automatically to find a record for a certain book. You have to search it yourself.

➢ New or obscure sites not yet indexed by a search engine.

6.6.3 How do I find information on the Hidden Internet?

That depends. If it's a password-protected site, you need to be authorized or you'll need to pay to get access. Don't hack! Many searchable databases can be identified either by a search engine or by hierarchical searches on the Net (see 6.5 and 6.6 above), and then you can search them directly.

The Hidden Internet lives, but there's no conspiracy. Really!

6.7 Evaluating information from the Internet

Let's be realistic for a moment (aren't we always?) and ask the question: *Why would people with data want to put it up for free on the Internet?* The answers are varied:

➢ They want to sell you something, and their web page is simply an advertisement or a doorway to a credit card purchase.

➢ They have something they want to say, and this a cheap and easy way to do it. Here you can have anything from, *"Hi, I'm Tim, and here are some pictures of my iguana Frank,"* to *"I was abducted by Martians, and I want to warn the world before they eat our brains."* Here too are the blogs and social networking sites like Facebook and Twitter, as well as human rights sites seeking to tell the world of abuses.

➢ A government or public agency will normally not charge for its information because it wants to make that information available. Here you can find everything from the ERIC Database to telephone and directory information, census data, and so on.

➢ An academic or educational body may see providing information as part of its mandate. Here you may get open access journal articles, electronic editions of out-of-print books, guides to this and that, occasionally even electronic dictionaries or encyclopedias.

➤ Sincere scholars and other individuals will have valuable information to share and want to make that information freely available for the edification of everyone.

But take careful note of one foundational rule of life: *Few people, except those related to the last three reasons above, provide information for free on the Net unless they can't find anyone to pay for it or they have the financial resources to give it away freely.*

What does that mean for you, the Internet searcher? It means several things:

➤ A lot of what you hoped might be on the Net is not there or you have to pay for it - the full text of most journal articles, the full text of recent books, a vast array of reference tools, etc.

➤ Most keyword searches through search engines also bring you many less-than-wonderful websites that you have to weed through to find a few gems.

➤ It's difficult to evaluate the quality of the material you find on the Net. Let's consider this point a bit more closely. In normal publishing, there are gatekeepers to make sure that material that is inferior doesn't get published (at least we hope there are gatekeepers). On the Internet, anybody who wants to say anything has the chance to say it. Unless it is criminally obscene, violently racist, or a clear and present danger to society, no one challenges it. Thus people can tell lies on the Net, and they probably won't suffer any nasty consequences.

So what happens when you download a document that has no clearly named author but seems to be reliable information about B.F. Skinner's behaviorism? How do you determine whether it's good or bad information? Here are some clues:

➢ Dig deeper for the name of an author and/or organization responsible for the information. One way to do this is to recognize that Internet URLs are hierarchical and that the slashes in an address (/) define levels of the hierarchy. For example, the website advertising this book has the URL

➢ **http://acts.twu.ca/library/textbook.htm**. If I chop off the portions **/library/textbook.htm**, I have the root left: **http://acts.twu.ca**, which is the educational institution that has allowed me access to their website and has thus viewed me as a credible person. Chopping back on a URL will often lead you to the source behind the document you're interested in, though sometimes it just reveals the name of a person's Internet service provider, which, if it's some generic vendor of web space, will give you no help at all.

➢ Look for signs of scholarship—good language level, analytical thinking, bibliography and/or footnotes, logical organization.

➢ Look for signs of a **lack** of scholarship—lots of opinion without the support of evidence, indications of paranoia (as in *somebody's out to get us,* or *we're victims of a conspiracy),* poor spelling and grammar, lack of references to other sources, poor organization.

➢ Ask yourself—does the author of this site have a vested interest in promoting a viewpoint or is he/she simply sharing information? Vested interests may be OK as long as you are well aware of what they are. A site selling Toyotas is going to be different in its very nature from a site offering independent reviews of Toyotas.

Ultimately, you will have to evaluate the information itself. Does it make sense? Does it ring true? Is there sufficient backing for viewpoints presented? Have you or your professor ever heard of the people involved? Remember that Internet data may lack all the proper signposts of good scholarly work and yet still be valuable. On the other hand, it may have footnotes and a bibliography but be totally uninformed. For proper evaluation, the buck stops with you actually reading the material and making sense of it.

If you want some help learning how to evaluate Internet resources, take The Internet Detective, a free website tutorial with quizzes. It's very cool (**http://www.vts.intute.ac.uk/detective/**).

6.8 Some more Internet addresses valuable for research purposes

In presenting the following addresses, I must warn you again that URLs, like phone numbers, go out of date fairly quickly. On the Net, something you found today might not be there tomorrow. So, some of these URLs might not work. If you have a problem, try searching for the title of the source, using a search engine. Or go to **https://sites. google.com/site/researchstrategiesweb/home/livelinks**, where I will try to keep all the web links for this book alive and current.

6.8.1 Reference sources

> *The Internet Public Library* (now *IPL2*):
  http://www.ipl.org/
> *Refdesk*: **http://www.refdesk.com/** (an amazingly detailed site that bills itself as "The single best source for facts.")
> A biography encyclopedia: **http://www.biography.com/**

6.8.2 Searchable library catalogs

> *WorldCat:* **http://www.worldcat.org/** (a union catalog representing holdings from a large number of libraries)
> *Library of Congress searchable catalog:* **http://catalog. loc.gov/**
> *Libdex:* **http://www.libdex.com/country.html**
  (A directory of library catalogs worldwide that you can identify by country).

6.8.3 Phone directories

➢ *Switchboard*: **http://www.switchboard.com/**. (Addresses & phone numbers—US plus Yellow Pages).

➢ *Canada 411*: **http://www.canada411.ca/** (Canadian phone numbers & addresses).

➢ A portal to international phone directories: **http://www. infobel.com/en/world/**

6.9 For further study

Study guide

1. What is the Internet? How does it relate to the World Wide Web?
2. Why are free journals not a prominent feature in the academic world?
3. What's the difference between a scholarly search engine and ordinary search engines? What are the names of some scholarly search engines, and what do they provide?
4. What are a few of the top search engines on the Net?
5. What are "subject trees" on the Internet, and how can they help you?
6. What are Internet portals, and how can they help you?
7. What is the Hidden Internet? How do you find information within it?
8. What are the key means by which you can evaluate the quality of information on Internet sites? What should you check first when evaluating a website? Why is more evaluation required for Internet sites than for regularly published books and articles?

Practice with the Internet

1. Try an identical search on several search engines (e.g., Google, Bing, Yahoo! Search, Ask.com). Why do some search engines come up with different results than others? Is it a correct assumption that **google.com** will most often produce better results than other search engines? [If you can't think of topics to search

try the following: Skinner and behaviorism and Walden; Lucrezia Borgia (or is it Lucretia Borgia?); Bill Gates and antitrust.]

2. Take the Internet Detective Tutorial: (**http://www.vts.intute.ac.uk/detective/**)

Assignment

1. Try a search on Google Scholar (**http://scholar.google.com**), using the topic: The March 2011 Tsunami in Japan. If your institution has links from Google Scholar to its own journals (called Library Links), make use of this feature (ask a librarian if unsure). Identify 6 journal articles or academic websites that are relevant to your topic.

2. Answer the following questions, using one of these search engines: Google, Bing, Yahoo! Search or ask.com. In each case indicate the keywords you searched with and URL(s) of the site(s) that had the answer:

    a. Where did the saying come from: "It takes a village to raise a child?" Can you find authoritative evidence to demonstrate that this is the source? How certain are you that the websites you looked at gave you an accurate answer?

    b. The following is a real question asked by an academic library user. Find the correct citation, including author, title, journal, volume number, date, and page numbers:

    > **A professor here needs help clarifying a citation. He already has a photocopy of the article, but needs to know the volume, issue, and date in which the piece was published. The information we have is:**
    > **Author: Joachim Begrich**
    > **Title: Das priesterliche Heilsorakel**
    > **Journal: Zeitschrift fur die altestamentliche Wissenschaft (ZAW)**

    c. Find the website for "Skeptical Science." What is the goal of this site? What would lead you to believe that the credentials of the authors on this site are strong or weak? What link did you use to find the list of authors?

d. The following quotation is plagiarized from a source on the Internet. Identify the author and title of the original source:

> **"Jack the Ripper! Few names in history are as instantly recognizable. Fewer still evoke such vivid images: noisome courts and alleys, hansom cabs and gaslights, swirling fog, prostitutes decked out in the tawdriest of finery, the shrill cry of newsboys—and silent, cruel death personified in the capeshrouded figure of a faceless prowler of the night, armed with a long knife and carrying a black Gladstone bag."**

How easy/difficult was it to identify the quotation? What does this tell you about the fate of those who plagiarize from the Net when a keen professor suspects some of their words are not their own? (Sorry to sound preachy, but it really is pretty easy to root out Internet plagiarists.)

7

Other Resources and Case Studies in Research

Sometimes you get desperate. All the normal research avenues narrow down to footpaths and then disappear entirely. You're running out of time and you have nothing to show for the hours you've spent. Now there's a need for innovative action. This chapter will try to steer you in new and potentially fascinating directions. Then, this being the most loosely organized chapter in the book, we'll look at some other helpful resources and try out a couple of case studies with actual research projects.

7.1 Seeing where you've been

Before you launch into new sources for research data, it's probably a good idea to rehearse where you've been. Maybe you've missed some important resources. Here's a strategies list to help you go back over your research methods to this point and check out possibilities that may have eluded you the first time you went through.

The Strategies We've Covered (Now for the First Time in One Place):

➢ *Get a working knowledge of your topic* (You want to use reference sources, print or online, and became familiar with the basics.) Ask yourself: Did your reference sources suggest related topics or give a bibliography that you've overlooked? Are there other sources of reference information to look at? (see below)

➢ *Assess the research topic, narrow it, come up with an analytical research question, and suggest a preliminary outline:* Did you set the topic so narrowly that you have a shortage of resources? Or, did you fail to set it narrowly enough, and now you have a fuzzy view of what your topic is? Often the problem with finding relevant sources is that you are not focusing clearly on what the research project is setting out to do. You need to be able to express your research question or thesis statement in ***one sentence*** that deals with ***one issue or problem that you're trying to solve***. Your outline, in turn, needs to be drawn directly out of your research question/thesis. More on all this in Appendix One.

➢ *Do a book search in a library catalog or discovery tool, using keywords and controlled vocabularies as needed:* Did you find everything that was relevant? If you began with a keyword search, you need to look closely at the catalog records you brought up. What controlled vocabulary subject headings were attached to the books you found? If you started with subject headings, did you identify the best ones for your topic? Looking at the records you've brought up may help you to discover other possible subject headings or narrower approaches to the topic. Did you consider more broadly based books that might *contain* information relevant to you? E.g., for a paper on euthanasia, perhaps some key works in medical ethics might have relevant chapters on euthanasia.

> *Do a search for journal articles:* Did you use the right journal databases for the topic? Did you investigate the searching requirements for those databases? Did you choose narrow enough keywords and use controlled vocabulary terms? Have you checked your library's journal holdings carefully to be sure the library either did or did not have the articles you wanted? Did you take the extra step of enlisting interlibrary loan to get the articles you didn't find in the databases you were searching?

> *Make a judicious search of Internet resources.* Here, use your best evaluative skills and be sure you know what your professor will allow you to include in your research project.

Does all this sound a bit too mechanical? A bit too much like "Five Steps to your Next Research Paper" which doesn't take into the account the reality that you may need to go back to earlier steps, skip a step, or do things in another order? Read the Clearing the Fog below.

Clearing the Fog – Step by step may not always be the best approach, but it can help you find your way

Throughout this book I have suggested a step-by-step approach to research. Why? Because learning a task often works best if you follow the same pathway every time until you master all the parts. Having steps to follow helps you succeed until you know the path well enough to branch out a bit.

But there also comes a time, with the steps to good research clearly and solidly within you, when you may want to live a little more dangerously. Maybe you want initially to entertain two or three possible research questions and then explore a bit more before you settle on the final one you will use. Maybe you want to minimize the use of books and move quickly on to journal articles. Maybe you feel the need to go back to earlier steps and do them again or revise what you did. The research process can thus become a glorious tangle of adventurous moves in many directions at once.

Warning - If you try out this more risky approach to research too early, before you've understood the steps you ultimately must cover, you'll end up with what you had before you began learning how to do research – a tangled mess. Remember when you were running around like the proverbial headless chicken, banging into walls of confusion and disappearing down rabbit trails?

So master the essential steps first. Then, if you want to get adventurous and mix things up a bit, you'll actually still know where you are.

Now let's consider some further options you may not have thought of:

7.2 ERIC

One of the great untapped resources for research is ERIC (**http:// www.eric.ed.gov/**). No, this is not a professional hockey player with a lot of missing teeth. ERIC stands for Education Resources Information Center, a clearinghouse that makes available studies, reports, curriculum helps, etc. produced by educational institutions.

But don't think of it just as an educational database. Educators are concerned about virtually anything that might be related to education, from the effects of early poverty on graduates students' job performance, to the ramifications of teen alcoholic use. This means that a wide range of topics in the social sciences are covered, as well as quite a few areas of the humanities.

Rather than have schools, colleges and universities put their studies on the issues affecting their work into filing cabinets, never to be seen again, the U.S. government arranged to collect these studies and make them available to libraries. To do this, ERIC needed to have a two part approach:

➤ The reports themselves. They could be anything from a study of the effects of TV violence on high schoolers in Salem, Oregon, to an analysis of dyslexia in relation to reading speed in Podunk Junction, Iowa. Such reports could be under 50 pages in length, though they might sometimes go to 100 pages or more. Pre-1992 ERIC documents (i.e., these gathered reports) were once only available on microfiche. Now most of them have been digitized and, along with documents 1993 to present, are freely available in PDF full text (but see the ALERT below).

➤ A database with which to search the ERIC documents for topics of interest. Here the government had a stroke of genius—why not put the database for free on the Internet so that anyone could search it from anywhere? What is more, all ERIC documents for which electronic full text was available could be linked to the citations in the databases and downloaded by users for free.

One further bit of information which sometimes confuses users: As ERIC grew, the database added a journals component to enable people to identify journal articles in education. The confusing part is that *ERIC itself does not provide the electronic full text of many of these journal articles. You will need to locate the actual articles yourself.* Thus you have two databases in one – a documents database and a journals database. To distinguish ERIC Documents from ERIC journals, the former were designated ED—so that each ERIC Document has a code number that looks like this: ED213562. ERIC Journals are designated EJ, as in: EJ498231. You can find both EJs and EDS in a single search, though it's possible to pre-set your search for only journals or only documents.

The ERIC interface at **http://www.eric.ed.gov/** has been updated as of August 2013 and now begins with a keyword search and then provides limiter links on the results page (similar to what the EBSCO databases do). You can then narrow down the search by date range, subject heading (descriptor) and so on:

| Collection | Thesaurus |

"short term memory"   🎤   Sea

☐ Peer reviewed only   ☐ Full text available on ERIC

PUBLICATION DATE	
In 2013	126
Since 2012	491
Since 2009 (last 5 years)	1440
Since 2004 (last 10 years)	2049
Since 1994 (last 20 years)	2283

DESCRIPTOR	
Short Term Memory	2508
Cognitive Processes	955
Memory	700
Recall (Psychology)	558

Using Visual Strategies to Support Verbal Comprehei
Lecas, Jean-Francois; Mazaud, Anne-Marie; Reibel, Esther; Re Therapy, 2011

It has been frequently reported that children with Down syndrom while having relatively good performance in visual short-term me detrimental effect on various high-level cognitive processes, mos

Descriptors: Comprehension, Down Syndrome, Short Term Memor

Association between Early Attention-Deficit/Hypera Term Memory
Gau, Susan Shur-Fen; Chiang, Huey-Ling – Research in Develo

Alternatively, you can do a Thesaurus (subject heading) search. ERIC's thesaurus is very well constructed and can really help you formulate a focused search.

ERIC has now also begun creating "brief, plain-language summaries of key education issues and topics" (ERIC Database). These documents will be done by leaders in the field and will provide links to other resources in the ERIC database.

Some database vendors (e.g. EBSCO) provide their own interface for ERIC, with additional search options.

Don't ignore ERIC. It is a very good resource for many kinds of research. The fact that you can access its index and much of its full text for free on the Internet makes it all the more helpful.

ALERT: In 2012, ERIC encountered a problem due to "personally identifiable information in some documents." Thus the ERIC folks removed much of the full text availability of its pre-2005 documents, and ERIC staff members are checking each document for such information before returning it to the database. Hopefully, by the time you read this, most of the documents will be back. Near the end of 2013, there were about 30,000 documents processed and 240,000 documents to go. The most recent update before publication of this edition said that the ERIC reintroduction process would be mostly complete by summer 2014. Thus, by the time you read this, the problem may be resolved.

7.3 Government documents

Governments produce vast hosts of information which can often be found in libraries, be purchased, or be discovered free on the Internet (depending on what the information is). Publications put out by governments cover potentially every area of life. The only problem is that they are notoriously difficult to find. If you are in a library that has government documents, rely on your reference librarian to guide you through the maze.

For US government information on the Internet, the Federal Digital System (FDsys, formerly GPO Access) is the place to go: **http://www.gpo.gov/fdsys/search/home.action**. This site can help you find materials by topic. It even offers you guidance on locating documents in libraries. (In case the address goes out of date, just Google FDsys.) For state and local government information, try the portal produced by the Library of Congress: **http://www.loc.gov/rr/news/stategov/stategov.html.**

If you are blessed enough to live in Canada, as I am, the Internet site you want is: **http://publications.gc.ca/site/eng/home.html**.

For other country governments, try: **http://libguides. northwestern.edu/content.php?pid=236155&sid=1953042** (Use the alphabet tabs at the top to find specific countries).

Not everything you need in government information, however, is on the Net. As with every other source of information, some is online and some is only accessible in print. Certain libraries are designated as depository collections that receive print and digital versions of government information. To locate the depository library near you in the US, go to **http://www.gpo.gov/libraries/**, and in Canada to **http://dsp-psd.pwgsc.gc.ca/Depo/table-e.html.**

7.4 Doctoral dissertations

It sounds so intriguing, so right - if you want the best cutting edge research on a topic, why not locate a few doctoral dissertations? But the realities can be a mixed bag.

The primary searching tool for dissertations is *ProQuest Dissertations & Theses Database,* an electronic tool available in larger libraries but few small ones. It's fully searchable and you can easily locate citations and abstracts (summaries) of doctoral work on your topic. ProQuest offers with its databases the full text of close to a million dissertations, for those libraries that can afford to provide this feature. (There is a PDF tutorial at **http://proquest.libguides. com/pqdt/pqdt).** For older dissertations not available in full text, you may be able to use interlibrary loan (not always successful) or buy the dissertation yourself from ProQuest.

Increasingly, doctoral dissertations are migrating to the WWW. Here are a few places to look for them:

> ➢ Open Access Theses and Dissertations - **http://oatd.org/** (over 1.5 million full text dissertations)
> ➢ PQDT Open - **http://pqdtopen.proquest.com/** (ProQuest dissertations that have been released to open access)
> ➢ Networked Digital Library of Theses and Dissertations - **http://www.ndltd.org/resources/find-etds** (hundreds of thousands of dissertations, mostly in English but many in other languages; click on titles to access full text; get links to other electronic dissertation sites as well)
> ➢ OpenThesis - **http://www.openthesis.org/**
> ➢ Google Scholar (a good source for dissertations if you can wade through all the stuff that is not dissertations). Note that a dissertation may be cited without the full text actually being available, so GS is a spotty resource for finding dissertations.

A suggestion: Before you go on a long quest for a dissertation, search for the author's name in your catalog and/or a larger catalog like WorldCat (**http://www.worldcat.org/**). It's possible that the dissertation was later published as an academic book which might even be in your library collection.

7.5 Bibliographic managers

For some time now there have been programs and apps available to help you save your citations to books, articles, websites, and so on. These *bibliographic managers* enable you to collect citations in specified folders and generate bibliographies in most any format you want. What is more, many of them are not only web-based, but offer the option of adding a plug-in to your word processing program so that you can create automatic citations and bibliographies without having to type in the information yourself. Let's take a quick look at each of them:

7.5.1 EndNote (http://www.endnoteweb.com/)

EndNote has a downloadable software version that is avidly used by many scholars (**http://endnote.com/**). This tool allows you to import citations from various databases, search databases from within EndNote (though the search interface is not as sophisticated as searching a database directly), store citations in designated folders and even attach PDFs to citations. Buying the software version gives you access to Endnote Basic, a Web-based version, which is likely more practical for beginning researchers. In fact, you can sign up for EndNote Basic on its own as a free product. Since it is all Internet-based, it doesn't take up room on your hard drive (leaving you space for a few more videos). You can configure Google Scholar to create an export link to EndNote (click the wheel icon to the right of Scholar results). Most journal databases support downloads to EndNote.

What is more, you can download Word templates from EndNote to enable you to format a research paper properly. Even better, you can download a plug-in that enables you to zap citations right into your research paper and format them as well as create a bibliography in the bibliographic format of your choice.

Many EndNote Basic users have had free access to a somewhat beefed up version of it through an institutional subscription to Web of Knowledge, from which you can set up an EndNote account. This lies between the free Web version and the for-purchase software version in sophistication. As of 2013, EndNote Basic, the free Web version, is available through **http://endnote.com/basic**.

7.5.2 RefWorks (http://refworks.com/)

RefWorks provides most of the features of EndNote except the Word templates. It also has a plug-in to download WWW citations. Many library catalogs and most journal databases have direct download to RefWorks functionality. Like EndNote, you can configure Google Scholar settings to export citations to it, and it has a word processing plug-in to insert citations into your paper as well as create a bibliography. Most people use RefWorks as part of an institutional site license, though individual subscriptions are available. If you start with RefWorks as part of an institutional license, you are automatically given lifetime access as long as your institution subscribes, so you can continue using this tool even after you graduate.

7.5.3 Zotero (http://www.zotero.org/)

If your institution doesn't have access to RefWorks, and you want to use a bibliographic manager, do not fear. You can use EndNote Basic, or try out Zotero, which is free and offers most of the strong features provided by commercial bibliographic managers. It will capture book, article and website citations and will even store PDF full text. Like the other two managers above, it has a download for working with Word documents. Zotero operates as a plug-in on the Firefox browser, for which there's a free download on the Zotero home page. It is also available as Zotero Standalone, a download that allows you to use it in other browsers, like Chrome and Safari (search <Zotero Standalone> with your favorite Internet search engine).

Happy researching with tools like these. They can be a great help.

7.6 Consulting with friends, mentors and librarians

We live in a highly consultative age, and the tendency to run our ideas past other people is pretty strong. There are real and obvious reasons why trying out aspects of your project on others can bring fresh perspectives and help you make early or mid-course correctives. Being more of a solitary researcher myself, I may be too anti-social to write about collaboration, but here goes anyway.

7.6.1 What are good friends for?

Meetings of minds are usually helpful, at least in theory. Running ideas past your friends is generally a good idea. Be open to their suggestions. At the same time, recognize that you may already know more about the subject matter than your friends do. Thus taking advice from a friend because he/she seems smarter than you, or more experienced, or whatever, may not be the best choice. Trust your instincts and filter advice from friends carefully.

7.6.2 Consulting professors

Your profs are a breed to themselves – intelligent and articulate, but they usually have far too much to do (which, I think, leads to the mythology of the absent-minded professor). If you are going to consult with a professor, have a clear question in mind and focus on being brief and to the point. For example, you might ask something like this: "You listed a research topic as 'Charlemagne,' and I was wondering what you'd think of me approaching it this way…" Consult your professor if you are unsure of what to do or unclear about what is being demanded, if you have thought of an approach to an assignment which may not be exactly what the professor is asking for, or if you are stuck somewhere in the research process and need advice to help you get unstuck.

Avoid the false assumption that, if you don't understand a professor's assignment, you are a dimmer bulb than are your fellow students. Professors, at least in the belief of their students, are notorious for setting assignments that are confusing and for not being clear enough on ultimate expectations. It may not be at all surprising that you need clarification.

7.6.3 Encountering librarians

Research shows that many students have a very limited perspective on what librarians can do for them. Some believe librarians are helpful only for book and paper issues, because they know almost nothing about technology. Not so. Most academic librarians are techno-geniuses. Others see librarians as "generalists" who know a little bit about everything but, unlike professors, don't know a lot about any specific topic. Not so again. Actually, most librarians have a good idea how most subject disciplines work. If you need to use almost any database, a librarian is likely to offer more help than anyone else can. And if you are working on a highly specialized topic, a librarian has the skills to help you manipulate that topic so you can actually advance significantly beyond where you are. Librarians are amazing people. Consult them frequently. They don't usually bite.

7.7 Case studies in research

It's all very well to read about the theory of research, but hands-on experience teaches us that we live in a complex world. Methods that may have worked perfectly well in one research project are disastrous in another. A keen mind and a brave heart are needed if you want to succeed in actually carrying out a research project. The moment you've been waiting for all along is here. Let's do some research.

7.7.1 "Arctic Ice Issues Resulting from Climate Change"

There is no question that the loss of Artic ice is creating serious problems, from rising sea levels to serious challenges for humans and animals in Artic regions and around the globe. You could compile a survey of all these problems, along with a suitably pious call for more action on climate change, but that would be similar to gathering books and articles, then giving a monkey some scissors, paste and blank paper. You need something much more dramatic.

What you do depends on what subject discipline you are working in. Possible research questions, each of which would be its own topic:

➤ Why are governments so slow to act with regard to climate change when the evidence from loss of Artic ice is so compelling? (Political Science, Economics)

➤ What process is required to enable former hunters in the Eskimo (we Canadians call them Inuit) communities to find a viable way to sustain their lives in the north? (Geography, Sociology, Economics)

➤ How can the Arctic polar bears be saved in light of diminishing Arctic ice due to climate change? (Ecology, Zoology)

➤ Or, if you really want to go down this much traveled road again: Is the loss of Arctic ice in recent years primarily the result of human activity or of natural phenomena over which humans have little control? (Not sure what discipline this falls into)

Since I like polar bears (though I would not want to meet one face to face – they are nasty and unreasonable), let's go with the question: **How can the Arctic polar bear population be saved in light of diminishing Arctic ice?**

Reference Sources

The natural temptation is to go first to Wikipedia. And that may indeed be a helpful first step. The Wikipedia article on "Polar Bears," has a section on climate change, along with some high powered citations of recent studies.

But let's balance that with something created in a more traditionally peer-reviewed manner: *Encyclopedia of Global Warming* (2010). Sure, it's a bit dated, but there is a cool picture of a polar bear on the front cover and an article on the influence of global warming on these amazing white beasts.

Topic Analysis

We seem to have a fairly firm research question, but we need to determine what we actually need to accomplish in order to answer it. This is a "problem to solution" kind of project, which usually demands that you determine what the problem is, then look at options for a solution.

In the case of our topic, we need to establish that climate change is, indeed, creating a problem for the survival of the polar bear population (there's nothing as bad as getting deeply into a project, only to find out there is no problem at all). In the case of polar bears, some people are claiming that bear numbers are actually increasing. Is that the case? An article by Peter Dykstra (**http://www.sejarchive. org/pub/SEJournal_Excerpts_Su08.htm**) argues that the view that populations are growing is tainted by the fact that there were no accurate counts of polar bears in earlier decades.

Having determined that there is a problem (or at least a potential one) we need to discover the extent of that problem and determine what negative effects on polar bears result from climate change. Only then can we begin looking at solutions, which might range from "do nothing," to "create supported refuges for polar bears," to "send them to Antarctica."

The best way to visualize this is with a preliminary outline:

Introduction – The Current Plight of the Polar Bear Due to Climate Change
   I.   The Effects of Climate Change on Polar Bears
      A.
      B.
      C.
   II. The Seriousness of the Problem
   III. Possible Solutions
      A.
      B.
      C.
      D.
Conclusion – A Proposed Protection Plan for Arctic Polar Bears

Why go to all this work? Because we now have a road map for the things we need to discover, and the things we need to think about, on our way to answering our initial question: "How can the Arctic polar bears be saved in light of diminishing Arctic ice due to climate change?" No road map, and you will be lost before you gather your first book or article.

Book Search

Having the most recent stuff is important, so I apologize in advance. By the time you read this, two or three years may have passed. In any case, the results below were fairly up to date when I put them together. Focus on my method more than the actual titles as you read on.

If you are searching a library catalog or using a discovery search tool, you are likely going to start with keywords. So what keywords should you use? Let me suggest that you choose words right out of your research question, e.g. **"polar bears" and (climate change OR global warming)**. I left out "Arctic ice" so as not to overload the search and eliminate good sources that might have great things to say about the effect of climate change on polar bears, even though the topic of "ice" doesn't come up specifically.

Here are some results from a keyword search for books:

> ➢ Freeman, M. M. R. (2009). *Inuit, polar bears, and sustainable use: Local, national and international perspectives*. Edmonton, Alta: CCI Press.
> ➢ Derocher, A. E., & Lynch, W. (2012). *Polar bears: A complete guide to their biology and behavior.* Baltimore: Johns Hopkins University Press.
> ➢ Ellis, R. (2009). *On thin ice: The changing world of the polar bear.* New York: Alfred A. Knopf.
> ➢ Stirling, I. (2011). *Polar bears: The natural history of a threatened species*. Markham, Ont: Fitzhenry & Whiteside.
> ➢ Waring, R. (2009). *Polar bears in trouble*. Boston: Heinle/Cengage Learning.

Some of the books are more directly relevant to the species threat situation, but all of them should be useful in some way or other. The problem is that we can't be sure we've found everything we could. Keywords are tricky and may have us missing out on some good titles. This is where opening up the full catalog record for one of the relevant books above may lead us to a strong subject heading. I chose the title: *On thin ice: The changing world of the polar bear*, and I identified these subject headings, which I probably wouldn't have thought of otherwise (lacking imagination):

Polar bear—Effect of human beings on
Polar bear—Climatic factors—Arctic regions

With these subject headings in hand, we should be well placed to identify relevant books whose titles might not clearly reveal their subject matter.

Journal Article Search

Half the battle with finding journal articles is identifying the right database to use. That's not as much of a problem if your library has a discovery search tool like Summon™ Primo, or EBSCO Discovery Search, but focusing on a database relevant to the subject area you are working with can really help when the discovery search has pulled in 352,498 results, most of them not relevant (that does happen). In this case, a tool like the database Science Direct should work well to cover aspects of ecology, biology and so on in the problem of threatened polar bears.

A search on **"polar bears" and (climate change OR global warming)** produces articles like these:

➢ Dyck, M. G., Soon, W., Baydack, R. K., Legates, D. R., Baliunas, S., Ball, T. F., & Hancock, L. O. (2007). Polar bears of western Hudson Bay and climate change: Are warming spring air temperatures the "ultimate" survival control factor? *Ecological complexity*, 4(3), 73-84.

➢ Meek, C. L. (2011). Putting the US polar bear debate into context: The disconnect between old policy and new problems. *Marine Policy*, 35(4), 430-439.
➢ Molnár, P. K., Derocher, A. E., Thiemann, G. W., & Lewis, M. A. (2010). Predicting survival, reproduction and abundance of polar bears under climate change. *Biological Conservation*, *143*(7), 1612-1622.
➢ Stirling, I., Derocher, A. E., Gough, W. A., & Rode, K. (2008). Response to Dyck et al.(2007) on polar bears and climate change in western Hudson Bay.*ecological complexity*, *5*(3), 193-201.

These, and the other articles I found, looked promising as I did my searches. But I wasn't really getting at the issue of a solution to the polar bear survival problem. So I tried **Polar Bears AND management**, but I found nothing new. Then I tried **Polar Bears AND survival**, and again found nothing new. Clearly, I am going to have to go through my existing resources and pull out what they suggest about possible solutions. As with many things in research, the answer is not just going to fall easily into my hands (sigh…)

Google Scholar may actually have some promise. A search on **Polar Bears AND survival** got me, among other citations:

Derocher, A. E., Aars, J., Amstrup, S. C., Cutting, A., Lunn, N. J., Molnár, P. K., Obbard, M. E., Stirling, I., Thiemann, G. W., Vongraven, D., Wiig, Ø. and York, G. (2013). Rapid ecosystem change and polar bear conservation. *Conservation Letters*. doi: 10.1111/conl.12009

Summary

There appear to be sufficient resources out there (I found more than I listed above), though not much of it deals directly with a solution to the problem. That will require more digging, but more digging is what the fun of research is all about.

Let's try another topic, this time in the area of history:

7.7.2 "The First Crusade"

For a course on Medieval History, you've been asked to write a research paper on the First Crusade. Since the issue of the Crusades in general is a hot-spot in international politics these days (long memories and ongoing tensions, etc.), you decide to work on the research question: *"Was the actual motivation for the First Crusade primarily religious or political/economic?"*

The rationale here is that the first of the crusades may have been guided by a quest for territory and power rather than liberation of the "Holy Land" from Islam. That would speak to current issues regarding the Crusades in general. You could, of course, find another topic, because this one is awfully controversial, but the key to solving problems in our world is understanding the issues as well as you can. So it's probably a good idea to press on.

Reference sources.

For a topic like this, any number of reference sources would give you a working knowledge, even general encyclopedias like *Americana* or *Britannica*. There are also specific dictionaries and encyclopedias related to the era of the Middle Ages. In this case, we have access to something even more direct: *The Crusades: An Encyclopedia* (2006). This resource has detailed information on the rise and carrying out of the First Crusade. As can be expected, there is also a fairly lengthy Wikipedia article (with the usual cautions about Wikipedia not to be forgotten). The above sources have abundant citations to other works that should be checked out.

Topical analysis.

My initial research question suggestion - *Was the actual motivation for the First Crusade primarily religious or political/economic* – now needs some nuancing. It appears that there are multiple suggestions as to the motivation, so we can now move to a more basic question that does not prejudge the options: *What was the primary motivation behind the First Crusade?*

A preliminary outline at this point needs to be quite open until we have nailed down the three or four most likely options. That's fine as long as we can fill in the blanks as soon as possible:

Introduction (Basics of the First Crusade)
  I. The Statement of Pope Urban (which initiated this crusade)
  II. Alternative Motivations
      A.
      B.
      C., etc.
Conclusion

Book search.

While there are many books on the Crusades in general, it's better to attempt a narrower approach initially and search for books on the First Crusade. Amazingly we find success from the beginning – how rare is that? An initial keyword search on book titles brings up a number of books specifically on the First Crusade (at this point, because books are blunt instruments, I won't seek for books more specifically on the *purpose* of the First Crusade). What is more, there are a number of primary sources – actual accounts of the First Crusade from people of that time. History professors love primary sources, so you will look good just by having them in your bibliography. Here are some titles:

➤ *The First Crusade: the call from the East* (2012)
➤ *The Chanson d'Antioche: an old-French account of the First Crusade* (2011 - primary source)
➤ *The social structure of the First Crusade* (2008)
➤ *The Gesta Tancredi of Ralph of Caen: a history of the Normans on the First Crusade* (2005 – primary source)
➤ *Fighting for Christendom : holy war and the crusades* (2004)
➤ *The First Crusade and the idea of crusading* (2003)

And so on.

There are many volumes specifically on the First Crusade. If we fall short, books on the Crusades in general will fill the gap. What is missing, however, is specific material on the motivations for the First Crusade, though most of the books above will include information on that issue. Journal articles, however, being more specific to particular aspects of a topic, may be more fruitful.

Journal databases

We have lots of choices for journal databases, from a religion source like ATLA Religion Database, to various historical databases to a broad search tool like EBSCO's Academic Search. Let's choose the latter in this case, because there is the potential for a number of motivations for the Crusades, coming from different areas of study like religion, political science, geography, and history. The broad subject coverage of Academic Search (or a similar database from another database company) is more likely to provide lots of good options to consider.

In the case of Academic Search, we want to do more than treat it like Google, so we'll start with a keyword search and see if we can narrow down our results. The initial keyword search is First Crusade. I had hoped we could try a narrower search – First Crusade AND (motivation OR purpose), but it brought disappointment (databases can do that).

Initially we have close to 700 results. Too many. So we use EBSCO's left column features and limit to the subject heading - First, 1096-1099 – and to academic journals only. Always look for limiters if you have more than 50-100 results. In this case, we get down to 25 quite focused journal articles. Looking at them, we can see why the (purpose OR motivation) limiter didn't work. The article titles are much more subtle in looking at motivations. Consider these article titles from the set of results:

> ➢ "A Warlord's Wisdom: Literacy and Propaganda at the Time of the First Crusade" [**Propaganda** implies motivation being promoted.]
> ➢ " Christians, Muslims, and the `liberation' of the Holy Land." [**Liberation** is a loaded term, since it has quotation marks around it, implying a motive that was promoted.]
> ➢ "Destruction or Conversion Intention and Reaction, Crusaders and Jews, in 1096." [See term **Intention**.]

➢ Iuvenes and the First Crusade (1096-99): Knights in Search of Glory? [**In search of glory** as a motivation."]

➢ "'Let Not a Remnant or a Residue Escape': Millenarian Enthusiasm in the First Crusade." [**Milleniarian Enthusiasm** as a motive.]

➢ "The Call of the Crusades." [**Call** implies motive.]

➢ "The Pilgrimage Origins of the First Crusade." [**Pilgrimage** as motive.]

➢ "The Roots of Lay Enthusiasm for the First Crusade." ["**Roots**" implies a motive.]

While bound to be a lot more clunky in its results, you might want to try, with Google Scholar, the narrower search we first tried on Academic Search (which failed, much to our embarrassment): "First Crusade" AND (motivation OR purpose). A search on these terms in GS's advanced search, limiting only to title words, gets us two doctoral dissertations, neither of them full text online. Searching on full text rather than title words, we find a whole bunch of books and a number of journal articles.

One more element remains – locating a copy of the sermon by Pope Urban II that largely initiated crusade activity. Sadly, the actual sermon is lost to history, but there are firsthand accounts of it. Here Wikipedia helps direct us to *The Medieval Sourcebook* where there are five such accounts with bibliographic data for the published volumes in which these translations first appeared: **http://www. fordham.edu/halsall/source/urban2-5vers.html**.

Conclusion

In the examples above, you probably hoped for easy and tidy results. Research isn't like that. Every project has its hazards and obstacles. There's rarely anything tidy about gathering information on a narrowed down topic. That's why we've looked at so many strategies. While you won't use them all in every research project, you need to have them in your arsenal just in case your next research adventure turns into a fight for your very life. Who said research is boring?

Clearing the Fog – Research is like a box of chocolates

"My momma always said, 'Life was like a box of chocolates. You never know what you're gonna get.'" – *Forrest Gump* (Movie, 1994)

Every new research experience is exactly that - new. While I've provided you with steps to follow, several key principles may help you navigate the reality of the many differences in what you experience, depending on your topic:

> ➤ No author/scholar is obligated to be interested in, or write about, any topic. Thus you may find that some topics bring up fewer resources than you were expecting. A possible solution is to go broader – If you can't find a book on your favorite 1970s rock group, for which you have to write a historiography, maybe a few books on the history of 1970s rock will contain useful information on your group. Journal articles may be your best option, because they tend to be narrower in focus.

> ➤ Newer topics tend to have much less material on them, and a lot of that material lacks the level of sober reflection and evaluation you may be looking for. This means that you are going to have to provide more of your own analysis of what is going on rather than relying on other scholars to do this for you (this is a good exercise and builds character, so hopefully you'll enjoy it).

> ➤ It's a real challenge to figure out how narrowly or broadly you are working. I have seen students start far too broadly on a topic and end up with a survey instead of an analytical research project. I have also seen researchers start so narrowly that there is little or nothing to be found when it comes to searching for resources. A lot of researchers, as well, have a narrow research question but do searches that are too broad (instead of searching directly on the name of a 1970s rock group, the researcher searches on "Music.") A cure for this is to use search terms, whenever possible,

that *actually come out of your research question.* Only if this doesn't succeed should you create slightly broader searches.

7.8 For further study

Study guide

1. Summarize for yourself the research strategies covered so far.
2. What is ERIC, what kinds of documents does it provide access to, and what subject areas does it cover best?
3. Where do you find the ERIC database? In what format is the text of most ERIC documents from the early 1990s to the present?
4. What is the Eric Thesaurus?
5. What's the difference between ED and EJ in ERIC?
6. How useful is the Internet in finding government documents?
7. What's the main problem with locating doctoral dissertations? What avenues can you follow to get your hands on one if you want it?
8. What kind of help can you expect from a librarian as opposed to the help you get from a professor?
9. If you can't find books or articles by a person you are researching, what other option do you have?
10. If you are doing research on a person (like a president of the US), would writings by that person be considered primary or a secondary sources?

Practice with resources introduced in this chapter

For practice with ERIC, see the Assignment below. For some of the other resources listed in this chapter, try these searches:

1. From **http://www.gpo.gov/fdsys/**, using the search box, find the 9-11 Commission Report and locate the link to the additional chapter: "We Have Some Planes."

2. For Canadians, or those interested in Canadian things (and who isn't?), go to **http://publications.gc.ca/site/eng/home.html** and enter the site.
   a. Do a search (left column) to find a document for finding a job.
   b. Under the same site, find documents on residential wood heating

3. Go to **http://libguides.northwestern.edu/content. php?pid=236155&sid=1953042** (Use the alphabet tabs at the top to find specific countries). Find information on the Estonian president (choose your language on the site from the upper right options of Estonian, English and Russian).

Assignment

1. Do a search for a topic relevant to ERIC using the Thesaurus function, adding at least one keyword to limit your search and further limiting to ERIC Documents only. List at least 10 relevant documents that you retrieved in your search.

2. Go through each of the cases above (7.8) and learn what you can.

3. Try out a few of the topics below, narrow them, then locate materials in various formats (books, journals, good websites). Obviously you won't have time for a lot of in-depth work, but see what you can accomplish in an hour or two:

Youth crime
Anti-Semitism
Causes of World War One
Anorexia
9/11
The Crusades
The Euthanasia Debate
Family Violence

Homelessness
Issues Facing the Modern City
Hurricane Katrina
Moral Development of Children

8
Learning How to Read for Research

It's all very well to amass an enormous bibliography and have all your sources scattered artfully on your desk or screen. But if you're assuming that your essay or research report is now as good as written, you're going to suffer a grave disappointment. Obtaining the research materials is only half the battle. Now you have to read them and evaluate them. This chapter majors on the joys of reading and note-taking.

8.1 Reading for the connoisseur and the glutton

With a tantalizing heading like the one above, you may want to head for the nearest cafeteria. But read on—food for the mind is better than French fries.

Our generation is very big on what is commonly called "escapist fiction." This kind of book makes no claim to be great literature with deep themes but does promise to take you out of yourself and into a far more exciting world. I, like many librarians, enjoy reading mysteries, adventure fiction, spy novels, and so on. I've even been known to write and publish such fiction in my spare time. This does get me dubious glances from some people, but I am amazed at how many seemingly sophisticated academics read the same stuff.

The advantage of a thriller is that it gives you a way to escape. You can sit back and let it happen without pondering or analyzing too deeply. Let the skilled thriller writer feed you the adventure until you scream for mercy. Escapist fiction is for gluttons.

I do not, however, call a well-crafted mystery novel "escapist" in the same sense. The writer of this kind of work dares you at every point not only to figure out who did it, but why and how whoever did it did it. In other words, such a writer does not want you to swallow the novel whole (as in a thriller) but to read it with discernment, pausing to think over clues with reserve and intelligence. The well-crafted mystery novel is for connoisseurs.

Where is all this leading? Simply to a foundational statement: *Research is not for gluttons.*

Consider the problem you face as a researcher: You have twenty-five scattered sources and seven websites waiting to be read. They comprise 3,423 pages in total. At an average rate of one page every two minutes, this will take you 6,846 minutes to read, or, in more familiar terms, 114.1 hours. If you skip classes for two weeks (or take a vacation from your job) and read 8.15 hours per day, you will have it all read. But wait a minute (even though you have none of these to spare) - I haven't allowed you the time you need to take notes on what you're reading nor to ponder its value. You'd better plan on three weeks.

Before we get too far into the realm of the ridiculous, I think you can see that there is no way you will be able to read and take notes on 3,423 pages for one research project. The approach that works so well for devouring spy novels - gluttonously reading without much thought - is going to sink you when you try to read research materials. There has to be a way to determine what's important and what's a red herring (or a blue elephant).

Let me show you the connoisseur's approach to reading:

8.1.1 Be ruthless

You may not like what I have to say now, but I do have to say it. *Any book or article you read for research purposes must be used and left behind as quickly as possible, even though you can never take anything out of context.* Forget that the author probably worked long into the night, leaving a weeping spouse and children waiting outside the study door. Forget that for perhaps years the author was utterly consumed by the burden of this topic until it could be rendered into print.

You need information. The source you are reading has information. The problem is that it has too much information that is not relevant to your research topic. Thus you need to use every skill you have to sift quickly through what you don't need and find what you do need.

At this point I must warn you not to show this chapter to anyone with an academic title. Such a person may very well burn your copy of *Research Strategies* right in front of you (if you have the print version) or confiscate your e-reader (if you have an electronic version). Professors are purists, and rightly so. They have written one or more theses for which they actually did read all 3,423 pages plus 74,689 more. They got into the hearts and souls of the authors they were reading.

You, on the other hand, are writing a paper that is due, along with two others, in seven days. *Be ruthless.* Read what you need and abandon the rest. It's your only hope.

One big note of caution: I am not urging you to read out of context. You have to read enough of an author's work to have a good idea of his or her main message. It's all very well to be efficient and discerning (the connoisseur) rather than a mindless sponge (the glutton), but be very sure you have grasped, not only what the author is saying, but why the author is saying it.

8.1.2 Get to know the material without reading it all

No, this is not an incentive to do skimpy research. This is an attempt to show you how to zero in on what you need without missing anything important. Here are the steps to take, first for books, then for articles:

Books

> ➤ At the start, have a good look at the title page, preface, foreword, and introduction, even if you are planning to keyword search in an e-book. A book is not just a series of paragraphs. It is not just a chunk of content. There is usually a motive and a plan, so the preliminary pages can give you solid clues as to why the book was written and what it intended to do. Title pages are often ignored because they seem to have so little information on them. But they can be important. Be sure to look at both the title and subtitle, since increasingly titles are there just to look cute, while the real purpose of the book is revealed in the subtitle. Consider these gems:
>
> *Lifestyle: Conversations with Members of the Unification Church*
> *Passages: Predictable Crises of Adult Life*
> *Sex in the Snow: Canadian Social Values at the End of the Millennium*
>
> The preface, foreword, or introduction will often tell you what the author was attempting to do in the book. There you can look for a thesis statement, as well as for a description of the approach to the subject and of the material to be covered. Reading a good preface could give you all the clues you need to get into the really important data.
>
> ➤ **Second**, check out the table of contents. This table forms the skeleton upon which the body is hung, the

keystone that supports the building, the street signs that give meaning to the metropolis, the - but why go on? The point is simply that the table of contents provides you with the basic structure of the book in its proper order. Here you find the good, the bad, and the useless for your purposes. There was a time when tables of contents gave you main headings, subdivisions, and even short paragraph summaries of the main arguments. Now chances are that most chapter headings you see will be cute but relatively uninformative. Still, it is worth your while to check out the table of contents. It may help you zero in on the chapter that you really want. And it gives you a sense of the writer's whole development of the topic.

➢ *Third*, have a look at the index. Indexes can be good, atrocious, or nonexistent. Their real value (when present) lies in their ability to locate specific information when the book itself covers a broader topic. But beware of two problems:

- Indexes often list many page numbers after each topic heading, forcing you to do a lot of looking up to find what you want. Comparing chapter headings with page numbers in the index might help you speed up the process by identifying the most relevant sections.

- When you have located a relevant page by using an index, beware the natural tendency to take information out of context. Remember that the paragraph you are reading on page 294 was preceded by 293 pages.

➢ *Fourth*, be sure to give the book a run-through, even if you are only going to use a part of it. If you fail to do so, you may miss completely the overall intent of the volume and thus misunderstand what you are reading in one portion of it. A run-through includes:

- Reading opening and concluding portions of each chapter to see what the author intended to cover and what he or she concluded.

- Considering the subheadings in the body of each chapter.
- Going over any summary or conclusion chapter at the end of the book.
- Possibly looking up a book review or two if the book is confusing or potentially controversial.
➢ *Fifth*, when it comes to reading the appropriate portion(s) of the book, be a connoisseur of the argumentation, not a glutton who does not evaluate what s/he's eating as long as s/he's got food in front of her or him. There is only one way to read when you are doing research—*by asking constant questions*. Questions form absolutely the most useful key to good analysis. Ask yourself:
- What is the author saying?
- What point of view or background is the author coming from that might influence what is being said? Thus, what biases do you discern?
- Is the author really dealing with the issues or are there some things missing or minimized in the argument?
- Is the evidence presented fairly? Is there enough evidence? Does the evidence support the author's case? Is there counter-evidence that needs to be considered before you automatically buy into the author's argument?
- How do this author's approach or beliefs compare/ contrast with other things you've been reading? (Here you should be able to group authors by what they believe so that you can see who supports whom and who opposes whom. This supports the concept that research is a conversation).

And so on. Don't merely absorb (gluttony). Analyze. Get involved. Ask probing and constant questions of everything you are reading. It will help your research immeasurably. What's more, your questions will help you start preparing your research for the final writing process.

Articles

With a journal article, or an essay within a book, you lack some of the more familiar signposts—tables of contents, indexes, sometimes even subheadings in the text. To add to the problem, the writer may argue a complex point over several pages without stating a conclusion until the last moment. How do you get a grasp of the article's message in short order and make good use of it?

> ➢ *First*, find an abstract (a summary of the article) if you can locate one quickly. The most generous journals actually provide their own abstracts in the text of their publications. If this is not the case for your article, the article may well be abstracted in a journal database. With a good abstract, you can discern the author's main points and conclusion.

> ➢ *Second*, watch for key propositions. *Key what?* **Key propositions**, despite the strange name, relate to a simple concept: *A key proposition is a statement of what the author believes to be true.* Whether or not it is actually true is something for you to discern, but it is what the author believes to be true. Most pieces of expository writing, whether books or journal articles, have several key propositions dotted throughout with, hopefully, a big key proposition at the end. There are two ways in which an author might present key propositions. Some authors start with a question, present various lines of evidence, then state a key proposition:

Question→ Evidence→ Key Proposition

> Others start with a key proposition (in the form of a thesis statement), present evidence for it, and then re-state the proposition:

Key Proposition (Thesis) → Evidence→ Restated Key Proposition

Your task is to identify how your author presents key propositions, and then *find them*. Key propositions form the foundation or the skeleton of the article. Everything else is introduction or evidence. With the key propositions identified, you can get to the heart of what the author is trying to say. [Note: The above procedure works just as well with books]

➢ ***Third***, check out the author's conclusion at the end of the article carefully. What is the author's bottom line as far as beliefs or final thoughts are concerned? Presumably everything else in the article has some relation to that final statement.

➢ ***Fourth***, if the article you are reading still gives you very few clues, read the whole thing. There are times when you just have to muddle through, but it won't hurt as much as you think it will. As you go, try to abstract the article for yourself on paper. It will help your understanding, and if you ever have to refer to it again (in a week, by which time you've forgotten you ever read it), you'll be one step ahead.

8.1.3 A final word on analytical reading

We have been dealing with hard realities here—too little time and too much to read. Perhaps professors or employers one day will let students work on fewer but larger projects where they have the hours to do the job right. Until that happens, you will need to know how to practice discriminating reading.

Remember that books and journal articles are sources of data. Develop those skills that will help you extract data with the greatest speed and efficiency. But beware of quoting an author out of context because you did not read enough to get the author's overall message.

Clearing the Fog – On using more than the first three pages

In a study of student research, The Citation Project found that 77% of all student citations relate only to the first three pages of a source, regardless of its length (Sandra Jamieson and Rebecca M. Howard, "The Citation Project: Preventing Plagiarism, Teaching Writing: Initial Data from the Citation Project Study of Student Use of Sources in Researched Papers from Sixteen US Colleges and Universities," 2011, **http://site.citationproject.net/wp-content/uploads/2011/08/Sources-Cited-in-the-Paper.pdf**).

This means that many academic students are really only interacting with sources enough to get a general idea of what is in them and to (dare I suggest it) mine for a few cool quotations.

In this section of *Research Strategies*, I've offered several efficient ways for you to interact with the whole of your sources without having read everything. So imagine this scenario – the really crucial information is on page 5 but you only read to page 3 and missed the point of what the author was saying. Unknown to you, your professor read the same article last week and remembers it well.

Even if you don't get busted by your prof for only skimming the first three pages, the point is that doing a decent job of research means you actually have to have significant interaction with your sources. Train yourself in the methods I've suggested above, and start reading past page three. It will open up whole new worlds for you.

8.2 Evaluation of research resources

Much of what we might call "evaluation" is part of analytical reading – trying to discern what the author is saying and how credible the author's arguments appear to be. But I also want to provide you with some clues regarding the overall evaluation process.

Evaluation has to do with determining the following:

➢ The qualifications of the author. The first criterion that comes to mind is how many academic degrees an author has, but that may not be the only measure of qualification. If your family doctor starts writing books about medieval art, her medical degree is not going to make her as competent as someone with a degree in medieval art. If an author is writing on a subject area but lacks clear qualifications to be writing in that field, the product is going to be shabby.

➢ The biases of the author. Bias is not necessarily a bad thing, because none of us are 100% objective. It may, indeed, be the bias of the author that is most important to you. For example, if you are writing on prejudice against Chinese-heritage people in 19th century San Francisco, reading primary sources (e.g. newspaper articles) by biased people of the time may well make your case. What is important here is that you *identify* the biases of authors so that you can walk into their works with eyes wide open.

➢ The level of expressed opinion as opposed to evidence. Opinion is not fact, but constitutes views that are unsupported by evidence. As you know, just because you read something in a published work, you can't assume that it's bound to be correct. You need always to ask, "How do you know that to be the case? Where's your evidence?"

➢ Whether or not the material is relevant to the problem you are addressing. Here you should take note of the fact that *relevance is not the same thing as quality.* A book or article may be highly relevant yet not up to par by the measures of scholarship. On the other hand, a book or article may be oozing scholarship but really have nothing much to say directly about the issue you are addressing.

A couple of great resource for evaluation:

http://www.lib.berkeley.edu/TeachingLib/Guides/ Evaluation.html
http://www.virtualsalt.com/evalu8it.htm

8.3 Note taking

You may be aware of those rare people who never annotate or take notes on the data they are discovering in research. Instead, they gather all their books and articles around themselves just before they start writing their first draft, then they cite and quote their sources simply by hauling books out of the pile and looking up appropriate passages. Or they open multiple windows of online articles and navigate skillfully among them. Such people, of course, have photographic memories and the organizational skills of Noah loading the ark. Or they are really only using one source for most of their data while occasionally referring to others to cover up the narrowness of their approach. Perhaps (heaven forbid), they're writing their research paper out of their heads and citing the occasional book or article only as some sort of weak signal to the reader that they did some actual research.

For most of us, it's crucial that we distill out of what we are reading the essential things we are going to have to include in our research paper. We don't have the minds, nor the stamina, to retain everything, unaided by notes. Trying to teach someone how to take notes is almost like trying to teach a baby sparrow to fly. Most of what it takes comes from within, not from instructions. I can try to help you by flapping my arms and showing you the motions, but you have to develop the will and skill to soar for yourself.

Generally I recommend taking notes from (or annotating) one source at a time, covering all of that source (book, article, etc.) before moving on to the next one. The alternative is to create note documents for each subject you are dealing with (or separate subject files on your device), then to record notes from various sources into these subject designations. This latter method may be used later in your process but is not recommended as a starting tactic, because it drags your notes out of their original contexts, thus losing the threads of thought of the authors you are reading. It's better to cover one book or article at a time, keeping all the notes for it in one place.

One of the biggest problems most students face is that they take too many notes that will later go unused. The key to this difficulty is to have a good research question and preliminary outline as soon as possible in the research process. If you are one of those people who only discerns your outline for the first time while you are proofreading the final copy of your paper, you have probably wasted a lot of time taking notes that ended up being junked. After all that needless effort, your paper is probably not very good anyway, because its structure was never planned. On the other hand, if you have a fairly solid idea of what you want to accomplish with your research project, you are less likely to take notes on irrelevant information.

Once you have a clear vision how you want your research materials to help you deal with your question, you next have to decide on a note-taking style.

8.3.1 The determined photo-copier/printer/e-doc highlighter

For some students, note taking is easy. You just annotate or highlight the PDFs you've gathered. Or, if you are doing analog, you arm yourself with fourteen dollars in dimes or a charged up printing account, then photocopy or print everything that looks important, taking all 140 copies home and assembling your essay out of them. Would that most of us could afford this method. Using the scan to e-mailed PDF function on many photocopies is often free, making that the better financial option for turning print into digital. Or people snap pics of their favorite pages with their phone or other mobile device and download the whole mess later. You can also use speech recognition software, available on most devices and operating systems, to read text into a word processor. In each case, you end up with the full text of the resource and then must figure out what to do with it.

A bit of advice here:

> ➤ If you are using a printing device, scanner, phone, or speech recognition to record pages, make sure that you have also recorded the *author, title, place of publication, publisher and date* for every book or article you've retrieved (*author, title, journal name, volume number, date and page numbers* for journals). You'd be surprised at how many people I find wandering the library, wayward

copy in hand, looking desperately for whatever source they took it from.

➤ Use a highlight pen on your paper copies or print-offs as soon as you have made them, while the information is still fresh in your mind. PDF in Adobe Reader has a comment function for your e-resources notations. For phone scans, use an OCR app (Apple, Android or Windows Surface) to turn the print into searchable text as PDF. You want to mark the passages that were of the greatest importance to you so that you will not, later on, wonder why you retrieved this material in the first place.

➤ Remember that you are at a disadvantage if you print, scan or snap. "Me?" you grin. "I'm the one who snagged all this stuff in a tenth of the time it takes these longhand scribblers and clickety-click keyboarders around here." Yes, but recognize that you have probably interacted with your material at a far more superficial level than have those "longhand scribblers and clickety-click keyboarders." When you go home tonight and try to wade through all your retrieved stuff, you may find that you've entered a strange and cruel world in which no landmarks make sense to you and the reasons why you printed/copied/ digitized/snapped even half of the stuff totally escape you.

➤ Once you have PDFs or other types of docs for your material, make sure you name them consistently and file them for clear and easy retrieval. I prefer using author name as the first part of the PDF file name, then a space-dash-space and the first few words of the title (e.g. **Smith – The apple pie conundrum**).

➤ Sometimes the option of creating separate notes can become attractive. With note-taking, you can copy/paste excerpts from your full text PDFs to a Word document, and add your own comments and summaries, thus establishing a condensed version of the original source (making sure that you stamp each set of notes with the correct bibliographic information.)

Here is an example of notes excerpted from large documents, showing this file name convention:

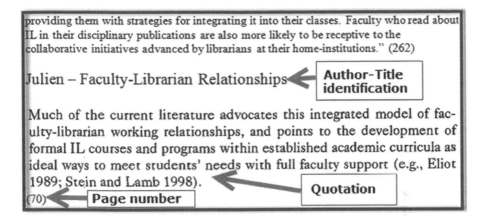

There are cool Net-based programs that can help you with note creation. Evernote (**http://evernote.com/**) is a free resource for gathering and accessing your notes. You can also download the app, Evernote Web Clipper, to save anything from the Web without having to leave your browser (**http://evernote.com/webclipper/**). Evernote will enable you to get to your cloud-based notes from any device. For a tool to annotate and store web pages, try Scrible (**http://www.scrible.com/**). The tool Catch, described in the 4th edition of *Research Strategies*, has shut down. This is a useful lesson - make sure you subscribe to the e-mail updates most of these free online programs offer you.

Just be careful that you tag or otherwise identify each of your notes consistently so that you can identify them easily. Chapter 9 offers some tips on organizing notes.

One word of caution: Because it is often so easy to input notes, you need to be careful that you keep your notes to a minimum. Simply pulling everything you've been reading into a pot of notes is probably counterproductive.

8.3.2 The value of going all digital

I've been all digital in my own research work for some time now, getting PDFs of articles and scanning portions of hardcopy (books, etc.) to PDF. I use a bibliographic manager (see 7.6 above) to keep track of citations, and a separate folder in My Documents to keep the PDFs. All PDFs are labeled with author - title format (e.g. Smith - Finding reality in the digital world). Then I create a notes file (Word Document) so that I can summarize portions of what I am reading and copy/paste relevant excerpts from my PDFs into my notes, making sure I identify each document in turn and retain page numbers (see illustration above). Some PDFs are image files that won't copy/paste well. For those, I use screen capture (built into most device operating systems) to snare relevant portions that I then put into my notes document. At the end, I have a collection of key information from my sources without having to type anything.

But be cautious here: If you collect a lot of PDFs without excerpting notes from them, you may have difficulty pulling out the information you need, since you have to search each PDF separately. A free resource to help you with this is Qiqqa (**http://www.qiqqa. com/**), a simply amazing PDF manager that enables you to store and annotate PDFs. It also provides unique search capabilities. If you are working with your original PDFs rather than taking shorter notes, give Qiqqa a try (requires a no-cost software download).

8.3.3 The quoter

Some people still prefer a low-tech approach with paper and pen or, lacking a portable scanner, they are using their own fingers to type material into electronic files. Often the plan is to get down information that is verbatim, that is, pull direct quotations out of their sources. There are some advantages to copying material word for word into your notes, and (inevitably) some disadvantages.

Advantages

> - You won't have to go back to the book or article later on if you need a suitable quotation. It will be right in your notes.
> - A quotation method can give you greater accuracy, since you have the actual words of your sources. This is especially helpful when a topic is new to you. When you

don't fully understand a writer's argument, you can copy out a paragraph that states it. Later, when you are more in tune with the subject, the paragraph may make more sense. If you had tried merely to summarize it before you understood the material, you might have misinterpreted the argument and carried that misinterpretation into your notes.

➤ The mere act of hand or keyboard copying helps you get to know the material more intimately, since copying demands that you read more slowly and, in fact, that you read each word several times. In understanding, you will be far ahead of the photocopier or scanner when your notes are complete.

Disadvantages

➤ The process can become fairly laborious. It's easier to photocopy or scan.
➤ You must be very careful to quote enough to catch the context. Alternatively, you could summarize the context in your notes, then directly copy the portion that is most important to you.

8.3.4 The summarizer

This person reads a chunk of material and then summarizes it in his or her own words. The point is to condense several pages into a paragraph of notes or a paragraph into a sentence.

Advantages:

➤ This method is quicker than quoting.
➤ The process of summarizing forces you to think about the material and make it your own.

Disadvantages:

➤ The method does not work well if you are dealing with difficult material that is hard to condense.

> ➤ You will have to go back to your book or journal article if you find later that you need a quotation.
> ➤ You have to be very careful that you understand the things you are reading. If you misunderstand, you have no way of checking for the accuracy of your summaries later on, other than going back to your source material.

8.3.5 The paraphraser (*not recommended* in most cases)

The difference between summarizing and paraphrasing is that the former *condenses* material while the latter *rewrites each sentence in the reader's own words*. For example, perhaps the original book or article said:

> *The rate of increase in building costs is rapidly making home ownership impossible for the average middle class family.*

A paraphrase might say:

> *The speed of growth in the cost to build is quickly making owning a home impossible for the average family with a middle income.*

But a summary might say:

> *The rising cost of construction is squeezing out middle class of would-be home owners.* [i.e., an **interpretation** rather than a paraphrase]

With a paraphrase, you can expect that your paragraph of notes will be as long as the book's paragraph, if not longer.

Possible advantage:

This method can be helpful if you are working through difficult material. Sometimes just the task of rewriting each sentence in your own words makes the writer's meaning clear.

Why, in most cases, paraphrasing is a bad idea:

➢ While sometimes recommended by professors, this method leaves you particularly open to a charge of plagiarism (see the end of this chapter), since you are still reproducing the writer's work, thought for thought if not word for word.

➢ In fact, people who paraphrase tend to change far too little of the original to qualify the result as plagiarism-free. Most paraphrasing that I see appearing in research papers is out and out theft of most of the original author's words as well as his/her thoughts.

➢ The method is laborious. Not only do you have to rephrase each sentence, but your notes will be as long as your original source, maybe longer.

So paraphrase only if you need it to explain a piece of writing to yourself. Word to the wise: *Avoid letting paraphrased material appear in an actual research paper you have written. Paraphrased material only puts you at risk of a plagiarism accusation. Summarize instead.*

8.3.6 Which method is best?

You can use any or all of these methods, except paraphrasing, to advantage. I suggest that you keep all methods available, using each as appropriate.

8.4 Further notes on note-taking

➢ Make sure you leave nothing out of your notes. Keep track of full information on author, title, place, publisher, date, volume number, page numbers, etc. You don't want to have to relocate a book or article you've already read. Chances are someone else will have it by now and you'll never find out what page that key quotation came from.

Other than a cold shower, there's nothing as subduing as having to throw out perfectly good notes because you don't have enough source information to use them in your bibliography. Bibliographic managers are great resources for keeping track of your bibliographies (7.6 above)

➤ If you are quoting, use quotation marks in your notes. If you copy/paste in an electronic environment, keep track of page numbers. If the material you are reading turns a page in the middle of your quotation, put a slash mark or some other indicator into your notes to tell you where the page turned in the original.

➤ If you are summarizing, conscientiously try to work at using your own wording. If you find that your wording is turning out like a clone of the original, then quote directly or photocopy/print. With summaries, indicate in the margin of the notes the page numbers you are summarizing (in case you want to go back to the book or article later).

➤ If an insight comes to you as you are reading, include it in your notes. Put square brackets around it and end the statement of your insight with a dash and your initials, like this:

[*Schwartzburg agrees with Smith on this point. Does Flutnof?—WB*]

An "insight" is simply anything that occurs to you while you're reading, as, for example, the discovery that this writer agrees or disagrees with someone else, has omitted something, has made a statement that you would like to challenge, has given you a good idea you want to follow up, and so on.

Clearing the Fog – What if I'm not an organized person?

All of this talk of pre-planning how you are going to create your notes and use them effectively may have you feeling a bit queasy. You, in fact, may find the whole idea of *method* to be a limiting factor. You are used to glorious chaos out of which emerges fresh ideas. Creating notes by set methods and organizing them (we'll get to note organization in the next chapter) seems much too structured, the kind of thing a librarian might do.

If you are a person who finds organization to be a burden, I suppose you can carry on as before. But how has that been working for you? As projects get bigger and more detailed, are you noticing that the anxiety regarding your "just wing it" approach is growing? Have you wasted a lot of time finding and re-finding material that you know is there somewhere? Do you often feel utterly lost?

Is the problem less that you hate organization than that you struggle with *doing* organization? If so, try this approach. First, before you ever start on a project, say to yourself, "I need to plan and organize my research." Rather than telling yourself that you can't create such a plan, let alone carry it out, ask yourself a set of questions. The answers will create a roadmap for you to follow:

> ➤ *What format do I intend to use to hold the notes I need to take for this project?* Rather than having some notes in paper, some on PDF and some on your phone, decide on one resource format and then determine how you will convert everything to that format. For example, you may say, "I want to have everything in PDF." Clearly, your article downloads will be PDFs. You can scan print material to PDF (see suggestions above). In the end, you will have only one type of format to deal with. If you use my naming convention (Author, space dash space, First part of title, e.g. Jackson - Finding a Path in Research), all your PDFs will organize in a documents folder in alphabetical order by author.
> ➤ *Where do I intend to store my notes?* This could be a binder for print, a documents folder for PDFs or one of

those note programs like Catch or Evernote. Keep your storage place consistent.

➤ *What rules do I intend to follow in note-taking?* Decide on a method in advance, and follow it. See the examples above.

There – you have a plan. Now all you have to do is stick to it.

8.5 A gentle warning about the horrible crime of plagiarism

Just to end the chapter on a cheery note, let me caution you about the academic crime of *plagiarism.* Plagiarism, to put it simply, is passing on someone else's work as your own. The following examples, if they describe your actions, place you very obviously among the guilty. You are plagiarizing if you:

➤ Get your whole essay from a friend or a paper mill online and then pass it off as your own original work.

➤ Quote directly from a book, journal, newspaper, friend's essay, etc. without using quotation marks and a note to indicate that the material is not yours;

➤ "Borrow" text from the WWW or some other digital source by copy/paste without indicating the source;

➤ Paraphrase an author, sentence by sentence, without acknowledging the author as the source of the material;

➤ Use a unique idea from an author without indicating the source of the idea. When you can't find the same idea in two or more independent sources, then it's unique and you have to tell the reader of your research project where the idea came from. (Concepts that are unique to an author need to be acknowledged, while more generally used information does not).

Plagiarism is an academic crime because it is the theft of someone else's creativity, and because it gives the impression that someone else's words or ideas are your own. Most astute professors catch offenders quite easily (especially those who skim their papers off the Internet), and then feel hurt that they have been lied to. This can result in anything from a zero for the paper to expulsion from the institution.

8.5.1 Why get stressed about plagiarism?

With easy access to the WWW and to online full text journals, plagiarism is increasing. A lot of students struggle with why plagiarism is such a big deal. We download music all the time, and the WWW is full of free information. What's the difference between downloading a song and downloading text to put into a research paper? The following may provide some answers:

➢ There is a difference between free access and the ability to claim that you are the author of the information you copied from the Net. If you download a song, you may "own" it, but you can't legally claim that you wrote it or sang it. If you download text from a freely available source and then neglect to indicate who authored that text, you're not only taking control of the information, you're executing a fraud by leading the reader to believe you actually wrote the stuff.

➢ Intellectual property is a big deal in Western society. To be able to write something and put my name on it is something I value, and my right to claim ownership is protected by copyright law. When someone else takes my material and puts his/her name on it, my intellectual property has been stolen.

➢ When you take someone else's words or ideas and pass them off as your own, you rob those words of their power, because your break the connection between the creator of the information and the information itself. To say that a known authority in the field wrote that: _____ (you fill in the blank) is much more powerful than saying or implying that you wrote the same thing. The power of information comes from the power of the person who authored that information.

➢ Research writing is a conversation. As you address your research question, you know that there are other voices out there who have already expressed points of view about possible answers to your question (the sources you are using – books, articles, and so on). Research involves dialoguing with those sources, agreeing with some, disagreeing with others. If you steal text or ideas from those sources and pass them off as your own words or ideas, you kill the dialogue and leave yourself as the only authority on the topic. A prof can see through that sort of thing in an instant. It's much more powerful to write, "Jones has argued _____ but Smith has countered with the argument that _____. In considering Jones' view, it appears that she has neglected to take into account the evidence that _____." Focusing on the dialogue - That's the key to good research writing.

8.5.2 About getting caught

Just at the time when it's easier than ever to steal electronic text and paste it into your research project, thus deceptively passing it off as your own, it's easier than ever to get caught. If you plagiarize an author's unique ideas, chances are your professor already knows what those unique ideas are. But even if you steal text, your professor can catch you very easily.

For material from the WWW, a simple Google search on a string of text from your paper (using quotation marks) will likely find you out pretty quickly. The same can be done with full text searches in journal databases or Google Scholar. For books, both Google Books and Amazon A9 have a lot of electronic full text available for searching.

Even if you take text from a print book or journal not available electronically, you are still at risk. Case in point - I was reading a student paper that just didn't seem right, so I googled a string of text.

The source the student was using wasn't available electronically, but the text I googled was in a website as a quotation from the print source. Once I knew what hardcopy book had been plagiarized, I got it off the library shelf and tracked down the rest of the massive amount of plagiarism in the paper.

Many institutions are using plagiarism detection services like Turnitin. Students submit their papers electronically, and the degree of correspondence between those papers and other electronic sources (including their bank of student papers) is analyzed. The professor gets a report.

So it's getting easier to be caught at the plagiarism game. The results are pretty awful. If your professor is really merciful you'll have to rewrite your paper. Normally the paper gets a zero, with no chance for a rewrite. But many institutions don't just stop there. They record your plagiarism infraction in your academic file, and you may be given a failing mark for the course. You could even be suspended or expelled. Overall, plagiarism can look like an easy way to get a paper done, but the rewards are not worth the penalty.

For a PowerPoint on plagiarism: **http://www.acts.twu.ca/ Library/plagiarism.ppt.**

See also the 10 minute video by Conrad Van Dyk of Concordia University College: **http://youtu.be/50zeD7uQiQs.**

For an article expanding on my approach to plagiarism, see Badke, William. "Give Plagiarism the Weight It Deserves." *Online* 31.5 (Sep. 2007): 58-60.

8.5.3 International students and plagiarism

International students face some unique challenges with the plagiarism issue. In many cultures, information is perceived as the property of the community more than it is the property of the individual. In fact, when other people in a community copy or freely use the information of a great scholar, they are honoring that scholar. If information is seen as communal property, using someone else's words or ideas does not appear to be a serious problem.

Yet even in societies where information is communal, it remains wrong to pretend that other people's words or ideas are our own. Even information that belongs to the community still had an author. If you leave the impression that you are the author, you are committing fraud.

Unfortunately, as well, international students who struggle with English are more likely to be caught when then plagiarize than native English speakers. Why? Because the style of English in the plagiarized material is obviously different from the style of an English used by a second language writer. It is not that international students plagiarize more often than domestic students. It is that international student plagiarism is easier to detect.

For a handbook to guide you in every aspect of your academic life as an international student, including plagiarism, see William Badke, *Beyond the Answer Sheet: Academic Success for International Students.* Lincoln, NE: iUniverse.com, 2003.

For more information on, and examples of, plagiarism see APPENDIX ONE, section A1.5.4.

8.6 For further study

Study guide

1. What's the difference between connoisseur and glutton reading?
2. In what way do you need to "be ruthless" in research reading?
3. What are the four steps to discovering the overall message of a book quickly?
4. When you get to the fifth step (actually reading material you need), explain the best way to go about it.
5. What is an abstract, and how can it help you?
6. What are "key propositions" and how does finding them help the reading process?
7. What's the secret to avoiding the trap of taking too many notes that you will later not use?
8. What are some of the risks for those who take most of their notes by photocopying their sources?
9. What are the advantages and disadvantages of taking notes using the methods of quoting, summarizing and paraphrasing?

10. What are the 4 further instructions the author gives about key elements of note-taking?
11. Define plagiarism and explain why it is such a serious offence. You might want to supplement your knowledge with the following websites:

http://library.camden.rutgers.edu/EducationalModule/
Plagiarism/
http://www.csub.edu/ssric-trd/howto/plagiarism.htm
http://www.hamilton.edu/writing/style/plagiarism/plagiarism.
html

Practice / Assignment

1. How is your research reading going? Is it efficient and effective? Go over the suggestions in the first part of this chapter and discover ways in which you can improve your research reading methods.
2. Assess your methods of note taking. Are they working for you? How would you improve them? Do you see ways to improve efficiency by using your electronic device (phone, tablet, or laptop) in note taking?

9

Organizing Your Resources to Write your Paper

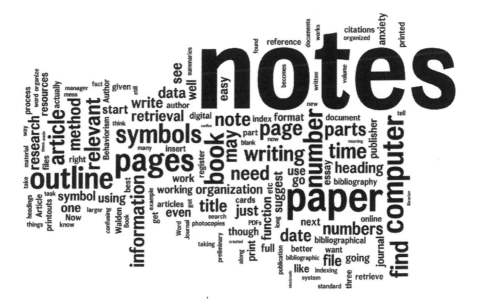

"I have seventy-five pages of notes not counting the photocopy I left on the copier and the two pages which I think fell behind my desk. And I've got at least 7 journal articles printed off, but no notes for them. I've got a bunch of PDFs, but I forgot to put them in one folder, and their file names tell me nothing about what they are. What a

mess! How am I ever going to make a finished research project out of this chaos? Will there ever be meaning to my life?"

Yes, there will. Take heart. There is a way to organize your disastrous jumble of resources or the chaos of notes in your laptop or tablet, no matter how incomprehensible it now seems to be.

I hesitate whenever I suggest "my" method for organization. What if your mind, heaven forbid, does not correspond with mine? What if I'm totally out of touch with the logical categories you most enjoy?

Still, someone has to suggest something. Librarians, even though dull, are undoubtedly logical and thus better equipped than, say, Renaissance painters, to suggest methods of organizing information. I am giving you only a couple of approaches to the problem, because throwing too many methods at you can be confusing. If you don't like what I suggest, ask your favorite professor or another librarian to suggest a better plan.

My first system can be called a "register method" of resource organization. A "register" is an index of some sort that enables you to organize data. Consider an auto parts store. The parts are laid out in bins on row after row of shelves. The fact that the water system thermostats are next to the distributor caps that are next to the spark plugs is not nearly as relevant as the fact that each bin has a number on it.

When I walk in and ask for a thermostat for a 1949 Wuzzly Roadster, the parts person does not immediately proceed to the shelves and start looking. He or she searches a database to find the bin number for that model of thermostat. Then it's an easy task to find the bin with the right number on it and deliver the part to me.

Here's the point of the analogy: The rows of auto parts are your jumbled mess of notes and printouts, in print or online. The bin numbers are codes you insert into these resources, such as page numbers and other symbols. The parts book or digital index represents an indexed outline by which you can retrieve your notes in a coherent way. This is how it works:

9.1 Your notes, photocopies and printouts

9.1.1 Organizing digital notes

I am presuming here that you have captured excerpts, produced summaries, and so on so that you are not working with the full documents you acquired in the process of your research, but with notes on them. If you are working with full documents, go back to 8.3.3 for some guidance. If you have created a digital document containing notes taken from your original PDFs (through copy/paste, plus your own annotations), take advice from the following:

> ➤ Some people prefer to print their digital notes onto paper. In this case, your device is just an input medium, and notes should be handled as in 9.1.2 below.
> ➤ If you are planning to retain your notes in their electronic format, you need to determine how you want to set them up for easy retrieval of the information you need. The best solution here is to create a single Word file of notes, using copy/paste from electronic sources as well as your own summaries and comments. I've created such note documents up to 400+ pages worth, so I know that they work and that retrieval is still possible, no matter how big the document becomes. *Presumably I don't have to stress the importance of backing up this file as you go along. Lose it, and you lose everything.*
> ➤ Your word processor's "find" function (in the "edit" menu) will become a retrieval tool, though in the organizing process you will need to input some codes (see 9.3 below).

9.1.2 Organizing your paper-based notes

Many students still base their notes in hardcopy, thus printing articles, taking photocopies of book pages and writing or typing/printing summaries. Some write notes on 3 x 5 or 4 x 6 cards. This is, in my humble opinion, a grave error. If God had meant us to write out notes on cards, he would not have allowed us to invent standard notepaper or printers that take standard paper sizes. Does not nature itself tell you that eyes, hands and pens were made for writing boldly on decent sized paper instead of scraping one-sixteenth inch high letters on miniscule cards? Are not printers set to standard size paper by default?

Save your note cards for the next part of my system if you wish (though there are much better ways), and produce your notes (if you are using print or printing electronic notes) on normal paper, hole-punching them and keeping them together in a binder. Be sure, however, to follow a consistent method. As you begin taking notes on each book or article, be very certain that you include full bibliographical information in the notes (author, title, place, publisher, date, volume number, and page numbers).

When you have completed creating your notes for a particular item (even if those notes are ten pages long), simply leave a few lines blank, then start notes on your next book or article, being sure again to enter full bibliographical information first. (If you are using a device, see the alternatives below.)

One of the important things you need to do is *number the pages of your notes consecutively.* If you have fifty pages of notes on ten pages, then number your note pages from one to fifty. (If using a device, see below). If you have photocopies or journal article printouts, put them in the right places in your notes and number them along with the notes, even if you end up with 150 pages numbered consecutively.

9.2 Your bibliography

As you gather sources, you have to keep track of them, including enough bibliographical information so that you won't need to go on a desperate search for a lost date or volume number when you start writing your paper. The best resource for this task is a bibliographic manager like EndNote, RefWorks or Zotero (See Chapter 7 for explanation of these tools). If you do not use a bibliographic manager, you may want to enlist a software or online style formatting program or at least construct a separate Word file with the bibliography in proper format (on format and formatting tools, see APPENDIX A – A.1.6).

Here's the minimal information needed for your citations:

Book - Author(s), title, city of publication, publisher, date.

Journal Article - Author(s) and title of article, journal title, volume number, date (e.g., (2013), (January 1999) or (Spring 2000)), and page numbers where the article is found.

Journal Article from an Electronic Periodical Database - everything listed under Journal Article above plus (possibly) the date you accessed the article, and either the persistent link / journal home page, or the DOI, depending on what bibliographical style you are using. For example:

> Badke, W. (2010). Foundations of information literacy: Learning from Paul Zurkowski. *Online, 34*(1), 48-50. Retrieved from http://www.infotoday.com/online/.

> Weickert, T., Goldberg, T., Egan, M., Apud, J., Meeter, M., Myers, C., et al. (2010). Relative risk of probabilistic category learning deficits in patients with Schizophrenia and their siblings. *Biological Psychiatry, 67*(10), 948-955. doi:10.1016/j.biopsych.2009.12.027.

Essay in a Book - Author(s) and title of essay, title of book, editor of book, city of publication, publisher, date, and page numbers where the essay is found.

Reference Book Article - Title of article, author(s) if given (often an abbreviation of the author name is provided at the end of the article), title of reference book, edition of reference book; and (sometimes) city of publication, publisher, date. Note that most basic reference book articles are not cited in bibliographies, though longer articles from substantial reference works may be.

Website - Author (if given), title, publisher (if given), Internet address (URL), and date you most recently accessed the information.

Clearing the Fog - How can I learn to read citations well?

So you've got a bunch of citations, but they are just *so* confusing. It's not just format - MLA, APA, Chicago, etc. - it's the fact that there are so many details. Is this a citation to a book or an article or an essay in a book, or just what? Websites are recognizable for the most part, but other academic literature can be a nightmare to decipher.

Being helpful as always (I'm a librarian, after all), I've compiled a graphic that spells out the main elements of book, essay and journal article citations. Don't worry about the format. Just have a good look at the various parts of the citation and what they mean. I hope this clears out some fog.

Book:

Essay in a Book:

Journal:

9.3 Your subject index

Note taking and printout gathering are easy. Retrieval is hard. The biggest problem most students face is that they've ended up with a ton of PDFs (or many pages of notes and printouts), but now that they want to write the research paper, they can't retrieve the data they need from these resources.

Virtually anyone, even a seasoned author, gets writing anxiety - that moment when you are finally staring at a blank screen (with the cursor blinking in taunting fashion) or a blank piece of paper, and your mind tells you that this essay will never happen. You may have written brilliant works in the past (or not), but this one simply will never see the light of day. You are doomed.

Now, imagine that you have the further problems that your full text resources or notes are a mess, you're not sure you did enough research, and you can't find even the data you remember noting down. Writing anxiety now becomes writing crisis. The only way to save yourself from all this *angst* is to get organized before you write.

Sure, I know you're thinking, *"My paper is due in 3 hours. I don't have time to get organized."*

My response is that **you don't have time NOT to get organized.**

Let me suggest a method that will break the back of writing anxiety and actually save you time in the long run. This procedure can be done with physical paper or an electronic document. Here are the steps:

- ➢ Open a new Word document (or take a good-sized piece of paper) and type/write your preliminary outline on it, leaving lots of space between each heading or subheading. (This assumes that you actually **do** have a preliminary outline. If not, you've probably already lost a lot of time researching things that aren't relevant to your topic, which may explain in part why your unfinished paper is due in three hours [not meaning to be cruel; just saying].)
- ➢ Determine a symbol to represent each heading or subheading. These symbols could be the letters and numbers used in your outline (I, A, 1, a, etc.) or special

symbols not normally used in written work: #, $ % +, etc. The latter usually function better.

> If you are working with notes in paper form, read through your notes. Every time you discover data that is relevant to one of your headings in your outline, write the location (page number of notes) under that outline heading. In your notes, insert your symbol for the relevant outline heading so that you can use your outline to find the exact location of the data related to it. (If this is confusing, see the example below.)

> If you are working with electronic files, type the symbols (%, #. %, or whatever) into the spots in your online file that are relevant to your outline. The "find" function in your word processor can then locate any symbol and its relevant notes any time you need them. *Just remember to insert a space after the symbol so that the "find" function can actually find it.*

For example:

% Darwin's approach to natural selection made it possible... etc.

If you are working with a PDF file, use the Comment function on the top right of the screen to insert your symbol where you want it (choose the "Sticky note" icon; you can then see your symbols in the right column and quick connect to the related text).

Thus, with this exercise of organization, you cross-reference your notes with your outline so that you can retrieve the relevant notes as you write your paper. The outline may then look something like this:

The Limits of Behaviorism: *Walden Two* in Perspective
I. An Introduction to Behaviorism
4, 7, 12, 17 [page numbers of relevant notes only needed if your notes are in print; for electronic files, only the symbol # is necessary].

II. B.F. Skinner's *Walden Two*
$ 3, 18, 3

III. *Walden Two* as a Demonstration of the Limits of Behaviorism
% 6, 12, 14-17

In the above example, note that my symbols are #, $ and %. If I had subheadings, I could create more complex symbols like &1, &2, and so on. These symbols will also be inserted in the appropriate places in the printed notes or electronic files for easy retrieval of data.

Below is an illustration of a pages of notes, with #, $, and & symbols attached to the relevant parts. If those notes are in digital form, you can use the "Find" function in your word processor to find them (as long as you ensure there is a space after each symbol). If they are in print form, you have page numbers of your notes, and the symbols just tell you where on the page you will find what you need.

This review begins with the simple premise that expertise is something people have or hold. 18

Codes from outline added to your notes

$ These studies [cited – BB] consistently assert that expertise ma repressive and productive, and it reproduces these relations wh (i.e., experts and laypeople). 18

& After all, to be an expert is not only to be authorized by an in to make determinations about what is true, valid, or valuable

Why go to all this trouble? Simply because it saves time and alleviates writing anxiety. Consider this awful alternative: You begin writing the actual paper and get to heading number one: "An Introduction to Behaviorism." Now you have to do a keyword search on "behaviorism" with your find function (with unpredictable results) or rummage through all forty-seven pages of your printed notes, looking for material on this aspect. Having found your material and written this section of your paper, you come to your second roadblock: The next heading is "B.F. Skinner's *Walden Two.*" Now you have to go through your notes again in a second desperate search for relevant information. Then comes heading number three, and the whole nasty quest starts over again. In the process, you will have plowed through all your notes three times and restarted your writing anxiety three times.

Thus, setting up an outline-based index to your notes before you start writing saves you having to re-read your material every time you start a new section of your paper. Besides, you are left with a warm and comforting sense that you actually know where you are going before you start. When was the last time you had a feeling like that?

9.4 A Second Method for Note Organization

This one is more complex and works best for larger projects up to a thesis or dissertation. But it takes some effort to make clear. You might find this PDF helpful in clarifying it: **http://tinyurl.com/ l3ste3z**. Method number two works only if all your resources are digital. That is, you have PDFs of articles, you've digitized book pages, and so on.

The first step is to get everything into a single document. That means writing a citation and then putting excerpts from your PDF for that citation in a word document until you have relevant notes for that resource, then inserting the next citation and pulling excerpts from the next PDF to add to your word file.

Second step: Create a second word document. This second word document will be populated with notes relevant to each heading in your outline. Here are the steps:

Put your outline at the top of this second word document. Then put *another* copy of your outline below it. We will call these the "upper outline" and the "lower outline." The upper outline will serve as a hyperlinked index to the lower outline. The lower outline will have notes from your *first* word file pasted into it under each outline heading. The reason you need an index at the top (the upper outline) is that it will become increasingly difficult to find the headings in the lower outline as the space between them becomes filled with notes relevant to each heading. Thus:

Word document #1 - Your notes arranged under each resource you are using, e.g.

Smith, The Effects of...
Notes

Jones, The Trouble with.....
Notes   And so on.

Word document #2 - Your notes pulled from Word document #1 and placed under the various headings of your outline, e.g.

Upper Outline which you will hyperlink to your lower outline

Lower Outline Heading 1
Notes, notes, notes

Lower Outline Heading 2
Notes, notes, notes And so on.

Go through your original Word document #1 and find material relevant to your outline. As you find relevant information in your original notes, copy it and paste directly into your Word document #2 under whatever heading is relevant in your lower outline. Make sure you include citations for these excerpts. In essence, you are creating notes for each of your headings, pulling them as excerpts from your original master notes list.

Here is a screen shot of the upper and lower outlines, along with notes:

Preface

Portion of upper outline

PART ONE: The Problem ⟋

The Cost of Information Illiteracy
Illiteracy in Academia
The State of the Art in Information Literacy

PART ONE: The Problem

The Cost of Information Illiteracy ⟵ **Lower outline and notes**

Feldman, The Hidden costs of information work (2005)

"With the economy now becoming information-based rather than industrial, the n
is to make information work more productive." (1)

"During the summer of 2004, IDC surveyed 600 U.S. companies in three size cat

In Word document #2 you have two copies of your outline, one
above the other (the upper and the lower outlines). Now, you turn the
upper outline into a hyperlinked index to the sections in your lower
outline. Here are the steps:

1. In front of each heading in the lower outline (the one with
   excerpts of notes), create a **bookmark**, using the Insert
   function in Word.
2. Then create a hyperlink to each bookmark in the upper
   outline so that the upper outline becomes a set of links.

Then, when you need to find the notes below, related to a particular
outline heading, you can click on the relevant upper outline heading.

In summary, it works like this. First click on the "bookmark" tab
and insert the bookmark where you want it:

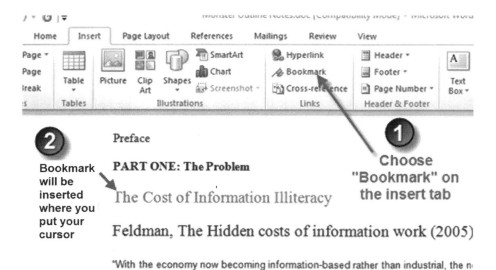

Second, create hyperlinks from the upper outline to the lower outline. The upper outline thus becomes a hyperlinked index to your lower outline.

Finish the process as below:

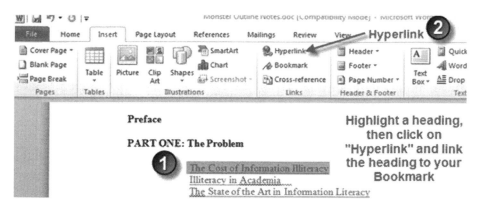

9.5 Indexing your notes for larger assignments

There may well come a time when you are asked to produce a really large research paper such as a thesis, dissertation, or book. Now the process of note organization becomes crucial, because retrieval is much more complicated.

In general, the procedures described above will work just as well on longer papers as they do on shorter ones, though my method two is better for larger assignments. A few tips for such projects (beyond the obvious that you should always back up your files):

> ➢ Do your indexing as you are going along in your research rather than waiting to the end and being faced with the task of indexing a massive electronic file or dozens (even hundreds) of printed pages of notes.
> ➢ Make especially sure that you are managing your bibliography well. The larger the bibliography, the more the risk of losing things. Here a bibliographic manager (7.5 above) is well worth the effort it takes to make it your friend.
> ➢ If your preliminary outline should change as you are going, don't panic. Go back over what you've already indexed and transfer your old indexing, as best you can, to the new outline. Sometimes this will mean going back over your notes again and making changes to symbols embedded in them.

Research may be fun, but nobody said it was easy. Come to think of it, though, isn't the challenge what makes it so much fun?

9.6 For further study

Study guide

1. Write out an explanation of the "register method" of note organization, including a good description of each of the parts.
2. If compiling your resources together is easy, what is hard? Why?
3. In using a device as your note taking tool, what options do you have for retrieval?
4. Why go to all this trouble to organize notes and establish retrieval procedures?

Practice/Assignment

Assess your past method(s) of note organization. Would the register method work for you? Are you brave enough to try our second, all electronic method? Can you think of another method that you'd prefer?

10

Tips on Research Writing

Research doesn't mean much if the presentation of your results is flawed. The kiss of death is to have a research paper returned with the comment: "Excellent bibliography, but your argument could have been developed more logically."

Two writing problems stand out as the most challenging: Getting your research question and outline straight, and writing persuasively. Let's deal with each in turn.

10.1 The final outline

Earlier, I argued that you need to have a preliminary outline pretty much from the beginning of the research process to act as a guide for the gathering of resources. In the early stages, organizing your outline is not crucial, but eventually you are going to have to structure it in a final form. Outlining is a major problem in any research presentation. If you are attempting (in real uneasiness, no doubt) a thesis or dissertation, the problem only compounds itself.

Let's visualize what we're dealing with first and then look at some possible solutions. The reason why the outline is so troublesome is that people receive information in sequence rather than absorbing all of the facts at the same time. Simply because a twenty page paper may take fifteen minutes to read means that some information must be presented before other information is given.

Let's look at it another way. Putting forward an argument (that is, the statement of a response to your research question) is like building a house. You have to lay the foundation before you can move to the upper stories. Everything you build rests upon whatever you've already laid down.

Perhaps the best way to learn outlining technique is to look at specific steps and see these illustrated with examples.

10.1.1 Step one: The research question/thesis statement

As we have seen, the first step toward putting together even a preliminary outline is figuring out what issue you want to deal with. This involves narrowing your topic and stating a **single** research question. For our purposes, let's choose the topic of "Burnout in the Workplace." Our narrower focus will be "preventing burnout," and our research question is, "How can today's office worker use warning signs to resist burnout in the workplace?" A corresponding thesis statement would be something like: "Today's office worker must be alert to the signs of burnout and take specific steps to counteract their influence."

10.1.2 Step two: Preliminary outline headings

Now you need to assess your question or thesis statement to determine what data you are going to need to answer it. For our example, presumably you'll need an introduction to burnout, explaining what it is and raising the issue that there must be means to resist it. You might, as well, assume that resisting this problem will involve recognizing the warning signs of coming burnout and taking some counter-measures to overcome those signs or to prevent them happening in the first place. Thus your preliminary outline (in no particular order) has three possible headings already: Knowing the Warning Signs of Approaching Burnout, Counter-measures, and An Introduction to the Problem of Burnout.

10.1.3 Step three: Organizing the headings

This is usually the hardest part. What you want is a logical order that is helpful to the reader. Above all, you want to avoid the impression that your paper lacks direction or that the direction it is taking is strange and hard to justify. The transitions in a good outline should not be all that noticeable because your goal is to take the reader from introduction to conclusion as comfortably as possible.

A few tips

> ➤ Get general and introductory matters out of the way first. Just as you needed a working knowledge of the topic when you started your research, you now need to give your reader a similar working knowledge, including background information and a clear statement of the question you're dealing with. In the case of our burnout example, you would probably have to define burnout, demonstrate what a problem it is, and then ask what things could be done to resist burnout in the workplace (your research question).
>
> ➤ Look for a natural order to your headings, if you can find it. In our burnout example, it seems more natural to discuss first the need to recognize the warning signs of

burnout and *then* to consider possible counter-measures to resist burnout (i.e., knowledge before action seems like a natural order).

➢ Here are some other possibilities:

- In a historically-oriented paper (e.g., "The Early Conquests of Alexander the Great"), you might simply want to move the paper along chronologically.
- In an analysis of issues related to a topic, you can follow an ascending or climactic order, looking at smaller factors or arguments first, then moving up to the more crucial factors. Your last section could begin,

   "The most serious difficulty with _____, however, is _____."

   Ascending or climactic order adds power to a paper by leading the reader into increasing levels of tension, much like an action movie builds to a climax. Resist giving away the most exciting parts of your paper early on—if you use up the good stuff too soon, you'll have little left to keep the reader interested in the rest of what you have to say.
- You need to include all relevant points of view on an issue, not just the one you support. When a research project ignores opposing arguments, the reader feels cheated, and the case you are making is weakened, not strengthened. An argument that pays no attention to other voices will not stand up to a challenge. Research, remember, is a conversation.

Comparing and contrasting

If you are comparing or contrasting two or more viewpoints, there are a couple of ways to go about it. Now's a good time to get your wits about you, so go have some coffee or take a walk, then read on

If the two views you are discussing are relatively simple to explain and analyze, try a *longitudinal method* by which you discuss all aspects of view A and then moved on to discuss all aspects of view B. Suppose, for example, you were dealing human cloning and covering both sides— **<Go Ahead>** and **<Wait a Minute: What Do You Think You're Doing?>**

Your outline might look like this:

I. Introduction to Human Cloning
II. The Go Ahead Position
      A. All Science is Legitimate.
      B. We Can Trust Scientists Not To Put Us At Risk.
      C. The Benefits of Having Clones Outweigh The Risks.
III. The Wait A Minute Position
      A. Is all Science Legitimate?
      B. Can We Trust Scientists Not To Put Us At Risk?
      C. Do The Benefits Outweigh The Risks?
IV. Conclusion

You can see that we are presenting one position in total, then the other, using our discussion of the second position as a base to deal with the arguments against the first. Thus the Go Ahead position will be described as objectively as possible. The analysis will come with The Wait a Minute Position.

But suppose that the arguments are getting complicated, and you're afraid your reader will have forgotten what the first position said about the legitimacy of science before you have time to discuss it in the second position. In a complex situation, you'll need a *cross-sectional approach*, which deals with both sides of each sub-topic in turn:

I. Introduction to Human Cloning
II. Is All Science Legitimate?
      A. Yes
      B. Maybe not
III. Can We Trust The Scientists?
      A. Yes

B. Not always
IV. Do the Benefits of Having Clones Outweigh the Risks?
    A. Yes
    B. Maybe not
V. Conclusion

If you want to see the two approaches side by side, here they are. Note how differently they are structured, despite the fact that they are dealing with the same subject matter:

Longitudinal Approach   Cross-Sectional approach

Longitudinal Approach	Cross-Sectional approach

I. Introduction to Human Cloning
II. The Go Ahead Position
  A. All Science is Legitimate
  B. We can Trust Scientists not to Put us at Risk
  C. The Benefits of Having Clones Outweigh the Risks.
III. The Wait a Minute Position
  A. Is all Science Legitimate?
  B. Can We Trust Scientists not to Put us at Risk?
  C. Do Benefits Outweigh the Risks?
IV. Conclusion
	I. Introduction to Human Cloning
	II. Is all Science Legitimate?
	  A. Yes
	  B. Maybe Not
	III. Can We Trust Scientists?
	  A. Yes
	  B. Not Always
	IV. Do the Benefits of Having Clones Outweigh the Risks?
	  A. Yes
	  B. Maybe Not
	V. Conclusion

Now you have the chance to deal with both sides of each issue in turn. By the time you get to your conclusion, your reader should have a cumulative understanding of the issues and of the reasons for your position.

A couple of other tips:

➢ Avoid stringing out a list of 7 or more main headings without subheadings, because this tends to obscure the unity and coherence of your paper (just like leading someone down a winding path creates more confusion than leading the same person down a straight city block with sights to see on all sides). How do you cover the ground without multiplying your outline headings? You do it by using fewer main headings and adding subheadings to them. Thus you *group* your points, arguments, etc. within 3 to 5 main categories and let subheadings pick up the detail. This makes a tighter structure that has more of a chance of achieving unity in the paper. See the outlines above for examples of useful ways to do this.

➤ Attempt objectivity at the beginning and do your analysis later. Here I need to get on a soapbox for a few moments:

Why does objectivity come before analysis? Because every view needs to be heard before you criticize it. Suppose you are doing a paper on the well-known (at least to me, since I created him) social scientist Horace Q. Blowhard, who has had the audacity to argue that the death penalty should be instituted for traffic offenses in order to restore public order. Your paper, entitled "Why Don't You Stand In Front of *My* Car, Horace?" intends to say terrible things. But how can you do this most effectively?

If you are still unclear about the fine points of research maturity, you may want to begin your paper with the words, "Horace Q. Blowhard truly lives up to his name. If there were ever a reason for tar and feathers, Horace (no friend of yours or mine) would be it." From here, your outline would be:

I. Condemnation of Blowhard
II. Some of the Vilest of his Views
III. Concluding condemnation.

But this is utterly the wrong approach. O ye contenders for justice and all it for which it stands, halt and listen: *No one deserves to be torched verbally or in print before he or she has been given a fair and objective hearing.* Not even Horace Q. Blowhard.

I know what you're thinking now—When did true objectivity ever exist? All of us are subjective, so why not just state our views without worrying about truth and fairness to other viewpoints? Why try to give anyone an objective hearing? My answer is that, while this is neither the time nor the place to get into the murky depths of Postmodernism, all of us know that it's possible to hear someone, understand that person, and treat that person's views fairly. Sure, our presuppositions will get in the way to some extent, but our goal still needs to be to understand the positions of others as best we can *before* we level either praise or crushing criticism. A good measure of objectivity is still possible for most of us.

Devastating attacks do not come before we have explained the position of our opponents. They come after, when both you and the reader have enough knowledge of the opposing position to determine whether you are launching the right missiles. Anything less than this is poor sportsmanship, bad form, bigotry, whatever you want to call it. Mature writing makes sure every view has been heard fairly before it is analyzed.

Clearing the Fog – What about creativity?

All this planning, let alone outlining, before you write the paper, may seem to be stifling those creative urges that make for great writing. My pre-planning process could resemble one of those old time paint-by-number kits where the "art work" was outlined in advance and a number system told you what color of paint to use in each of the lined sections. Boring. Uncreative. Even soul-destroying.

If you have to plan everything in advance, isn't the writing just going to be a dull process of filling in the blanks? What about people who actually learn by writing or who problem-solve best in the act of writing up the final project? Won't all of that creativity just be suppressed?

Surprisingly, no. And this for one strong reason – your research question/thesis/outline are works in progress until you turn in the final project. Only then is it too late to change them. You can come up with new ideas, revamp your outline, and even tweak your research question or thesis as you are writing up your project. No one will see earlier versions of your planning elements, so if you want to change them as you write, do so (but carefully, and with a lot of thought).

Why plan anyway? Simply because, when you aim at nothing, you are bound to hit it. You do not want your goal to be mush, because the chances of your creativity then turning the mush into substance are slim to none. Having a clear goal in mind gives you something to revise as need be, without having to re-invent everything from the beginning.

Please do plan and organize. It won't hurt your ability to be creative. Only a novelist writes with a murky outcome in mind (and I think it's the rare novelist who has no idea where the story will end up.)

10.2 Some tips on research writing

10.2.1 Introduce your paper well

Introductions serve two purposes:

> ➤ They give you a chance to provide your reader with a working knowledge of your topic.
> ➤ They let you state your (*single*) research question or thesis statement.

One thing to avoid here is the temptation to multiply your research questions along the lines of:

> "Why, then, did Skinner write *Walden Two?* Did he indeed believe that he could create Utopia with behavioristic methods? Was he blind to the problems in his approach? Did he later change his mind?"

What you've done is create a shotgun blast heard around the world, not one goal but many. You reader has no idea what your real intention is because you have so many of them. The paper itself will be as superficial and as scattered as your introduction. Keep your goal singular.

Sometimes a real life illustration is helpful to get the topic going. For example, if you are doing a paper on a historical figure, you might want to begin with an anecdote from that person's life that typifies what you want to say about him/her. Beyond that, stick with the purposes of an introduction - to provide a working knowledge and to state your research question.

10.2.2 Be focused at all times

There is something almost magical about creating a successful research paper. If you have a solid, narrowly-focused, analytical research question, you can pretty much see in your mind's eye the problem to be addressed. If you have a well-structured outline, you can also see the path through the paper to a conclusion before you even start writing it. Don't begin writing the paper until everything comes into focus and you have that "Aha" experience that tells you that you know pretty clearly what you plan to do. If it's all fuzzy, it will remain fuzzy through the writing process, and the product will be fuzzy too (a triple fuzzy can't be a good thing).

If you keep the narrow focus on what you are doing, magic will happen.

10.2.3 Always describe before you analyze.

You thought I had long since fallen off my soapbox. Don't worry. I won't bring it up again. But do it. Your writing will look more mature.

10.2.4 Avoid ridicule.

When you disagree with a certain author or viewpoint, you need to maintain a level of respect and decorum. Your opponent is not a "moron," "idiot," "stupid" or "useless." (Believe it or not, I've seen all of these terms in student papers). This kind of language reminds me of an elementary schoolyard with two kids arguing about an issue until one of them runs out of ideas and says, "Oh yeah? Well, I think you're stupid." Ridicule is the lowest form of argument. It reveals a lack of ability to address the issues in a mature, intelligent manner. Such language only reflects badly on you.

10.2.5 Be logical.

By this, I mean that, whenever you are traveling along a certain train of thought, make sure your reader is in the caboose behind you. Don't flit around. Don't jump to another track without warning. Always remember that you are writing for someone who doesn't know where you're going. Lead your reader along gently, step by step. Stay on track. For example, when you move on to a new area of discussion, use a transitional clause such as, "Turning to the issue of...," "Having considered Smith's approach, it is necessary to go on to that of Brown, who...." For guidance on creating transitions, see the helpful site, "How to use paragraph transitions" (**http://www.whitesmoke.com/how-to-use-paragraph-transitions**).

Keeping a clear sense of your research question and outline is a great help here. If you have a single focus for your paper and understand the steps you need to take from question to solution, it's easier to help your reader stay with you. To make sure you're really on track, ask yourself with each paragraph in your paper:

> ➢ Is this paragraph in the right place in my paper (i.e., does it match the heading it's under)?
> ➢ Does this paragraph contribute to the solution for my research question?

There are times when I come across a research paper with a "bulge" in it. What's a bulge? It's a chunk of information that has little relationship to the paper topic. How did it get there? The researcher worked for a long time on something that, as it turned out, didn't really relate to the final paper. But no one wants to admit to wasting time, so the researcher simply plugged the less-than-relevant material into the paper anyway. This turned what might have been a lean and mean research essay into an ugly project with an unsightly bulge in the middle of it. The poor reader is left to figure out what the bulge has to do with anything else.

10.2.6 Be explicit.

I don't know how many students there are out there (good, otherwise intelligent students) who believe in ESP. They assume that their professors can read their every thought even if it is never expressed. Thus we get a gem that looks something like this:

"In looking at the issues of Nicaea, we must focus of the Arian Debate. The facts are well known and thus we move to the specific role of the famous Athanasius in dealing with…"

What's a Nicaea? What's an Arian Debate? Who's Athanasius and, if he's so famous, why have I never heard of him? Be clear.

You might counter-argue, being a clever person, that if this were a paper, say, in pre-medieval European history, the professor indeed would know all this. If you're writing for your professor, why would you have to explain these terms? But consider the problem of the professor, who has two options when reading a sentence like the one above – either you know what you're talking about and you're sparing the prof a tedious explanation, or you don't understand the topic well enough to explain it. In the face of no clear explanation, your professor may well choose the second option and think you're trying to hide your lack of understanding with bafflegab. It is better to be clear about what you know, even if you know the professor already knows it.

There's a balance, of course. You have limited space to get your ideas down, so too much explanation can be counterproductive. Find a healthy mid-point where you show what you know without showing off what you know.

10.2.7 Aim for clear writing rather than erudition.

The mark of an educated person is not the length of words and sentences used but *the ability to communicate complicated information in plain language.* Be concise. Say what you mean. Avoid like the plague every long word where a shorter word would work as well. Try never to be ambiguous. Writers often struggle with just what sort of language to use in order to be clear to the reader. A resource to help you choose the right language to use is the Academic Phrasebank (**http://www.phrasebank.manchester.ac.uk/**).

10.2.8 Watch out for flawed arguments.

These include:

> ➤ *Misrepresenting authorities.* If you are appealing to someone's work as support for your argument, be very

sure that you represent that person accurately. Don't quote out of context, suppress information that would give a more honest picture, or do anything similar. This sort of misrepresentation is best left to the tabloid newspapers, which do it with better skill than the rest of us.

➤ *Arguments from origins.* Just because a viewpoint arose from a dubious source, it does not necessarily mean that the idea is wrong. If a nasty government that exploits the poor of its nation comes up with a wonderful invention to help end famine in the world, is the invention of no value simply because the government it came from is exploitative? Of course not. Those who know about such things are going to have to examine this invention and make their own assessment, regardless of its origin. Similarly, we can't always determine the value of an idea simply by considering the person who suggested it. While it might seem legitimate to doubt the advice on marital harmony put forward by someone who has been divorced seven times, you have to look at the person's material itself. The concepts may be sound even though the author does not exemplify them.

➤ *Arguments from insufficient evidence.* I am constantly amazed at the way some researchers skip over weighty problems without making their case. They use expressions like, "It is obvious that…" or "Such a view is unacceptable today…" or "In my opinion…" even though much more effort is needed to convince the reader to buy into what you are saying. My reaction when I see statements without sufficient evidence is to assume one of three things: the writer hasn't done enough research to discover that a controversy exists, the writer has no evidence to offer and is trying to bluff through the problem, or the writer is has inflated sense of self and believes that merely stating an opinion is all any reader needs in order to be convinced. Only if the writer is a seasoned scholar in the field should you consider accepting a controversial or unproven idea without evidence. Even then, that seasoned scholar could be biased.

How much evidence is sufficient? Enough to be convincing. When you write a research paper or report, you need to imagine a reader who is slightly hostile, who is *not* prepared to believe you. Thus you must present sufficient support for your argument that your hostile reader will at least say, "Well, you make a good case." You don't need absolute proof, just enough evidence to get your reader to take your view seriously.

If you don't have enough evidence to do this, then you will have to be a lot more humble about sharing your views. Admit that evidence is scarce and that, therefore, any position you are taking on the matter is tentative.

Sometimes, the evidence is not available at all. If that's the case, admit it. Write something like, "There continues to be much debate over this issue, and no consensus seems possible until more evidence is found." (Don't suicidally write: "I can't understand this issue, so I haven't made up my mind.")

10.2.9 Know when to quote and when not to quote

You should quote:

> ➢ When you want to back up your view with that of a prominent scholar who agrees with you.

> ➢ When something someone has written is catchy or memorable in its wording. For example, Bruno S. Frey, in his book, *Dealing with Terrorism: Stick or Carrot,* gives the following clear analysis of the difference between deterrence and brute force:

>> "Deterrence is not necessarily the same as using brute force. Deterrence involves the *threat* of damage to an adversary. It would be most successful if it were possible not to actually carry it out." (p. 28)

In a few short sentences, he explains a crucial distinction in such a way that little more needs to be said.

You should not, however, quote:

➢ When you can say it just as well in your own words.
➢ When the material you want to quote is over 5 or 6 lines long (unless it is absolutely crucial in its original wording and is necessary for the central theme of your paper).
➢ When you already have a quotation every page or two in your essay. You don't want to fill your paper with quotations. Your reader primarily wants your wisdom, not the words of everyone else.
➢ When the conventions of your discipline frown on quotation (sciences and often the social sciences). Check with your professor on this.

10.2.10 Know some basic principles for quotations.

If you are quoting, make it a habit to present your own material first, and then *back it up* with a quotation. Quotations should not normally be used to present new data. Here the issue is one of authority. Every time you present new data with a quotation, you are deferring to the authority of your source. That knocks the wind out of your own authority as an author. Let's put it this way: *Whose paper is it?* It's yours. Stand on your own two feet and make your own statements. Quotations are for backup and support.

Thus the pattern you should use is something like this: Present, in your own words, some data or a viewpoint, and then follow up with something like "As Joseph Schwartz has argued...", then quote from Schwartz in support of your data or viewpoint. Even if you are just presenting the views of someone (e.g., B.F. Skinner), present those views in your own words first, then if you need to, follow up with a quotation from Skinner that summarizes his position well.

Never, never, never, ever write a paper that strings together long quotations interspersed with only a few lines of commentary by you. Such papers are doomed, since your professor knows that her ten-year-old son could paste together the same quotations just as well. A research paper should state your case primarily *in your own words*, showing that you can present data clearly and use that data analytically to answer an important question. Use quotations sparingly, merely as support for what you are saying.

If you have a book or article that quotes another source, and you want to use that quotation, the rule is to find the original source that the quotation came from and quote that source directly. Until you go back to the original source, you can't know for sure whether the quotation was accurate or was quoted in its proper context. Only if you can't find the original source should you use the book or article in which you found the quotation. Even then, you need to indicate what you are doing, e.g.:

> [3] Raymond Sludge, *The Red Rose,* 47, as quoted in
> Horace Roebuck, "Roses are Forever," *Flower Journal*
> 42 (May 2000): 76.

But think twice before you use this option. Some professors will punish you for doing so (and, of course, professors are the ones with all the power).

10.2.11 Know the uses of footnotes/endnotes/citations.

These days, most students are using short forms of citations (e.g., Jones, 241) instead of the more traditional footnotes and endnotes. In this case, only the first of the purposes below is going to interest you. But don't forget that you can still add footnotes related to the other purposes below, even when you're using a short citation method.

The purposes of Footnotes/Endnotes/Citations include:

> ➤ Citing works you have quoted or borrowed ideas from. Most students are aware that direct quotations need to be noted/cited. But you need also to cite or note borrowed *ideas* if they are relatively unique. Here's a (perhaps simplistic but helpful) rule of thumb: If you use an idea that you can only find in one or two of your sources, it's better to cite the source(s). If the material is found in three or more sources and you can't see that these are borrowing

their idea from a single source in the past, don't bother with a note/citation. An exception might be a view held by three or four people, yet the view is controversial and you may want to indicate to the reader where you got it from.

➤ Stating further bibliography for the reader who may be interested in pursuing the matter. This procedure, which might look a bit tedious, shows the extent of your research and could earn you appreciation from the reader (and a higher grade if the reader is a professor). Even if you are using a short citation format in the body of your paper, you can still add further bibliography as a footnote or endnote.

➤ Citing sources that agree with your position. This is especially useful if you know you've gone out on a limb and you suspect your professor is ready to cut it off at the trunk. The support of five other scholars who agree with you may not prove your case, but at least it shows that you are not a flake. Begin this type of footnote/endnote with something like: "So too Steven Johnson, [etc.]" or "This position is also held by…"

➤ Defending a certain position against possible objections. Here you are not sure someone will object to what you are saying, but you see a potential flaw in your argument. It's better for you to point out the problem yourself and respond to it before your reader can raise it as an issue. A format for this could begin, "It might be objected that… but [then give your response to the possible objection]." This type of note shows your reader that you are not trying to present a whitewash with only your side represented. If, however, you find that the argument you are presenting is important for the whole thrust of your paper, include it in the actual text of your paper. Notes are for additional or less relevant material.

➤ Dealing with a related side issue that might spoil the flow of the essay itself if it were to appear in the text. This use is rare, but you may want to add to the depth of your paper in this way. Be careful, though, that you don't make the multiplying of notes a habit. I once spoke with a world famous scholar who admitted to me that he had a problem with his use of notes. I refrained from chuckling only because I'm a polite librarian. One of this scholar's most celebrated works was published as two equal length volumes. The first volume was the text of his book and the second was his endnotes. I'd say he had a serious problem (though his notes were often fascinating). Avoid having the same difficulty yourself.

Clearing the Fog – Becoming a better academic writer

Very commonly in my experience, students struggle with how to present their research in such a way that it looks intelligent and mature. How do you become a better academic writer? I could simply throw that old adage at you – "Practice, Practice, Practice" – but we all know that practice can simply mean repeating the same mistakes. There's no progress in that.

Let me suggest a couple of approaches to help you improve your work. First, pay attention to the comments of your professors on previously submitted research projects. Most of us hate reading the comments. Why open yourself up to esteem-destroying criticism? But good comments can do a great job of awakening you to mistakes you are making and ways you can correct them.

Second, read *published essays/articles* on the topics you are writing about. Yes, actually read them, and do so very analytically, asking as you go:

➢ How does the author introduce the paper?
➢ How much basic information does the author provide at the beginning?
➢ How is the paper structured? Can you follow the line of argument?
➢ What kind of transitional language is used to guide you through the paper?

> ➢ How and under what circumstances does the author use citations?
> ➢ How does the author use persuasion?
> ➢ How does the author deal with opposing viewpoints?
> ➢ What is the nature of the conclusion the author makes?

These are just a few of the questions you can ask. The more analytical reading of published academic work that you do, the better you will be able to model such mature writing in your own work.

10.2.12 Watch your conclusions.

A good conclusion briefly summarizes the main focus of your paper and makes your final position clear. Avoid flowery, sentimental, or overly long conclusions. Say what you need to say and end it mercifully. In general, half a page at the end of a fifteen page paper is more than enough.

10.2.13 Give your final paper a professional look.

Your final project should avoid typographical or spelling errors (use your spell-checker). Find out what style manual your institution is using, and follow it rigorously for title page, outline page, page format, bibliography, etc. With bibliographies, make sure you follow the format rules you've been given. If you haven't been given any, then choose a single style (APA, MLA, etc.) and follow it (See **Appendix A** for more on style).

You may be using a bibliographic manager like EndNote, RefWorks or Zotero that has a bibliography generating function. While this is a big help, remember that no bibliography generator is foolproof. You will have to troubleshoot everything in the resulting bibliography. The best way to do this is to have a crib sheet for your style (a list of the most common examples of form – books, articles, web pages, etc.) and compare it with the bibliography that you've generated, fixing things as needed. For URLs to crib sheets on the Net see the Appendix, section A1.6.2 below

Word to the wise - Professors tend to assume that a sloppy product is evidence of a sloppy mind, so get your style in order.

Here's the final pep talk: Research can be exciting, even fun, so enjoy.

FUN??? Yes, as long as you see the path of discovery as an adventure. Research can be done well by virtually anyone, no matter what your initial ability may have been. I trust that I have introduced you to sufficient strategies that you can develop your skills and do first class work. The rest is up to you.

10.3 For further study

Study guide

1. What are the three steps to take in first establishing an outline?
2. In a research paper or report, what should you cover first?
3. Explain the longitudinal and cross-sectional approaches to outlining discussion of more than one view on an issue. Try each method with the following outline elements:

Topic: Physician Assisted Suicide
The points of view: Seeing it as a beneficial aid to sufferers vs. seeing it as wrong morally.
The subsections under each view: The problem of unbearable suffering, the wishes of the patient, the risk that we are playing God.

4. What are the two purposes of introductions?
5. Why describe before you analyze?
6. What are some things to remember if you want your paper/ report to flow logically so that your reader can follow it?
7. What's a "bulge" in a research paper or report?
8. What is the mark of an educated person?
9. Explain types of flawed argumentation.
10. When should you not use quotations? Do you agree with the author's position that your quotations should be few? Why or why not?

11. Why would you use "notes" or "citations" in your research paper/report?
12. What should you avoid in a conclusion?

Practice/Assignment

Take a research project you have recently done and run it by the suggestions in this chapter. What would you change in the way it's been written?

APPENDIX ONE – A Research Paper Clinic: More Tips and Troubleshooting for Development of Great Research Papers

[The following chapter was created for a seminar on research paper writing. It supplements the book *Research Strategies*, but in some cases overlaps with it. If you experience a measure of déjà vu while reading the Appendix, be thankful for the enhanced examples of research question development, as well as essay preparation hints more detailed than those discussed in the body of this book. Or use it on its own as a mini-workshop.]

A1.1 Research questions

A1.1.1 Why many research projects miss the target

You have likely been trained to see a research project as a way to force you to read a lot of material from many sources, then report on what you have read, covering whatever subject you have been given with as much depth as space will allow.

Thus, a paper on the causes of World War I would begin with a brief history of the events leading to this war, then would list several causes, and would perhaps conclude with a statement that war is bad and we should watch for warning signs so we can prevent war in the future. What would you say your research paper is about? "It's about the causes of World War I," you reply, looking at me strangely. You've read all about those causes in various books and magazines. You've put that material together (that is, you've synthesized it), and you've written a paper explaining the causes.

But your paper missed the target entirely. This is because a research project is not supposed to be *about* anything. Please understand this: If you were writing a genuine research paper, and I asked you, "What is your paper about?" you should be able to answer, "It's about nothing." That response, of course, would result in some questions: *"What do you mean, 'It's about nothing?' Does this mean there's no a topic? Are we in an episode of Seinfeld?"*

Certainly, you have a topic. The problem is that my question, "What is your paper about?" is wrongheaded. It assumes that a research paper is intended to explain a certain topic, using resources that you have studied. That's a false assumption. Studying up on a topic and compiling data about it is not research at all.

What, then, is the point of a research paper?

A research paper seeks to use data from various resources to answer a question or to solve a problem.

Data in this case is not an end in itself but a *means*, a *tool*. Research does not result merely in an explanation of a topic. It is a problem-solving exercise that takes data from various sources and analyzes it to help you answer a burning question.

A1.1.2 Getting focused by asking the right question

If you are merely reporting on what you have read, then you don't have to worry about the purpose of your paper. Your purpose is to explain to your reader everything you know about your topic.

But if you are in search of the answer to a question, you're not really interested in knowing everything about a topic, only what is relevant. Sure, you will provide some broader background information to make sure the reader understands the issues involved. But the data you find and use will be selective, because what you really need to know is *only that portion of the data that can help you answer the question.*

EXAMPLE:

Instead of describing the causes of World War I, find a controversy that can become a research question. For example, it is often argued that the murder of Archduke Ferdinand was the chief cause of World War I. Your research very early tells you that this is an overly simple explanation. True, this particular assassination did lead to a series of events that began the War, but lots of important people are murdered every year without the events turning into a worldwide conflagration. Thus you become interested in answering a question like this one: *Why did the murder of Archduke Ferdinand become the flashpoint that led to WWI?*

There are several assumptions here to test out:

➢ This was no ordinary murder.
➢ The murder must have meant something more to the various sides than is apparent.
➢ There must have been a background to this particular murder so that the sides that created a war out of it knew immediately what the murder meant.

When I teach research skills to students, I think I use one word more often than any other – "Focus." Most people approaching the research task are facing a crisis of lack of proper focus. This is what causes the anxiety, the belief that research is tedious, the shabby research papers and the punishment from the profs who have to read them. Focus, focus, focus. The more your project forms a clear, narrow and single-minded image in your head, the better off you are.

This is where the research question comes in (or thesis statement if you want to go that route). It identifies the research problem and gives you the direction your research needs to take to solve it. The research question, along with a preliminary outline, provides you with a roadmap to success for any project. But a badly constructed question will mess you up every time.

Back in Chapter Two we looked at bad and ugly questions. Let's pick up examples of those, see what they look like, and learn how to fix them.

A1.1.3 The question that isn't there

Questions that aren't there are not necessarily projects without questions. It's just that the questions don't lead to real research. These are the projects that simply compile information on a topic, then report on it. As such, gathering information is an end in itself, so there is no problem to solve.

Rubric:

Definition of good – The project not only has a question, but that question leads to a problem-solving exercise in which information is a tool, not an end in itself.

Definition of bad – The project has a fairly narrow topic but the question is merely informational in its goal. It simply asks you to look things up and report an answer.

Definition of ugly – The project not only merely gathers information, but is itself a survey of a broad subject area without any question to answer.

Examples of bad and their fixes:

"What were the events of August 1914 that led to the start of the First World War?"

Fix it by asking: *"Was the assassination of Archduke Ferdinand really as significant a cause of WWI as many scholars assume?"*

"What foods are good sources of low fat protein?"
Fix it by asking: *"Is tofu a viable option for the primary source of low fat protein in our diets, considering the problem we have with making it palatable?"* (or, *"...considering the problem we have with tofu allergies in the population?"*)

"Who are the Taliban?"
Fix it by asking: *"Is the military suppression approach to dealing with the Taliban of Afghanistan and Pakistan the best way to address the problem?"*

Examples of ugly and their fixes:

A survey of terrorism today.
Fix it first by narrowing to at least one arena of terrorism, then ask: *"Have the use of drone attacks proven ultimately helpful or harmful to the suppression of terrorism?"*

A description of Samsung's latest innovations.
Fix it first by narrowing to one area of operation, then ask: *"Why did Samsung succeed so well in its battle for market share with Apple in the mobile device arena?"*

A1.1.4 The fuzzy question

The fuzzy question is either unclear or ambiguous. It carries no certainty that there is a single, well-defined goal. When you ask it, your reader says, "Huh?"

Rubric:

Definition of good – The question is focused clearly. Not only does your reader have a solid understanding of your goal, but so do you.

Definition of bad – The project has a fairly narrow topic but the question does not provide a clear mental image of your goal.

Definition of ugly – Neither the topic nor its goal are defined clearly enough to be understood.

Examples of bad and their fixes:

"Was it good that the once secret documents from the history of the CIA were made public?"
Fix it by pondering: Good for whom? What do you mean by "good?" Who determines what is "good" and what is not "good?" Then ask, *"Was it beneficial for public confidence in the current CIA that the secret documents from its early days were released?"*

"What should we make of all the recent speculation about the nature and life of the historical Jesus?"
Fix it by determining what you mean be "what should we make of," then ask, *"To what extent can we say that the speculation about Jesus in the book/movie* The Da Vinci Code *actually has merit?"*

"How can we make sense of the harm reduction policies put forward by some experts who deal with users of illegal drugs?"
Fix it by deciding what sort of sense you want to make, then ask: *"If the harm reduction procedures for illegal drug users in Europe and Canada have been shown to reduce drug use, why are they not being implemented everywhere?"*

Examples of ugly and their fixes:

"Is Globalization a good thing?"
Fix it first by defining your topic. "Globalization" can be economic, political, religious, etc. Also decide what you mean by "good thing" and who determines what is and is not "good." Then ask, *"What evidence is there that the development of global free trade actually improves the economic life of the poorest producers of goods?"*

"Why are people so paranoid these days?"

Fix it by setting a definition for "paranoid." Are you speaking of a psychological condition or a mood of distrust? Next determine which people you are describing and make clear the nature of their paranoia. (Right now you have a generalization that can't be supported in that only a small portion of the population is likely to be "paranoid" by whatever definition you give to the word.) Then ask, *"If serious crime rates are going down, why do so many people continue to believe that there is more crime in their neighborhoods than there once was?"*

"What's the best solution to the problem of street people?"
Fix it first by defining what you mean by "street people" Do you mean homeless people? People who drink too much and hang around in public places? Street sex workers? Second, determine what the problem is and who is supposed to do something about it. Third, ask, *"To what extent are volunteer organizations which deal with people without permanent homes in _____ (an inner city) making more progress toward housing these people than are government sponsored programs?"*

A1.1.5 The multi-part question

One research question per project is the rule. You don't want multiple goals, which divide your paper up into mini-projects and destroy unity.

Rubric:

Definition of good – The question is absolutely singular – one goal expressed as one simple question.

Definition of bad – There are two or more related questions on the same topic so that it is unclear which question is the primary goal.

Definition of ugly – There are two or more questions really dealing with different aspects of the topic, so that no attempt to unify them into one question is going to succeed.

Examples of bad and their fixes:

"I want to look at the causes of WWI and discuss why war is a great evil and show how WWI could have been avoided."

Fix it by determining what your main goal is and eliminating any other goals or making them subordinate to the main goal: *In examining the causes of WWI, how could this war have been avoided?*

"What are the difficulties facing homeless children and how can we help further their education?"
Fix it by asking: *"Given the challenges facing urban homeless children, what is the best way to ensure that they get a good education?"*

"What are we doing about the use of illegal guns and how can we prevent so many young people dying in our cities?"
Fix it by asking: *What is the best way to decrease the number of shooting deaths among urban youth?*

Examples of ugly and their fixes:

"Will we find a cure for AIDS and how do we change public perception about it and how are we going to get the drug companies to supply cheap AIDS treatments to developing countries?"
Fix it by choosing one, dropping the others, then asking: *"How can governments and aid agencies convince the drug companies to supply cheap AIDS treatments to developing countries?"*

"Did Shakespeare actually write the plays attributed to him, and what are the basic features of his tragedies, and in what way could Twelfth Night be viewed as a tragedy rather than a comedy?"
Fix it by choosing one, dropping the others, then asking: *"How valid is it to view Twelfth Night as a tragedy rather than a comedy?"*

"What causes Fetal Alcohol Spectrum Disorder and how can we help women not to drink during pregnancy and how could the legal system do a better job of keeping Fetal Alcohol youth and adults out of jail?"
Fix it by choosing one, dropping the others, then asking: *"How could the legal system do a better job of keeping Fetal Alcohol youth and adults out of jail?"*

A1.1.6 The open-ended question

Open ended questions are like fishing expeditions. They are capable of having many possible answers. Often they begin with, "What were the results of…" or "What are the implications of…"

Rubric:

Definition of good – The question sets its boundaries clearly so that there is no risk that the answers will go off in several different directions at once.
Definition of bad – The question is fairly narrow, but it is capable of being answered in a variety of ways.
Definition of ugly – The question is quite broad and is capable of being answered in a variety of ways.

Examples of bad and their fixes:

"What were the implications for French industry of the end of WWII?"
Fix it by determining what sorts of implications there were and narrowing a bit further. Then ask: *"What was the primary reason why French automobile manufacturing rebounded after WWII?"*

"What are the implications of the Crusades for modern Arabs?"
Fix it by defining "implications" more narrowly and clearly, then ask, *"What is the best way for the West to overcome the perception of some Muslims, brought on by reference to the Crusades, that the West wants to destroy Islam?"*

"If we were to legalize all currently illegal drugs, what would that mean for our country?"
Fix it by defining "mean," then ask, *"How valid is the argument that legalizing all currently illegal drugs would cut crime and stabilize or diminish drug use?"*

Examples of ugly and their fixes:

"What trends should we be looking for in the world of technology over the next decade?"

Fix it by asking narrowing dramatically, then asking: *"With many initial MOOCs (Massive Open Online Courses) being seen as failures, what is the best future for the MOOC?"*

"What were the results of the housing crisis of 2008 and following?" Fix by narrowing dramatically, then asking: *"Have US mortgage regulations changed sufficiently to avoid another major crisis such as the one the housing market experienced in 2008 and following?"*

What does the rise of the Internet mean for information today? Fix by narrowing dramatically, then asking: *"How did the user created reference resource, Wikipedia, succeed in providing mainly reliable information despite its lack of traditional editors?"*

A1.1.7 The question that will not fly

This type of question is formulated by a creative person who wants to venture into the unknowable. Often such questions have been asked before (with no answer found), or they seek solutions that can't be tested or measured, or they look into a mysterious future. The cure for this kind of question is to resist ever writing a research project using one of them.

When will the next major earthquake hit San Francisco?

How many angels can dance on the head of a pin?

Are UFOs real?

There is no cure for questions that simply cannot be answered given our current state of knowledge. Questions that have no clear answers are doomed. Abandon them or foolishly devote your life to searching for solutions to things that can't be solved. If you choose the latter, you'll end up as a delightful eccentric, but your efforts won't even raise a blip on the importance scale.

A1.1.8 Thesis statements

Some professors prefer you to use thesis statements. Put quite simply, a thesis statement is a proposed answer to a research question. It's not a conclusion as such (which demands that you've gone through all the evidence) but a proposal, like a hypothesis in a scientific experiment, that needs to be demonstrated.

For example, you might ask: *"Are government sponsored programs or nonprofit charitable programs better able to address the needs of homeless people in city cores?"* The corresponding thesis statement might be: *"Non-profit charitable programs are better able than government sponsored programs to address the needs of homeless people in city cores."* This is not a dogmatic statement but a position you want to try to defend with evidence.

If you're not yet comfortable with doing research papers, the research question approach is best, because with a thesis statement there is always a tendency for you to be biased in favor of the evidence that supports your thesis, thus ignoring or misusing the evidence that doesn't.

If you do take the thesis method, e.g., "The following paper will argue that..." you need to be very careful to look at the counter-arguments as well. You might in the end discover that you're wrong.

A1.2 Practice with research questions

A.2.1 The questions:

Determine whether or not each of the following the research questions is a good one. Then check the key below to see what I thought of the question:

1. *Did Martin Luther, the German reformer, write anything criticizing the Jews?*
2. *What effect does homelessness have on the price of beds in Canada?*
3. *What's happening with Bill Gates now that he's donated so much money to educational technology?*

4. *Is there evidence that changes in emphasis in the _____ child welfare program in the past 5 years are the result of pressure from the press?*
5. *What happened in Iraq in 2003?*
6. *How could the looting of the museums in Iraq in 2003 have been avoided?*
7. *What are the main features of Fetal Alcohol Spectrum Disorder and what can be done both to treat and prevent this condition? Should all alcohol containers carry a warning?*
8. *What are the ethical implications of human cloning?*

A.1.2.2 Suggested key for the questions:

1. *Did Martin Luther, the German reformer, write anything criticizing the Jews?*
Bad question: Anyone with the works of Luther available can find the answer in less than half an hour (the answer is "yes," though you may want to ask, instead, why he took the stance he did toward the Jews). A research question is more than discovery of a fact. It has to deal with an issue that can be analyzed in depth.

2. *What effect does homelessness have on the price of beds in Canada?*
Bad question: This question is the never-will-fly variety. Even if there is some connection between homelessness and the price of beds, there is no conceivable way for you to find out the nature and extent of the connection. Sometimes two ideas simply have no obvious relationship or the relationship is such that no amount of searching will help you find out what it is. A similar sort of question might be one like this: *What has been the influence of the rise of the automobile on morality in the United States?* There may be an influence, but I can think of no survey or statistical tool that would give you an answer. The key to avoiding these kinds of questions is to ask yourself: Is there a reasonable hope that I can gather evidence that will lead to an answer? If there seems to be no hope, drop the question.

3. *What's happening with Bill Gates now that he's donated so much money to educational technology?*

Bad question: The point is fuzzy, not focused at all. What are you trying to discover? What Bill Gates does with his day? Whether he's enjoying his remaining money? Whether his financial give-away plan is the best use of his money? As long as your question doesn't indicate a point or a direction, you have no idea how to develop your paper. Besides, all aspects of Bill Gates' life are tracked so publicly that even a fuzzy question like the one above would likely be easily answered without much thought (though it could be answered in several possible ways). Here's a good focused research question to replace it: *Is Bill Gates' extensive plan to fund technology in education leading to an undue influence over educational methods in K-12?*

4. *Is there evidence that changes in emphasis in the _____ child welfare program in the past 5 years are the result of pressure from the press?*

Good question: Why? It demands research and analysis and there is evidence available to support that research. You would need to discover when various complaints about the child welfare were prominent in the press, and then see whether or not changes in procedure consistently followed such periods of complaint.

5. *What happened in Iraq in 2003?*

Bad question: This question likely wants the writer to recount the story of the Iraq War (which would only be a descriptive paper), but it's not clear from the question what the author is seeking. Many things happened in Iraq in 2003.

6. *How could the looting of the museums in Iraq in 2003 have been avoided?*

Good question: In hindsight, it should be possible to look at what happened and show what protection measures could have been in place to prevent the looting. Considerable writing has been done on the issue, so there should be lots of information.

7. *What are the main features of Fetal Alcohol Spectrum Disorder and what can be done both to treat and prevent this condition? Should all alcohol containers carry a warning?*

Bad question: This is your classic multi-pointer. With this many questions to answer, you will find that your project is cut up into a number of smaller projects and has no overall unity. Follow this rule—every research project must deal with only one issue expressed by one question. So choose one of the questions above and dump the rest.

8. *What are the ethical implications of human cloning?*

Somewhat good question: There's a lot to research and analyze but you may well find that the question is too open-ended, so that you run into far too many ethical implications to deal with. To solve this, limit your scope. For example, ask something like this: *With the high risk of early death of clones, is human cloning ethical?*

A1.3 Types of research papers

Here are some common research paper types:

A1.3.1 Descriptive paper

This type of essay aims at merely discovering and sharing information about something. It is not a true research paper but just a report on what you've read. Avoid this approach unless your professor explicitly asks for summary of reading or an overview without evaluation.

A1.3.2 Analytical or investigative paper

This type of essay seeks to find out the truth about something. It often focuses on questions like Who? What? When? Where? Why? or How? For example:

> ➢ *Why is the United Nations Organization so slow in responding to situations of genocide in the world?*
> ➢ *When did the Reformation actually begin?*
> ➢ *What is the truth behind the legend of Robin Hood?*

> ➢ *How were the pyramids of Egypt constructed in a time when machinery was so simple?*
> ➢ *What would be a better method to respond quickly to large international disasters before hunger, thirst and disease overtake the survivors?*

If you are writing this type of paper, you need to be sure that what you are investigating does not have an obvious answer but requires a lot of digging, study and analysis.

A1.3.3 Persuasive paper

This type of essay takes a position on a particular issue, seeking to persuade the reader of the truth of something and is generally expressed through a thesis statement rather than a research question. There are two major types:

> ➢ Cause and effect - This type has the goal of persuading you that something or someone was the cause of some event or situation. For example, consider these possible thesis statements:
>
> *Support for assisted suicide creates a slippery slope in which society loses its respect for life so that other euthanasia policies are allowed to flourish.*
>
> *The reason why terrorism flourishes is that we have not paid sufficient attention to the problems of injustice in the world.*
>
> Note that cause and effect is notoriously difficult to demonstrate, because two events are often related only by coincidence or because an effect may have several causes rather than just one. To show cause and effect, you have to demonstrate that the effect was caused by one factor out of all other possible factors. That's not easy to do.

➢ Evaluation - This type of paper seeks to persuade you that one view on a certain topic is better than another. For example:

The problem of homelessness is best solved by local non-governmental initiatives rather than federal programs.

Early intervention programs are a better way to deal with juvenile crime than punishment after the fact.

With persuasive papers, always be sure to include all relevant viewpoints in your discussion. Persuasion brings with it a temptation to ignore opposing arguments. Don't do it.

A1.3.4 Literature review

A literature review is usually just the first portion of a paper that plans to report a study or experiment done in a social scientific or scientific setting. Occasionally the literature review will stand on its own as a full article. A lot of students are confused about the nature of such reviews. The goal of a literature review is essentially to explain what has been done within a certain subject area, including the types of studies published, the key players in this field, and a sense of what still needs to be done. I like to think of literature reviews as narratives, starting with earlier research and coming down to the most recent.

But they must never be simply an account of studies (books, articles) with a bit of commentary. Instead, they need to revolve around themes or emphases. You might indicate what people were thinking about the subject at the beginning, then how the emphasis changed. You might spell out various schools of thought that developed around the topic and explain significant examples of the writings or experiments of the major scholars supporting those schools of thought.

Overall you want to group the various movements and stages in the topic's history so the reader will have a strong sense of the best work that has been done on the topic or issue. Then, near the end of the review, you need to point to something that still needs to be done. This could be a gap that remains in our knowledge or some flaw in the research to date that needs to be corrected. That gap or flaw then becomes a launch pad for further research.

Is a literature review the same as a research paper? To the extent that it has a clear goal and clear question (to determine what is lacking in this subject area that must still be investigated) it can either stand alone as a research paper or form the introduction to one.

A1.4 The outline as a research paper guidance system

Most struggling research papers have one of two problems—lack of a good, well-focused research question or lack of a proper structure that can take you from question to conclusion clearly and faithfully. In a research paper, the lack of structure is solved with the outline.

A1.4.1 Why worry about an outline early in the research process?

Many paper writers leave the outline to the end of the process. Some people even write the paper, and then discern an outline so that it can be included on a contents page. The real point at which outline construction needs to begin is *once you have a research question.*

> ➤ The points of your outline tell you what you need to cover, and thus the outline serves as a blueprint for your research. It also keeps you from missing anything.
> ➤ The outline gives body to your research question, showing the direction you have to take to reach your target. As you are doing your research, the outline will help you begin visualizing the completed product, thus giving your paper more depth and substance.
> ➤ It takes time for a paper to germinate in your thinking. The outline provides a structure to allow that germination to develop properly.
> ➤ The very structure of a research paper is crucial to making the paper work. If you get things out of order, or if the order is not clear, it won't matter how much good

information is there. The reader will see the paper as a failure. Thus, if you start thinking about structure and order early in the process, you are more likely to have the order right when you're done.

A1.4.2 Steps to a good outline

Use your research question to identify key terminology

Your research question expresses the goal of your essay. Embodied in it is the basic embryo of your outline. Suppose your research question was as follows:

Was the assassination of the Archduke Ferdinand as crucial a cause of WWI as is often asserted?

First, identify the key works in your question:

Assassination of Archduke Ferdinand
Cause of WWI
Crucial cause

Think through your goal
Now have a good look at your question and ask yourself, "What am I trying to accomplish?" In a few sentences, analyze your purpose, fleshing out your research question.

You could expand on it like this: Commonly the assassination of the Archduke is seen as the flashpoint that led to WWI. Yet one has to wonder how a single murder could have led to worldwide conflict. This murder must have meant something more than other murders did. If so, maybe the background or context to the assassination had more to say about the cause of WWI than did this single event.

Determine the scope of your paper

With your analysis of your research question before you, ask yourself: *What do I need to include in order to answer my question?* From your question, keywords and goal analysis above, you will need to:

> ➢ Present the common view that the assassination was a *crucial cause* of WWI
> ➢ Explain the historical and political context of the *assassination of Archduke Ferdinand.*
> ➢ Consider all the evidence with regard to the role of Ferdinand's murder in the events leading to WWI and determine whether or not it was *as crucial a cause of WWI as is often asserted*

You now have the elements of an outline. It may not be in the right order, and you may have to revise it, even add or subtract elements, but the basics are there. It might look like this:

> Introduction – The Common Interpretation of the
>   Assassination as a Crucial Cause of WWI
> The Historical and Political Context of the
>   Assassination of Ferdinand
> Determine if it Was as Crucial a Cause as is Often
>   Asserted
> Conclusion

Begin thinking about order

You don't need to make any final decisions about the order of your outline headings yet, but here are some tips:

> ➢ You will need an introduction that serves two purposes: to provide your reader with enough background information to be able to deal with your topic, and to declare your research question. Alternatively, you may want to formulate a thesis statement, which is a proposed answer to your question, along the lines of, "The following paper will argue that…"
> ➢ If there is any further development of background material that's more complex, it will have to go next as a separate section.
> ➢ Often you will find that you are dealing with more than one point of view. Once you determine which point of

view you are going to support, cover the view you do not support first, then cover the view you do support. Never reverse this order.

> Think about your reader. What needs to be covered before something else makes sense?

> Avoid stringing out your outline into 6, 7 or more points. A structure of 3 to 5 points works far better for the reader, unless you are working on a thesis or a book, where 6 to 10 main sections may be needed. Group things together so that you use fewer main points, even if it means that each main point has two or more sub-points.

Germinate

Memorize the outline you've created, even if it's still quite basic, and develop the habit of *germination*. What's "germination?" This is a hard thing to describe, but it's something like letting a seed of your research project grow inside of you. Take time through your day to think about your outline: *Would this order work better than that order? Have you left anything out? Have you included anything that really isn't relevant to your research question?*

Then, as you gather your books, articles, and so on, and start to read them, begin to write your paper in your head, thinking constantly about your reader: *At what points might your reader become confused? What would you change to make those points clearer? Are you being fair and complete by including all sides of an issue? Is your research question itself in need of some revision, and, if so, how will that change your outline?*

By the time you write your paper, your outline should be working well for you, and your paper should be already pretty much written in your head.

Why do you need germination? Because depth and maturity in a research paper comes through working on it over time. Without this process, you simply have another one of those projects that is dashed off superficially and lacks substance. Truly great writing needs germination. Your paper has to live and grow in you, or it will never have the power it should have for a reader. The best way to encourage it to grow is to build it around your ever-maturing outline.

Structure your final outline

Ultimately, just when you are beginning to enjoy framing your arguments in your head, your germination process needs to come to an end. This happens somewhere either just before the writing process begins, or during the writing. But one thing must be virtually complete before you start writing: your final outline, which forms the roadmap for the final composition of your research paper, telling you at each point what you need to cover to develop your paper from introduction to conclusion. A paper written without an outline firmly before you or in your mind is a paper destined to confuse your reader and resist your hopes to communicate what you have discovered.

I cannot stress this strongly enough—your outline is the crucial element in hitting the target your well-formulated question is aiming at.

So how do you go about structuring your final outline? If you have any uncertainty about your skills, follow a simple formula: Introduction, 3 or 4 points, Conclusion.

KEEP IT SIMPLE. If you find there is need for some complex discussion in point 2, then use sub points, like this:

I. Introduction – The Common Interpretation of the Assassination of Ferdinand as a Cause of WWI
II. The Historical and Political Context
    A. Prior to August 1914
    B. August 1914 and Beyond
III. Evaluation of the Significance of the Assassination
IV. Conclusion

A1.4.3 Practice with outlines

For the following questions, create a 3 or 4 point outline, then compare your outline with mine in the suggested key (remember that outlines may vary):

1. *To what can we attribute the fact that Martin Luther's attitude toward Jews grew more and more negative through his lifetime?*
2. *What is the best approach to reducing homelessness in an urban setting?*

3. *Is the growing influence of Google in the digitization of books really as bad for the world as many critics say it is?*
4. *Is there evidence that changes in emphasis in the _____ child welfare program in the past 5 years are the result of pressure from the press?*
5. *How could the looting of the museums in Iraq in 2003 have been avoided?*
6. *What is the best way to deal with non-violent teens in trouble with the law but afflicted with Fetal Alcohol Spectrum Disorder (FASD)?*
7. *What are the implications of human cloning for our definition of a "person?"*
8. *Was the religious "conversion" of Roman Emperor Constantine genuine or a fraud carried out for political reasons?*

A1.4.4 Suggested key for practice with outlines

1. *To what can we attribute the fact that Martin Luther's attitude toward Jews grew more and more negative through his lifetime?*

Possible outline:
Introduction [Explain who Luther was, and ask the research question]
I. Evidence of Luther's Growing Anti-Semitism
II. Possible Explanations
     A.
     B.
     C., etc.
Conclusion

2. *What is the best approach to reducing homelessness in an urban setting?*

Possible outline:
Introduction [Explain the problem of urban homelessness and ask the research question]
I. Current Approaches to Reducing Urban Homelessness.
     A.
     B.

    C., etc.
II. Critique of Such Approaches
    A.
    B.
    C.
III. A Proposed Best Approach
Conclusion

3. *Is the growing influence of Google in the digitization of books really as bad for the world as many critics say it is?*

Possible outline:
Introduction [Introduce the growing influence issue and ask research question]
I. Arguments that the Influence is Bad for the World
II. Arguments that the Influence is Good for the World
Conclusion

4. *Is there evidence that changes in emphasis in the _____ child welfare program in the past 5 years are the result of pressure from the press?*

Possible outline:
Introduction [Introduce the issue and ask the research question]
I. The Nature of Changes in the Program over the Past 5 Years.
II. Instances of Coordination between Press Pressure and Changes
        A. Incident One
        B. Incident Two
        C. Incident Three, etc.
III. Possible Alternate Explanations for Timing of Changes
Conclusion

5. *How could the looting of the museums in Iraq in 2003 have been avoided?*

Possible outline:
Introduction [Explain the problem and ask the research question]
I. An Account of the Looting and the Failure to Prevent it

II. Possible Alternate Security Measures that Could Have Been Introduced

    A.

    B.

    C. etc.

Conclusion [Take possible alternate measures and state an overall plan that might have worked]

6. *What is the best way to deal with non-violent teens in trouble with the law but afflicted with Fetal Alcohol Spectrum Disorder (FASD)?*

Possible outline:

Introduction [Explain problem of non-violent FASD offenders and ask research question]

I. Common Current Approaches to the Problem

II. A Critique of Such Approaches

III. A Suggested Better Approach

Conclusion

7. *What are the implications of human cloning for our definition of a "person?"*

Possible outline:

Note that this is still quite an open-ended question allowing for many possibilities. Thus a variety of outlines are possible. Here's one.

Introduction [State the problem and ask the research question]

I. Traditional Definitions of a Person

II. Elements of Cloning that Redefine "Person."

III. A New Definition of Personhood.

Conclusion

8. *Was the religious "conversion" of Roman Emperor Constantine genuine or a fraud carried out for political reasons?*

Possible outline:

Introduction [Introduce Constantine and his conversion; ask research question]

I. Evidence that the conversion was genuine.
II. Evidence that the conversion was a fraud with political motives
Conclusion

A1.5 Building the substance of the essay

In this section we will deal with the substance of this thing called a research essay. We will consider how it is put together and study the crucial elements that make a mature, thoughtful paper.

A1.5.1 Intent and direction

The best research papers are characterized by strong goal-orientation. This means that they have a purpose, defined by the research question, and a sense of movement from problem to solution.

A research essay is like the flight of an arrow from bow to target. When you aim the arrow, you see a target - a specific destination. You know that to hit the target you will have a launch, a period of travel through the air, and a conclusion when the arrow hits its mark.

But an arrow in flight is also subject to things like wind speed and wind direction. Similarly, a research essay cannot ignore the influencing factors: context of the issue and the various options that could be answers to the question. There needs to be opportunity for recognition and analysis of other points of view, even opposing ones, as long as you make sure you stay on target with your main intention—to answer the research question.

Here's an insight: *Every part of your paper needs to contribute ultimately to answering your research question. There is no room for irrelevant details, even if they are interesting.*

Keep your paper goal-orientated. Don't allow it to wander or lose its sense of purpose.

A1.5.2 Building the paper

There are simple procedures that make the difference between a well-constructed paper and a mess. Here are some of them:

Use your outline like a blueprint.

Careful structure will contribute more to the success of your paper than anything else. *Follow the plan.*

You may be the sort of person who resists structure and organization in your writing, believing that structure limits your freedom of expression. But remember this: Structure is not just for your benefit, but the benefit of your reader. The reader has a distinct disadvantage. He or she does not know where you are going in your paper. Without structure, much of what you have to say will remain foggy to the reader. With structure, your reader is never lost.

Beyond wanting to help your reader, you want to avoid leaving out anything that is important or including anything that is not important.

Carefully adhering to your outline as you write ensures that everything that needs to be in your paper is there. Write or print out your outline and keep it (along with your research question) ever before you as you produce your paper.

Build your paper from the paragraph up.

While sentences are the basic building blocks of communication, paragraphs are the basic building blocks of an essay. Each paragraph advances your argument, like steps in a staircase. Think of your paragraphs as the smallest sub points of each point in your outline. Each has a topic and a unity that advances whatever you are covering in the particular element of your outline.

A1.5.3 Using sources well

A research paper has some very definite features that make it different from an opinion piece or a speech. First, it is an investigation of a problem, leading to a solution. This means that there is room for actual application of your solution only in the conclusion section itself, and even then the application should be brief.

Second, if a research paper is an investigation leading to a solution, it is a journey that requires the help of others, that is, the help of the books, articles, etc. that you gather during the research process. While you could simply follow a logical process of argumentation, leading to a conclusion, you need to recognize that no topic is truly original, even if your solution may be. Others have also dealt with the issue and have put forward points of view and evidence for their own interpretations.

In fact, finding a solution to a research question most often involves weighing the conflicting interpretations of others and finding your answer as a result of your evaluation. This makes research a conversation between you and your sources. Spend a lot of effort on listening to and evaluating the publications of others.

Using sources can be tricky. At one extreme, your paper could be primarily a set of quotations from books and articles, with brief commentary from you. At the other extreme, you could virtually ignore your sources and do most of the analysis yourself. The ideal is somewhere in between, where you use your sources extensively but you still keep in control of the analysis.

How do you achieve the ideal use of sources?

Group your sources by the particular issues they address, and especially by the particular viewpoints they support. Thus you should have a group of sources that deal with or support view A., a group that deal with or support view B., and so on.

Keep your quotations to a minimum, usually only one quotation for every page or two. Keep the quotations under 5 lines for the most part. Instead of quoting, refer. Use language like: *Smith has argued that Constantine embraced Christianity solely because he saw its power as a political force in the Roman Empire.* You are not quoting. You are referring to or describing a viewpoint in your own words. You'll still need to provide a citation [either in the text – (Smith, 234) or as a footnote or endnote], but you'll avoid having your sources do all your speaking for you.

Recognize that the research paper is not supposed to be simply an account of what the world already knows but an analytical investigation of a problem while you are in dialogue with others who are also addressing the problem. Thus, your own analysis, indeed your own presence, has to be seen in the paper. This means that you control your sources. They do not control you. It is you who must lay out the information that your sources provide, e.g., *Smith has argued that...Jones provides a contrary view...Green has added a new voice to the issue by asserting that* [and so on]. You are using your sources to be sure, but you are controlling the process.

Almost never provide new information with a quotation. Use quotations to support a statement you have made first or to present a striking way in which an author has made a point.

Use sources that you agree with as well as sources you disagree with. A research paper needs to show evidence that you've investigated all relevant points of view and have treated your sources fairly. In general, even for writers with whom you disagree, explain what the source is saying before criticizing. Let your source be heard fairly before you evaluate it. When you do criticize, avoid the language of ridicule. Make your criticisms logical and fair.

A1.5.4 Avoiding theft of other people's work

Plagiarism is passing on the thoughts or words of someone else as if they were your own. It ranges from quoting others without acknowledging them to using other people's unique ideas as if they were your unique ideas.

It's relatively easy to make sure, when you quoting a source, that you include the required quotation marks and a bibliographical note. It's a little trickier, however, to determine if you've stolen someone's ideas. A general rule of thumb is that, if an idea is found in two or three other sources which are not all dependent on one earlier source, you can safely use it without acknowledging its source. To be on the safe side, make a bibliographical note if a source is stating a point of view rather than just well known information.

There is another source of theft that is often not recognized—the use of paraphrases by which you take your source, sentence by sentence and simply rewrite each sentence using different words. In this case, you are not interpreting and explaining your source, but using your source's paragraph structure and thoughts in something that is very close to quoting. This too is plagiarism.

Here's an excerpt from an article that I published on the Internet on the challenges regular users of university websites face in trying to navigate to needed information. The original paragraph is:

Many higher educational institution websites have been designed to attract new students and impress the constituency rather than to inform current students. A user's sheer frustration in trying to find a particular department, a faculty member's e-mail address, or a how-to for some obscure academic procedure, points to a website that is a barrier rather than a support (William Badke. "The key word is access." http://www. evolllution.com/opinions/the-key-word-is-access/).

A paraphrase, which would *not* be acceptable, might read:

A lot of websites of universities are set up to draw new students and impress supporters rather than give information to registered students. Students are frustrated trying to find departments, e-mail addresses for professors, and ways to carry out procedures. This makes the website an obstacle rather than a support.

Notice that I've borrowed sentence structure and even words from the original without really interpreting it. Now let me express the material in my own words:

Badke argues that university websites, created for recruitment and flying the flag of the institution, can prevent current students from finding the information they need. Such websites fail to provide access to a large user group - students.

What I have done is to *interpret* what I've read and to express it mostly in different words (though it's all right to use a few words from your source, maybe 5% or less). Remember that the point of a research essay is not simply to quote or interpret others, but to evaluate their work and provide your own arguments. Your own analysis is extremely important.

A1.5.5 Practice with essay structure

Let's walk through the development of a research paper around the following question:

Is there evidence that changes in emphasis in the _____ child welfare program in the past 5 years are the result of pressure from the press?

Introduction [Introduce the issue and ask the research question]
I. The Nature of Changes in the Program over the Past 5 Years.
II. Instances of Coordination between Press Pressure and Changes
    A. Incident One
    B. Incident Two
    C. Incident Three, etc.
III. Possible Alternate Explanations for Timing of Changes
Conclusion

Here's a way we could develop our ideas:

Introduction
It is common for government departments to take press criticism seriously, even to revise programs rather than have the press influence public opinion in a negative way. There have been changes in the _____ child welfare program over the past number of years, many of them appearing to be reactions to press criticism. Is there evidence that changes in emphasis in the _____ child welfare program in the past 5 years are the result of pressure from the press?

I. The Nature of Changes in the Program over the Past 5 Years
Survey, with documentation, the major changes that have occurred, using chronological order as your organizing principle. By doing this, you are showing evidence that significant and frequent changes have been made.
II. Instances of Coordination between Press Pressure and Changes
    A. Incident One
    B. Incident Two
    C. Incident Three, etc.

Now take each instance of change and follow this kind of structure - Incident One: Prior press reaction, timing of change, determination of whether or not the change is a correction of the problem raised by the press. Incident Two: Follow the same process as One, and so on.

III. Possible Alternate Explanations for Timing of Changes

Now provide analysis of any other possible driving motivations for the change. You have shown a correlation between press criticism and changes, but you have not demonstrated cause and effect until you've eliminated other explanations.

Conclusion

Summarize briefly what you have covered, and make a final statement either supporting or rejecting the implication of your research question.

A1.6 Bibliographic style

Many faculty members place an emphasis on papers being presented in a certain style (MLA, APA, Chicago/Turabian, etc.) which determines what the notes and citations to various sources of information will look like. This has long been an issue with students, both because perfect style is so hard to achieve, and because it doesn't make much sense to give so much effort to something that really doesn't seem crucial to the construction of a research paper. Good style is important, however, for several reasons:

> ➢ The reader has fewer distractions away from content when the style (even proper title pages and tables of contents) is consistent and clear.
> ➢ The reader is better able to navigate a properly formatted paper.
> ➢ Adhering to style helps to guarantee that nothing important in the paper will be left out. This is particularly true in notes and bibliographies, where sloppy style can result in dates, volume numbers, pages, and publisher information being omitted.
> ➢ Your professor wants proper style, and that makes style important in its own right (if, indeed, you're at all interested in getting good grades).

A1.6.1 Style software

Personally, I think students are often made to devote too much effort to getting the right punctuation in the right place in a bibliography. Most of your essay-writing effort should be focused on actually writing and revising the essay. But style is important, so what are you to do? The use of bibliographic managers like EndNote, RefWorks, or Zotero (see Chapter 7) has made formatting notes and bibliography a much less painful experience than it used to be. So have online and commercial style formatters.

My recommendation is to use the electronic style resources available to you to get the grunt work done. Then, armed with a crib sheet of style examples, clean up what the software could not.

There are several types of electronic style resource available to you:

Style formatters in most recent word processing programs – Check these out by looking for a tab that says "references" or something similar. You can set your format and create citations using fill in the blank forms. The program will generate a bibliography for you when you have finished typing the paper. But be careful – depending on the age of your word processing program, you may or may not be working with the most recent version of your style format.

Bibliographic managers – See 7.5 above. Most of these do not actually format your paper (title page, section titles, etc.) for you, just the notes and bibliographies (though EndNote has downloadable Word templates at **http://www.endnote.com/support/entemplates. asp**).

Style generators embedded in databases - Some journal database vendors (such as EBSCO and InfoTrac) have provided the ability to save or e-mail journal records in a variety of formats. The multi-catalog search tool WorldCat (**http://www.worldcat.org**) enables you to cite any book you find in a variety of formats (open a book record and click on Cite/Export icon). Google Scholar has a citation style feature (click on "More" or "Cite" under each citation).

Commercial style software - Commercial style software is available for a price. It enables you to format the whole research paper, not just notes and bibliography. Let's look at what a couple of these products can do, with the disclaimer that I have received no promotional fee from these products nor was I asked or coerced to promote them.

> *EazyPaper* (**http://www.eazypaper.com/index.cfm**) is a truly amazing research paper formatting program for APA, MLA and Turabian, written by a former student of mine, Michael Hu, a tech genius in his own right. Not only does it enable you to format papers, notes and bibliographies, but the formatting can be configured according to your professor's specifications. It will let you input references into a database, ready to be cited in your paper (though you can't direct download or import citations from journal databases). But what about all those references you stored in RefWorks or EndNote? How would you get them into EazyPaper? Easily. Just generate a bibliography of them, copy citations and paste them into the EazyPaper database. It will recognize the difference between an author and a title, etc. and generate records that you can then use for citations. In its Pro version, EazyPaper even allows you to search and download book records from a wide variety of libraries. Nice work, Michael.

EasyBib (**http://www.easybib.com**) is an online tool that creates citations in the main three formats, through basic input from you, and then generates bibliographies. It comes in a free and more advanced subscription format.

Noodle Tools (**http://www.noodletools.com/**) is an online resource that provides "integrated tools for note-taking, outlining, citation, document archiving/annotation, and collaborative research and writing." Thus it is more than a citation generator and is well worth checking out.

StyleEase (**http://www.styleease.com/**) is a basic program that helps you format your paper and notes/references. It allows you to compile a database of citations, though you have to enter the reference information box by box (author, title, etc.) rather than being able simply to paste a citation into the database. This is a reliable product for APA, MLA and Turabian formats.

Free internet-based citation format tools

If you lack access to a bibliographic manager and don't want to spring for style software, there are tools that can help you. By searching on the WWW for a style type with the word "template" (e.g., Turabian template, APA template), you can often find word processor templates that will help you format title pages, proper spacing, and so on. But be careful – some of these are generated by professors who have their own idiosyncratic rules for research paper style. Professors, being the truly special bunch that they are, may have you doing some very idiosyncratic things. Or, if you're skilful, you can create your own template.

There are a number of good citation generators online. Check out EasyBib in its basic, non-subscription, form (**http://www.easybib. com**), Citation Machine (**http://www.citationmachine.net/**) and KnightCite (**http://www.calvin.edu/library/knightcite/**). Each of these asks you to choose format and type of source. Then you to enter citation information and generate an accurate citation.

A newer really cool tool for Turabian, MLA and APA citation generation is eTurabian (**http://www.eturabian.com/turabian/ index.html**). This one may well be the winner, if all you want is a citation. While a bit complex looking, you can choose the style and type of resource, then enter information about it (author, title, ISBN, etc.) and get a full-blown citation without having to fill in all the blanks.

A1.6.2 Crib sheets

All of the major bibliographic styles have their own detailed books for sale which detail most aspects of formatting. If you are doing serious research, buy the book. You can often get a copy at a reduced price as an e-book (Kindle, iPad, etc.).

There are, however, a number of WWW-based crib sheets that give you examples of the most common formats. These can be very useful in conjunction with bibliographic managers or style software, just to check your results (especially important with bibliographic software).

Here are some web addresses, but recognize that URLs go out of date almost as quickly as yesterday's pop singers:

APA (6ᵗʰ ed., 2009)

http://library.nmu.edu/guides/userguides/style_apa.htm (interestingly, electronic styles are covered first)

http://www.wisc.edu/writing/Handbook/DocAPA.html

http://www.nova.edu/library/dils/lessons/apa/index.htm (video tutorial approach)

> A word about the DOI in APA 6. A DOI (digital object identifier) is a unique code assigned to each journal article published by many of the newer journals (it's like a barcode on a corn flakes box). Since each DOI identifies a specific article, APA 6 has determined that the DOI should be supplied as the last element in a journal article citation that you have retrieved in electronic format. Thus:

> Badke, W. B. (2005). Can't get no respect: Helping faculty to understand the educational power of information literacy. *Reference Librarian, 43*(89), 63-80. doi: 10.1300/J120v43n8905

> But, *if the electronic format journal does not yet use the DOI system*, you must do a search on the Net for the journal's home page and use the URL for that home page instead:

> Badke, W. B. (2000). Questia.com: Implications of the new McLibrary. *Internet Reference Services Quarterly,*

5(3), 61-71. Retrieved from http://www.tandfonline. com/loi/wirs20

MLA (7th ed., 2009)

http://library-guides.scottsdalecc.edu/content. php?pid=20236&sid=319995

http://owl.english.purdue.edu/owl/section/2/11/ (contains an overview and a specific description of citation format)

http://libguides.dixie.edu/content.php?pid=5025&sid=31250

Turabian (8th ed., 2013)

http://www.press.uchicago.edu/books/turabian/turabian_ citationguide.html (official Turabian site - quick guide)

http://writing.wisc.edu/Handbook/DocChicago.html

http://libguides.msubillings.edu/turabian

Additional Format Help and Sample Papers:

For Electronic Items in your Bibliography - all 3 Formats Above:

http://owl.english.purdue.edu/handouts/research/r_docelectric. html

APA (6th ed.) Sample Paper: **http://supp.apa.org/style/PM6E-Corrected-Sample-Papers.pdf**

MLA (7th ed.) Sample Paper: **http://owl.english.purdue.edu/ media/pdf/20091250615234_747.pdf**

Turabian (8th ed.) Sample Paper: **http://www.liberty.edu/media/2030/Turabian_8_footnote_bibliography_style.pdf**

A1.7 Conclusion

Research papers do not have to be the painful experience many people make of them. It is possible to develop significant skills in order to make the writing process much easier than you thought. We've seen a detailed explanation of them above, but let me summarize:

➢ Develop a well-focused analytical research question.
➢ Structure your paper with a solid outline that answers the question.
➢ Write intentionally, filling in the blanks in your outline with paragraphs that focus on your single goal, which is dealing with the research question.
➢ Use your sources skillfully and ethically at all times.
➢ Let the tools available for formatting help you produce papers that professors will find a pleasure just to look at.

Happy Researching!

APPENDIX TWO –
This Textbook and Information Literacy Competency Standards for Higher Education (ACRL)

Research Strategies conforms to the Association of College and Research Libraries, "Information Literacy Competency Standards for Higher Education." ["Information Literacy Competency Standards for Higher Education." American Library Association. 2000. **http://www.ala.org/ala/mgrps/divs/acrl/standards/standards.pdf** (Accessed 16 November, 2010). Used by permission.]

For a comparative index showing which portions of *Research Strategies* (5th ed., 2014) are relevant to the various ACRL standards, go to: **https://sites.google.com/site/researchstrategiesweb/home/acrl**

Note that, at the time of publication of this edition, the ACRL Standards are undergoing revision. For more information, see **http://acrl.ala.org/ilstandards/**. When they are in place, the above comparative online index will be revised to reflect the latest edition of the information literacy framework.

Index

Topic	Section
ACRL Information literacy standards	APPENDIX TWO
Ask.com	6.3.2
BASE	6.2.3
Bibliographic managers	7.5
Bibliographic style	A1.6
Bibliographic style crib sheets	A1.6.2
Bibliographic style software	A1.6.1
Bibliographies	9.2
Bing	6.3.2
Blekko	6.3.2
Boolean searching	3.2.2
Carrot2	3.3.2.1
Catalogs, Library	4.6.1/5.1
Citation searches	5.5.1; 6.2.3
CiteSeerX	6.2.5
Clustering search tools	3.3.2
Consulting with others	7.6
Controlled vocabularies	4.5-4.9
Databases	3.1
Discovery searching	5.1
Dissertations	7.4
E-book citations	5.2.2
E-books	1.5.1/5.2.2

EBSCO Visual Search   3.3.2.5
Electronic books   1.5.1/5.1.2
EndNote   7.5.1
ERIC   7.2
Evaluating information   1.7/6.7/8.2
Faceted searching   4.7/5.4.5
Federated searching   5.7
getCited   6.2.7
Google   3.3.2/6.3.2
Google Scholar   6.2.2
Government documents   1.5.3/7.3
Hidden Internet   6.6
Hierarchical searching   3.3/6.4
Information, History   1.1-1.8
Internet   6.1
Internet addresses for research   6.8
Internet searching   6.1-6.8
Internet, Hidden   6.6
Journal databases   5.3-5.7
Journal citation content   5.3.1
Journal content alerts   5.3.5
Journals   1.5.2/5.3/6.2
Key propositions   8.1.2
Keyword searching   3.1-3.5
Knowledge for All Project   6.2.2
Librarians   7.6.3
Literature review   A.1.3.4
Metadata   4.1-4.3
Microsoft Academic Search   6.2.4
Narrow topic   2.6.1
Note organization   9.1-9.4
Note taking   8.3-8.4

Notes (footnotes, endnotes, citations)	10.2.11
Open-Access Journals	1.5.2/5.3.1
Outline, Final	10.1/A1.4
Outline, Preliminary	2.7/A1.4
Paraphrasing	8.3.6
Peer review	1.5.2/5.3.1
Plagiarism	8.5/A1.5.4
Portals (Internet)	6.5
Primary sources	1.6
Printing press	1.3
Professors	7.6.2
Quoting	10.2.9-10.2.10
Reading, Analytical	8.1
Reference sources, Electronic	2.5.3
RefWorks	7.5.2
Repositories, Finding	1.5.2
Research case studies	7.6
Research, Inadequate	2.2
Research, Great	2.3
Rescarch Model	2.4/7.1
Research papers, Structure of	A1.5
Research papers, Types of	A1.3
Research questions	2.6.4/2.8/A1.1-A1.2
RSS feeds	5.3.3
Scirius	6.2.6
Search engines	6.3
Search engines, Scholarly	6.2
Search engines, Semantic	6.3.3
Secondary sources	1.6
Sources, Use of	A1.5.3
Subject headings	4.5-4.6

Subject tree searching (Internet)   6.4

Thesis statements   2.6.3/A1.1.8

Wikipedia   2.5.2

Working knowledge   2.5.1

Writing   10.2/A.1.5

Yahoo! Search   6.3.2

Yippy   3.3.2.2

Zotero   7.5.3

17100226R00177

Made in the USA
Middletown, DE
06 January 2015